DATE DUE

No Duty to Retreat

Also by Richard Maxwell Brown

The South Carolina Regulators

Anglo-American Political Relations, 1675–1775 (coeditor)

American Violence (editor)

Strain of Violence: Historical Studies of American Violence and Vigilantism

Tradition, Conflict, and Modernization: Perspectives on the American Revolution (coeditor)

Helldorado: Bringing Law to the Mesquite by William M. Breakenridge (editor)

No Duty to Retreat

Violence and Values
in American History
and Society

RICHARD MAXWELL BROWN

New York   Oxford
OXFORD UNIVERSITY PRESS
1991

To my wife, Dee

Oxford University Press

Oxford   New York   Toronto
Delhi   Bombay   Calcutta   Madras   Karachi
Petaling Jaya   Singapore   Hong Kong   Tokyo
Nairobi   Dar es Salaam   Cape Town
Melbourne   Auckland

and associated companies in
Berlin   Ibadan

Copyright © 1991 by Richard Maxwell Brown

Published by Oxford University Press, Inc.,
200 Madison Avenue, New York, New York 10016

Oxford is a registered trademark of Oxford University Press

Library of Congress Cataloging-in-Publication Data
Brown, Richard Maxwell.
No duty to retreat : violence and values in
American history and society / Richard Maxwell Brown.
p.   cm.   Includes index.
ISBN 0-19-504510-6
1. Violence—United States—History.
2. United States—History.
3. Values—United States—History.   I. Title.
E179.B88   1991   303.6'0973—dc20
90-19661

9 8 7 6 5 4 3 2 1

Printed in the United States of America
on acid-free paper

Preface

This is a book about violence and American values. The central concept upon which it hinges is the pervasive but little-studied theme of "no duty to retreat." Ancient English common law obliged one who was assailed and in fear of death or great bodily harm to retreat "to the wall" at one's back before killing in self-defense. Indeed, the common law required an individual in such a plight to forestall violence by fleeing from the scene if such flight could be safely made. This was the English doctrine held by Blackstone and his predecessors in the common-law tradition. In America a gradual legal revolution reinterpreted the common law to hold that, if otherwise without fault, a person could legally stand fast and, without retreat, kill in self-defense. This was a right to stand one's ground with no duty to retreat. Not merely a revision of an esoteric legalism but a significant development in American culture, no duty to retreat reigned mainly in the frontier states west of the Appalachian Mountains. By the early twentieth century a standard text on the American law of homicide declared that the duty to retreat was "inapplicable to American conditions," and in 1921 Justice Oliver Wendell Holmes of the United States Supreme Court incisively upheld the Americanized common-law doctrine of no duty to retreat.

Representing similar, widespread social values, the Americanization of the common law in favor of no duty to retreat helps explain why the American homicide rate has been so much higher than that of England during the nineteenth and twentieth centuries. It also helps explain why our country has been the most violent among its peer group of the industrialized, urbanized democracies of the world. The attitude of no duty to retreat has long since become second nature to most Americans and has had a deep, broad impact with a significant, although often intangible, effect upon our foreign relations and military conduct. Neglected by previous scholars, no duty to retreat is much more than a legal technicality. It is an expression of a characteristically American approach to life.

Chapter 1 traces the origins of the tradition of no duty to retreat in law and the American mind. Chapter 2 treats a prime exemplar and most potent symbol of the idea of no duty to retreat: the much misunderstood gunfighter of the American West. Focusing on two competing versions of the American dream, Chapter 3 is a study of the spirit of no duty to retreat in a California conflict of the late nineteenth century. In the breadth of crime, law, and society from the 1850s to the present, Chapter 4 deals with the renewed vigor of the no-duty-to-retreat attitude in recent years. The last chapter offers an assessment of violence and American values in relation to no duty to retreat and our foreign, military, and civil affairs. It concludes by addressing the future of no duty to retreat: As the twentieth century gives way to the twenty-first, is the no-duty-to-retreat tradition a hopelessly atavistic, obsolete reversion to America's turbulent past? Is the combative spirit of no duty to retreat bound to wither away in a more pluralistic, apparently post–Cold War America increasingly dominated by notions of peace, civility, and tolerance?

Eugene, Oregon   R. M. B.
November 1990

Acknowledgments

For research and writing I much appreciate the generous support of the Beekman Endowment of the University of Oregon and a sabbatical year from the University of Oregon.

For aid or encouragement in various ways I am grateful to Marinus Bakker, Edwin R. Bingham, Ruth and Norman Brittin, James W. Ely, Jr., Ted Robert Gurr, Frank H. Hoell, William L. Lang, Frank Latta, Taylor Littleton, Michael P. Malone, Louise Carroll Wade, Scott Wallace, Eddie Warmerdam, and H. E. (Hal) Weisbaum.

I thank the knowledgeable and helpful staffs of the Arizona Historical Society; Special Collections division of the University of Arizona Library; Bancroft Library of the University of California, Berkeley; California Historical Society; California State Archives; California Room of the California State Library; Federal Archives and Records Center, San Bruno, California; Hanford (Calif.) Public Library; Henry E. Huntington Library and Art Gallery; Indiana Historical Society; Indiana State Archives; Indiana State Library; Library of Congress; Visalia (Calif.) Public Library; and my home libraries—the Knight Library and the Law Library of the University of Oregon.

I am grateful, too, for the encouragement and the patience of Sheldon Meyer of Oxford University Press and for the expert aid of India Cooper and Leona Capeless in the process of publication.

The support of my wife, Estella Dee Brown, was crucial in so many ways.

Contents

No Duty to Retreat

1

No Duty to Retreat in Law and the American Mind

"A man is not born to run away."
Justice Oliver Wendell Holmes (1921).*

As far back as the thirteenth century, English common law dealt harshly with the act of homicide.[1] The "right to kill in self-defense was slowly established, and is a doctrine of modern rather than medieval law," wrote one authority.[2] On this issue Sir William Blackstone looked not to the future but to the past in his eighteenth-century summation of the English common law of homicide. At the core of Blackstone's view was the centuries-long English common-law tradition that supported "the idea of all homicides as public wrongs." In England the burden was on the one accused of a homicide to prove his innocence. The plea of self-defense was eyed most skeptically. The presumption against the accused killer stemmed from the fear, as Blackstone put it, that "the right to defend may be mistaken as the right to kill." Before the court in the English common-law tradition would countenance killing in self-defense two essential tests had to be met: that of retreat or avoidance and that of "reasonable determination of necessity."[3] The latter test meant that the accused must prove in open court his necessity to kill in order to prevent his own

3

death or serious injury at the hands of an opponent. The test of retreat or avoidance went back to the ancient English common-law doctrine that it was necessary to retreat "to the wall" at one's back before one could legitimately kill in self-defense.[4]

There was a logic behind the English comon-law requirement of a duty to retreat in a threatening situation: it was that the state—the Crown—wished to retain a monopoly of the resolution of conflict at the level of dispute between individuals. In effect the common-law doctrine said to the contentious Englishman: any quarrel that you have with another must be settled peaceably or in a court of law. Should your opponent threaten you, you must not defend yourself with violence until you have attempted to get away—to flee from the scene altogether. If you are unable to leave the scene, you may not *stand your ground* and kill in self-defense. Instead you must *retreat* as far as possible from your enemy: to the wall at your back. Then, and only then—with the wall at your back and all retreat cut off—may you legally face your opponent and kill him in self-defense. And even with the wall at your back, there must be necessity, which you must later prove in court: that is, the need to save yourself from grievous harm. Thus in English society of the medieval and early-modern periods, the state attempted to reduce the incidence of murder by shifting personal disputes from field and street to the court of law. The state—that is, the Crown—insisted on monopolizing for itself the act of homicide. As Blackstone noted, "justifiable homicide," for which the common law held that there was no guilt, was restricted to the execution of a criminal for a capital offense, the unavoidable slaying of a runaway criminal, and the killing of one resisting arrest by an officer of the law. Under the category of "excusable homicide" there was guilt, but it was slight. If one obeyed the duty to retreat to the wall and could prove a reasonable necessity to kill, the proper finding of the court would be excusable homicide, for which, by Blackstone's time and for centuries before, there was in fact no penalty.[5]

The English common-law "duty to retreat" was a powerful

means to produce a society of civility, for obedience to the duty to retreat—really a duty to flee from the scene altogether or, failing that, to retreat to the wall at one's back—meant that in the vast majority of disputes no fatal outcome could occur. It takes two to make a fight, and with one party having fled from the scene, no killing or injury could possibly result. Any grievance that lingered would have to be settled not by the arbitrament of death or wound but by the judicious finding of a court of law. There were, of course, many fewer situations in which flight from the scene was entirely blocked, and even in such cases one had to retreat "to the wall" (the legal phrase)—until one could retreat no further—before one could without blame stand one's ground and, if necessary, kill. At its nub, then, the duty to retreat was a command to avoid physical conflict between individuals. Compared to the United States of America, England has long had a very low homicide rate, and one reason, surely, is its deeply embedded doctrine of the duty to retreat.

In a minority of American states the English common-law doctrine of duty to retreat did survive, but one of the most important tranformations in American legal and social history occurred in the nineteenth century when the nation as a whole repudiated the English common-law tradition in favor of the American theme of no duty to retreat: that one was legally justified in standing one's ground to kill in self-defense. Recognized at the time as a crucial change in "the American mind," it was a combination of Eastern legal authorities and Western judges who wrought the legal transformation from an English law that, as they saw it, upheld cowardice to an American law suited to the bravery of the "true man." The centuries-long English legal severity against homicide was replaced in our country by a proud new tolerance for killing in situations where it might have been avoided by obeying a legal duty to retreat. This undoubtedly had an impact on our homicide rate, helping to make it the highest on earth among our peer group of the modern, industrialized nations of the world. It is impossible to say how many lives have been lost in this country as a result of the change in the law from the duty to retreat to the legal right to stand one's ground, but the toll of victims during the nineteenth and twentieth centuries may well be, indirectly but significantly, in the tens of thousands. The impact of this change in law is hardly restricted to the realm of homicide alone, grievous as that may be, for the metaphorical and symbolic impact of the transition from duty to retreat to standing one's ground is obvious and is crucial to the American identity. In the realms of both peace and war, it is not in the nature of America to approve retreat. Standing one's ground is an attitude that has deeply permeated our foreign relations and our military habits as well as the peaceful pursuits of daily life.[†]

The American theme of no duty to retreat was proclaimed as federal law by the United States Supreme Court in 1921, but long before then it had been written into the common law of a majority of American states. The roots of the transformation from the duty to retreat to standing one's ground went back to about the time of the American Revolution. Thus the Americanization of the common law of homicide in favor of no duty to retreat paralleled the rise of the independent American nation. Ironically, it was an English legal commentator, Sir Michael Foster, who, in an essay on the law of homicide in 1762, first undermined the traditional requirement of the duty to retreat. Foster was attempting to clarify the previous writings on the subject by William Lambarde, Edward Coke, and Matthew Hale.[6] During this century, there has been controversy among legal scholars over whether Foster actually clarified or distorted the traditional doctrine of the duty to retreat.[7] What he wrote, however, came to have greater impact on this side of the Atlantic than in his own country. In his 1762 essay on homicide, Foster declared that Coke, Lambarde, and Hale had not treated "the subject of self-defence with due precision" and went on to assert that "the injured party may repel force by force in defence of his person" against one attempting to commit a felony—such as a robbery or murder—upon him. In such a case, wrote Foster, the self-

[†]See Chapter 5.

defender was "not obliged to retreat" but might "pursue his adversary till he findeth himself out of danger, and if in a conflict between them he happeneth to kill, such killing is justifiable."[8] In 1803, another English commentator, Edward Hyde East, echoed Foster's view.[9]

What might have developed into a great controversy in England over the duty to retreat failed to occur in the absence of conditions like those of America where a turbulent new society made the issue an important one.[10] Whether it was a clarification or a distortion, the Foster-East doctrine had no practical impact in England, whose Criminal Law Act of 1967 retained the age-old duty to retreat,[11] but such an impact soon occurred in America. In a Massachusetts case of 1806, *Commonwealth v. Selfridge*, the Foster-East mitigation of the duty to retreat was cited and upheld.[12] Although the Selfridge case was not to be a legal landmark equal to later state supreme court cases west of the Appalachians, legal experts in the eastern United States absorbed the doctrine of Foster and East and incorporated it in their authoritative and influential textbooks, which were destined to pass through many editions in the nineteenth century. These textbook writers bolstered the Western judges whose sense of American society told them that the duty to retreat was improper. Francis Wharton published widely used textbooks on American criminal law and on the law of homicide. Not original in interpretation, Wharton's treatises merely blended the texts of English authors with notes of American cases.[13] The first truly original American work on the criminal law was published in 1856 by Joel Prentiss Bishop of Massachusetts.[14] By 1892 Bishop's textbook was in its eighth edition. Going back to the first edition of 1856 it had been Bishop's pride to have written his *Commentaries on the Criminal Law* for the practical use of lawyers, not just law professors and their students. It was, he claimed, a book based not on "mere dead cases" but on "the *living principles*" deduced by him as guides for future adjudications.

As for the law of homicide and self-defense, Bishop followed Foster and East in the turn away from the duty to retreat. Indeed, Bishop was such an ardent exponent of the Americanized doctrine of no duty to retreat that he wrote that "if a man murderously attacked by another flies instead of resisting, he commits substantially [the] offense of misprision of felony." Bishop noted that "misprision of felony" was an indictable misdemeanor; what he meant in nontechnical terms was that the law did not give one the option of flight or resistance but, rather, commanded resistance. Yet Bishop was using the concept of flight from the scene of a murderous assault as misprision of felony (and thus a crime in its own right) not as dogma but to make a strong symbolic point against the dictum of retreat. Thus, Bishop showed common sense when he admitted that "in strict law" one who fled would be excused from the offense of misprision of felony as a person "acting from the commendable motive to save life."[15] Although less original than Bishop in his approach to the common law of crime and homicide, Francis Wharton incorporated the Foster-East doctrine of no duty to retreat into his textbook *The Law of Homicide*.[16]

It was one thing for textbook writers such as Bishop and Wharton to promote the doctrine of no duty to retreat, but the decisive arena was the appellate decisions of state supreme courts. These tribunals were the courts of last resort for the common law of homicide and self-defense on a state-by-state basis. Following the westward movement of settlers from the Appalachians to the Pacific Coast, state after state saw its highest court repudiate the duty to retreat in favor of the doctrine of standing one's ground. State supreme court judges routinely cited the decisions of other state supreme courts in support of their own opinions. Two of the most influential state supreme court stipulations of no duty to retreat came in 1876 and 1877, respectively, in the "true man" and "American mind" decisions from Ohio and Indiana.[17]

The "true man" case was that of *Erwin v. State* in Ohio in 1876.[18] Some years before, a family dispute in Gallia County resulted in James W. Erwin killing his son-in-law, a sharecropper or tenant on land owned by Erwin. Between Erwin's home place and that occupied by his son-in-law was a storage shed. With a background of ill will between the two men, their dispute over who was entitled to possession of the shed festered. Erwin kept his farm implements in the shed; his son-in-law wished to store grain in it. On the day of the homicide, Erwin was in the shed tending to his tools when his son-in-law approached. A parley between the two turned into a quarrel. With an ax on his shoulder, the son-in-law, so Erwin later claimed, made for Erwin and the shed in a threatening manner, which Erwin countered with a warning not to enter the shed. Heedless, the son-in-law closed on Erwin, and the latter—far from fleeing the scene—stood his ground and dropped his daughter's husband with a pistol shot that soon proved fatal.

Under indictment in the Gallia County court, James Erwin was convicted of second-degree murder. He appealed his conviction to the state supreme court, partly on the grounds that the judge of the county court had wrongly instructed the jury that Erwin had a duty to retreat. The state attorney general held that the issue of duty to retreat was as yet undetermined in the common law of Ohio, so the supreme court undertook to settle the matter. In the court's decision, written by Judge George W. McIlvaine, the duty to retreat was struck down, the conviction of Erwin was reversed, and a new trial in the county court was ordered. With full cognizance of the facts of the homicide (as related above), McIlvaine seized on a rather innocuous use of the phrase "true man" by Sir Matthew Hale in his commentary upholding the duty to retreat. Finding that Erwin's son-in-law had, with ax in hand, been maliciously seeking to take Erwin's life or "do him enormous bodily harm." McIlvaine wrote, in words that must have been music to the ears of Erwin and his attorney, that while "the law, out of tenderness for human life and the frailties of human nature, will not permit the taking of it to repel a mere trespass, or even to save life" if the assault is provoked by the killer, it is much more tolerant if the killer was without fault in provoking the clash. But the court, speaking through McIlvaine, found that Erwin himself had been without blame and therefore as a "true man" was "not obliged to fly" from his assailant, the son-in-law. Thus McIlvaine, after a learned discussion of the views of Foster and Hale and the Massachusetts court in the *Selfridge* case, widened Hale's doctrine that a "true man" had no duty to retreat if assaulted by a thief (which Erwin's son-in-law was not) to the view that there was, generally, no duty to retreat in Ohio—that a *"true man"* (the assumption was that there was, or should be, no other kind) who was without fault in a confrontation was free to stand his ground against any menacing assailant, regardless of the consequences.[19]

 ·Lawyers, judges, and legal scholars had barely begun to digest Ohio's "true man" theme of no duty to retreat when, across the border in Indiana, the supreme court of that state found that the duty to retreat was contrary to "the tendency of the American mind." This viewpoint was at the core of the Indiana state supreme court's decision in the May 1877 case of *Runyan v. State*.[20] The Runyan case grew out of an episode of election-day violence resulting in the death of Charles Pressnall on November 7, 1876. Election-day mayhem was one of the most common forms of violence in nineteenth-century America,[21] and Indiana was a state unsurpassed for partisan rivalry between Republicans and Democrats after the Civil War.[22] At the presidential level, the election of 1876 was one of the most closely contested in American history and, due to disputes in four other states, was not settled until 1877 when a special federal electoral commission decided in favor of the Republican candidate, Rutherford B. Hayes.[23]

Meanwhile, voters were tense in central Indiana's rural Henry County where two neighbors, John Runyan and Charles Pressnall, prepared to experience the excitement of election day in the county seat, New Castle. Henry County was the model for the mythical "Raintree County" in the novel of that title by the late Ross Lockridge, Jr.[24] *Raintree County* appeared in 1948 as its author's post–World War II version of the "great American novel." Set in the middle and late nineteenth century, Lockridge's imaginary county was a close copy of the external features of Henry County. Lockridge's fictional story of Raintree

County was an expression of the American myth of greatness discovered at home, of the American dream and destiny in contrast to the harsh reality of America in the Civil War and post–Civil War periods.[25] On both sides of his family, the novelist came by his interest in history as a basis for fiction. His father, Ross Lockridge, Sr., was a researcher and writer of Indiana local history,[26] while his mother (born Elsie Lillian Shockley) came from a leading nineteenth-century family of Henry County.[27] Her father, John Wesley Shockley, was the inspiration for the protagonist of her son's novel.[28]

Although steeped in the history and lore of Henry County, Ross Lockridge, Jr., made no attempt to portray actual county events in his novel. Rather, he tapped the general historical reality of Henry County to lend authenticity and depth to his attempt to portray the American myth in the form of a fictional community. He drew on the look of the real Henry County as well, incorporating illustrations of county scenes from the *Illustrated Historical Atlas of Henry County* (1875)[29] into the endpapers of *Raintree County*. The first endpaper of *Raintree County,* for example, contains an exact reproduction of the *Historical Atlas*'s engraved illustration of Henry County's monumental, tower-topped courthouse in which the issue of the duty to retreat would be aired in the trial of John Runyan for the killing of Charles Pressnall.[30] The tragic death of Pressnall is not depicted or even hinted at in Lockridge's novel, but it is in keeping with a principal theme of *Raintree County:* the loss of innocence.

John Runyan and Charles Pressnall were neighbors on farms about four miles southwest of the county seat,[31] New Castle (called Freehaven in *Raintree County*). About thirty years old, Runyan came from a far-flung family in Henry County and as a youth had served as a private in the Union army during the Civil War.[32] Emerging from the war with a severely injured right arm, Runyan applied for and received a pension for Civil War service from the federal government.[33] Pressnall was a few years younger than Runyan, but he also served in the Union army.[34] Despite their residential propinquity and their wartime service in common, Runyan and Pressnall were divided by an important factor in a time of bitter partisan rivalries: politics. Runyan was a Democrat, and Pressnall, like so many veterans who wore the blue in wartime, was an enthusiastic member of the "Grand Old Party"—the Republican party—which formed a strong majority in Henry County.[35]

As Runyan and Pressnall went their separate ways to spend election day in New Castle, political feeling ran high among the people of the county and its county seat. The members of the Republican majority were anxious over the outcome, because the Democrats were a heavy threat to take control of the White House away from the Republicans for the first time since the inauguration of Abraham Lincoln in 1861. Indiana was viewed nationwide as a key to victory in the presidential election.[36] Staunch Democrats like Runyan had high hopes that Indiana and America would terminate sixteen years of Republican domination. Emotions were strong on both sides in Henry County, since, although the Democrats stood little chance of carrying the county, the votes cast by the minority party in Henry County might combine with Democratic votes elsewhere in Indiana to carry the state for Samual J. Tilden against Rutherford B. Hayes, and Indiana's electoral vote, in turn, might carry the nation for Tilden and the Democrats.[37]

Upon arriving in New Castle, Runyan and his brother-in-law, Henry Ray, along with a new resident of the county, one Cady— all good Democrats—found themselves the targets of a vendetta spearheaded by three hot-blooded Republicans: Pressnall; a strapping bully by the name of John Spell; and Benjamin F. Moore, who served in a dual capacity as assistant marshal of New Castle and constable of Henry Township.[38] Runyan, Ray, and Cady were victimized by threats and harassment all day long. Runyan in particular was bitterly resented by the Republicans. He was seen as a turncoat for supporting the Democratic party in spite of his status as a Union veteran who had been granted a Civil War pension by a Republican administration. Some of his Repub-

lican tormentors went so far as to denounce Runyan to his face as
a "damned rebel"—no doubt because Runyan's party was depend-
ing heavily on a sweep of the former Confederate states to win the
election of 1876. Moore joined in the cry by telling Runyan "he
ought not to be drawing a pension and voting the way he did."
Runyan was especially alarmed by the threats and curses of Spell,
who had a reputation for violence. Conscious of his crippled right
arm and fearing that Spell might therefore easily overpower him,
Runyan borrowed a pistol for self-protection.

About nine o'clock that night, Runyan and Ray decided to
make one last check for news of election returns before returning to their homes. They proceeded to the center of town, where
the telegraph office and the polling place were located near New
Castle's leading hotel, the Taylor House. Here people were milling about, among them the Republican factionists who had bul-
lied Runyan and his fellow Democrats during the day. Moore
roughly accosted Runyan and began an angry quarrel with him.
Incensed by the outbreak, Ray made a threatening movement
toward Moore. As Moore pushed Ray away, Runyan—fearful of
being separated from his brother-in-law—spoke up loudly. Pressnall harshly told Runyan to be quiet, the latter replied insult-
ingly, and Pressnall struck at Runyan two or three times with his
fists. Runyan warded off the blows and with his left hand
strongly pushed Pressnall away from him, six or seven feet into
the street, while reaching into his coat pocket with his right hand
for the revolver he had concealed there. With this weapon he
quickly fired a shot into Pressnall's chest. "My God you have shot
me dead!" exclaimed the victim, to which, according to some
witnesses—most of them allies of Pressnall—Runyan blazed
back, "Yes, damn you, I've shot you," and, eyeing others in the
crowd around him, "I can shoot more of you."

There was, however, no more violence. Runyan threw his pistol
away and was quickly overcome and arrested by his Republican
rival, Moore, in his capacity as peace officer. Pressnall soon died in
the Taylor House where he had been taken after the shooting.
Although the vigilante-minded talked that night and the next day

13

of lynching Runyan,[39] the law was allowed to take its course. In the February 1877 term of the Henry County circuit court, John Runyan went on trial before Judge Robert I. Polk[40] in the "large and commodious" courthouse recently erected in New Castle and later enshrined in *Raintree County*. Judge Polk instructed the jury that Runyan, like any other, had a legal duty to retreat before killing in self-defense. The evidence in the trial was clear that Runyan, far from retreating, had certainly stood his ground and killed Pressnal. Judge Polk's instruction to the jury was, therefore, a clear invitation to it to find Runyan guilty for not having obeyed the duty to retreat before killing his opponent. The outcome was a finding of guilt by manslaughter and a sentence to the state prison for a term of eight years.[41] Neither judge nor jury reckoned, however, with the mind and character of a newly elected member of the Indiana supreme court, William E. Niblack, who three months later would, on behalf of his supreme court colleagues, issue a ringing denunciation of the duty to retreat in an opinion overturning the conviction of Runyan.

Judge William E. Niblack was a seasoned politico and longtime former member of Congress who had emerged as a lawyer and local judge during the frontier period of his home region of southwestern Indiana.[42] A hardy pioneer, Judge Niblack's father, John Hargrave Niblack, had carried rifle and Bible with him in 1817 as he went west along the "mud-hole trace," a primitive trail slicing through the angle between the Ohio and Wabash rivers. The elder Niblack dropped off the mud-hole trace in newly formed Dubois County and laid out the county seat of Portersville, where he also built the county's first courthouse. For himself Niblack toiled as a tanner and miller and with his wife, Martha, reared a family on a farm away from town. Among their offspring was William E. Niblack, born in 1822—a lad who carried wood and water on the home place and when not thus or similarly employed attended a log-house school. There came a time when young Niblack wanted more out of life, and for two years he studied sporadically in the fledgling Indiana University. That came to an end when his father died. Back home to support his mother and family, Niblack worked as a land surveyor while on the side he learned law in a local attorney's office.

Moving to adjacent Martin County, William E. Niblack was soon in the midst of a flourishing career in law and politics. One after the other came stints as a circuit judge, state legislator, and seven-term member of the U.S. House of Representatives. Meanwhile, Niblack was admitted to the bar of the United States Supreme Court and, as an avid Democrat but one who strongly supported the Union in the Civil War, served three times as a delegate to his party's national convention and eight years on the Democratic National Committee. By 1877, the fifty-four-year old Niblack was one of the most revered political and legal figures in Indiana. A large, erect, handsome individual with a splendid physique, Niblack was saluted in 1880 in an Indiana biographical compilation as (in words that unintentionally but appropriately echoed the motif of the Ohio case *Erwin v. State*) a "true man." Proud of the maternal great-grandfather who fought in the Revolutionary War, Niblack would become a founder and president of the Indiana society of the Sons of the American Revolution, whose members nationally came to include Presidents Hayes, McKinley, and Theodore Roosevelt as well as Elihu Root, Henry Cabot Lodge, and many other eminent Americans.

Pictures of William E. Niblack reveal a person of thoughtful and intellectual mien with firm features suggesting a strong inner character. As a supreme court judge in Indiana, Niblack was praised for his judicial temperament and respected as a stern magistrate. Decisions written by him were notable for their purity, force, and directness of application. His judicial opinions represented sound legal learning and sprang from his "deepest convictions." In 1888, Indiana Democrats mentioned Niblack as a presidential possibility, and his death on May 7, 1893, was reported under the leading front-page headline of the *Indianapolis Sentinel*. In death as in life, Niblack was viewed as a paragon of the pioneer era of his state and nation.

More than any other of his state supreme court colleagues from the Appalachians to the Pacific who rolled back the English common-law doctrine of the duty to retreat in favor of the American principle of standing one's ground, William E. Niblack represented the frontier background and heritage which gave emotional fervor and depth to the doctrine of no duty to retreat. Speaking for the Indiana supreme court in its May 1877 term, Niblack presented his own deeply held views in the decision on the case of *Runyan v. State.* Runyan's attorneys had appealed his conviction in the Henry County circuit court on the ground, among others, that Judge Polk had wrongly instructed the jury that there was a duty to retreat. Niblack and his supreme court confreres upheld Runyan's appeal and sent the case back to the circuit court for retrial.[43]

In his opinion upsetting the conviction of Runyan, Niblack swept aside other considerations and focused on the issue of the duty to retreat. He quoted the lower court judge's instruction to the jury declaring that the law "is tender of human life, and will not suffer the life even of an assailant and wrong-doer [here he seemed to be referring, by implication, to Pressnall] to be taken, unless the assault is of such a character as to make it appear reasonably necessary to the assailed [in this case, Runyan] to take life in defence of his own life, or to protect his person from great bodily harm. And," the judge concluded, "if the person assailed can protect his life and his person by retreating, it is his *duty to retreat* and thus avoid the necessity of taking human life."[44] The circuit court judge's interpretation was, in effect, that Runyan had had a duty to retreat—by which he meant an obligation to fly from the scene, for in that way he could have protected his own life and person while not taking the life of Pressnall.

Niblack, on the other hand, roundly rejected Judge Polk's endorsement of the duty to retreat. He found that the latter had incorrectly stated the law of self-defense "as it is now recognized by the general drift of the American authorities." To support his own denial of the duty to retreat, Niblack asserted that "in cases of this kind" the right of self-defense is "founded on the law of nature; and is not, nor can be, superseded by any law of society." His citation of natural law revealed his depth of feeling, but

Niblack quickly resorted to both law and American values to support his contention that Runyan, as the victim of what Niblack saw as a felonious assault by Pressnall, was "not obliged to retreat" but could pursue his adversary until he, Runyan, was out of danger.[45]

Holding that Runyan's homicide was justifiable, Niblack noted that "a very brief examination of American authorities"—including both Bishop and Wharton—showed that the "ancient" English doctrine of the duty to retreat had been "greatly modified in this country, and has with us a much narrower application than formerly." Then, in a passage which was to be widely quoted in subsequent decisions upholding no duty to retreat, Niblack got to the heart of the matter: "Indeed, *the tendency of the American mind* seems to be very strongly against the enforcement of any rule which requires a person to flee when assailed"—even to save human life.[46] In effect, Niblack held that the duty to retreat was a legal rationale for cowardice and that cowardice was simply un-American.

The language of the supreme court in Ohio with its emphasis on the action of a "true man" and of the Indiana court with its repudiation of what it saw as legalized cowardice illustrates a running theme in the language of the American state supreme court judges who grappled with the issue of the duty to retreat versus standing one's ground: a concern for the values of masculine bravery in a frontier nation. For example, in an earlier case focusing on the retreat requirement, a Tennessee judge had scathingly referred to the defendant, a hunter named Grainger, as a "timid, cowardly man," and this case, *Grainger v. State* (1830)—which significantly increased the right of violent self-defense—was ever after referred to as the "timid hunter" case.[47]

Much later, a Minnesota case—*State v. Gardner* (1905)—emphasized frontier conditions that brought tough, brave men into conflict with a weaponry far beyond the deadliness of anything known in medieval times when the duty to retreat had been formulated.[48] The case arose from the killing of William Garrison by Joseph Gardner in an open field on July 18, 1904. Gardner appealed his conviction of murder in the Itasca County court to the Minnesota supreme court, for which Judge Edwin A. Jaggard wrote an opinion in November 1905 upholding Gardner's appeal.[49]

In his lengthy recitation of the facts of the homicide, Judge Jaggard stressed the wild, frontier character of northern Minnesota where the killing took place. Joseph Gardner, a homesteader who doubled as a rural mail carrier, was "a typical pioneer, industrious, courageous, and self-reliant." William Garrison was ten years younger than the forty-five-year-old Gardner. Well-built, strong, and active, Garrison—known for a "violent temper" and "quarrelsome disposition"—was adept at the use of his rifle, resided on his own land a few miles north of Gardner's home, and had openly expressed his hatred of and intention to kill Gardner.

The bad feeling between the two men originated in a dispute over a tract of good hay land which both claimed. The trouble came to a head on July 18, 1904. Shortly before noon on that midsummer day, Gardner's son informed him that Garrison had been over that morning demanding pay for six tons of hay cut by Gardner on the controverted land. Packing a rifle, as was customary in this frontier country, Gardner left to provide Garrison with documentary proof (from the county auditor) of possession of the land to support his harvest of the hay. Nearing the Garrison place, Gardner was angered to note that Garrison had cut hay that he, Gardner, claimed. As Gardner later testified, "I can't say I was extremely angry; I wasn't fighting angry; I was chewing the rag angry," and he began to curse as he approached Garrison's cabin, near which the latter was working on some poles. A shouting quarrel began:

GARDNER   *(with an oath):* "Who told you to cut that hay, Bill?"
GARRISON   *(leaping across the poles and toward the rifle that leaned against his cabin thirty feet away and with face distorted with passion):* "I'll show you!"
GARDNER   *(with another curse):* "Hold on!"

Rejecting Gardner's command, Garrison raced on for his gun. Gardner, certain that Garrison meant to shoot him, fired his own rifle at Garrison and, as Garrison dodged back and forth under fire, brought his enemy down with a mortal wound. As Garrison lay bleeding, Gardner, still in the heat of combat, roared "a horrible imprecation" over his victim and charged, "You have been working for this some time, and now you have it." Before dying that night, Garrison said of his slayer, "If he had not shot me, I would have shot him," and of his own weapon after the shooting, "I guess the cur got my gun." Thus a combination of murderous hatreds and firearms had produced a tragedy of the North Woods frontier.

On behalf of his supreme court colleagues, Judge Jaggard weighed the evidence presented in the county court trial and rejected the contention that the shooting of Garrison was premeditated. Rather, Jaggard focused on the county judge's instruction to the jury that Gardner had a duty to retreat. Accepting the self-defense plea of Gardner, Jaggard drastically qualified the duty to retreat. In effect, Jaggard held that the American combination of frontier conditions and lethal firearms had outmoded the duty to retreat in innumerable situations, an interpretation which supreme court justices in other states found persuasive. "The doctrine of 'retreat to the wall'," said Jaggard, "had its origin [in medieval England] before the general introduction of guns. Justice demands that its application have due regard to the general use of and to the type of firearms. It would be good sense for the law to require, in many cases, an attempt to escape from a hand to hand encounter with fists, clubs, and even knives, as a condition of justification for killing in self-defense; while it would be rank folly to require [an attempt to escape] when experienced men, armed with repeating rifles, face each other in an open space, removed from shelter, with intent to kill or to do great bodily harm." With Garrison having been only thirty feet from his gun and with Gardner being a hundred feet away from the surrounding forest, Jaggard opined that had Gardner obeyed the traditional duty to retreat he would have been hit by Garrison, "a dead shot," before reaching the safety of the woods. "What might be a reasonable chance for escape" in an encounter without firearms, reasoned Jaggard, might with them be "certain death." In conclusion he drove home the point that any "requirement of the duty to retreat" that turned self-defense into "self-destruction" was unreasonable and impermissible.

With the "true man" doctrine of Ohio and the "American mind" thesis of Indiana as well as the frontier-and-firearms contention of Minnesota ready to hand, energetic state supreme court justices the length and breadth of the land eloquently and feelingly put under siege the beleaguered notion of the duty to retreat. In *State v. Bartlett* (1902), the Missouri court viewed standing one's ground as a sacred right of human liberty "as dear in the eye of the law" as human life and magisterially declared that the "idea of the nonnecessity of retreating from any locality where one has the right to be is growing in favor, as all doctrines based upon sound reason inevitably will."[50] Still operating on a high theoretical level, the supreme court of Washington found in 1917 that standing one's ground was "more in keeping with the dictates of human nature" than the requirement to retreat or escape from an adversary.[51] Taking the highest ground of all was the Wisconsin supreme court, which in 1909 announced that self-defense was a *"divine right"* by which a man might "stand his ground" in preference to the obsolete " 'flight' rule" embodying the "ancient doctrine" of Blackstone and "early common-law writers." "Retreat to the wall," said the court, "may have been all right in the days of chivalry, so called" but "has been pretty generally" and "in this state very definitely, abandoned."[52]

The soaring judicial rhetoric in Missouri, Washington, and Wisconsin was in touch with the times. The sun was setting on the duty to retreat in America, but as the nineteenth century turned into the twentieth it still had its defenders in a minority of states and among the academic halls of ivy. A few loud, firm voices denied the premise that the duty to retreat was a cowardly betrayal of the American mind. One of the most indefatigable of these pro-duty-to-retreat spokesmen was a stern, remarkably industrious state supreme court judge in Alabama. Another was a brilliant, trenchant scholar in the august precincts of the Harvard

Law School.[53] The former was George Washington Stone. Serving on Alabama's highest court for twenty-seven years (1856–1865 and 1876–1894), as late as 1910 Stone held the record among English and American courts of last resort for the most opinions—2,449—written by one judge.[54] Many of Stone's opinions were in support of the duty to retreat. Yet he was no hidebound traditionalist. Broadly, Stone was a business-oriented supporter of the modernizing "New South" trend of the late nineteenth century. In legal terms he was committed to procedural reform in the interest of a more efficient, effective judiciary, but even more basic was his deep reverence for the principles of the "grand, colossal system" of the old English common law.[55]

Of these enduring principles, none was more dear to George Washington Stone than the "sacredness" of human life.[56] Thus Judge Stone led his colleagues on the Alabama supreme court in a tireless attempt to curb the street fights and personal disputes that took so many lives in Alabama and the South. Stone's judicial strategy was to narrow the law of self-defense. He detested above all the popular belief that killing in a mutual fight was not murder or manslaughter, a view upheld in the neighboring state of Mississippi in the influential 1856 case of *Ex parte Wray*.[57] As a result of a personal dispute, Jacob Wray accosted Clarke Brown and struck him. When Brown fought back with a whipstock, Wray killed him with a bowie knife. In its decision affirming Wray's innocence, the Mississippi supreme court greatly expanded the common law of self-defense by annihilating the traditionally rigorous requirement that one claiming self-defense must demonstrate the necessity of the killing. Instead, the Mississippi court emphasized the principle that killing in a *mutual* fight—such as that between Wray and Brown—was no crime.[58] In an early decision during his second term on the Alabama supreme court, Stone angrily denounced the principles in the *Wray* case, which in Alabama as well as Mississippi were "annually rushing scores if not hundreds of our citizens into eternity, red with their own blood causelessly shed."[59]

Buried in the case reports heard upon appeal by George Washington Stone and his peers on the Alabama supreme court were numerous examples of the tragic, needless homicides that afflicted Alabama, the South, and all of America. Stone was dedicated to the erection and support of a judicial barrier of law to forestall the sort of human catastrophe involved in an episode that came before Stone and his court in 1877 in the case of *Judge v. State*.[60] The court reporter caught very well the language and emotion of the time and place as the defendant, Alexander (Alex) Judge, and the deceased, Robert Wallace, had confronted each other one rainy morning on the cotton plantation of William H. Locke.[61]

Alex Judge was a field hand on Locke's plantation; he served in a plowing squad supervised by Wallace. Judge was the bigger of the two men. The work on the plantation was lagging too much in the view of owner Locke. On the morning of the killing, Locke had instructed Wallace "to hurry up idle hands" and report the dilatory to him. Wallace took these instructions to heart. At about eleven o'clock, the plowmen were allowed to stop work and take shelter from the rain. When the shower ceased, the men were sent to a nearby lot to round up their mules so they could get on with the plowing. Judge was a "little slow," and Wallace remarked to him, "Alex, go and get your mule," to which Judge replied, perhaps insolently, "Ain't I gwine?" Wallace, growing angry, retorted, "If you are, you are going blamed slow." "If you want me to go faster, make me," was Judge's defiant reply. Wallace had had enough: "Alex, next time I speak to you, and you answer me that way, I'll knock your blamed mouth wide open!" Judge looked back at the foreman but said nothing. To drive home his point and further assert his authority, Wallace added, "Alex, if you want a difficulty you can get it right now." "If you want one, you can get it," was Judge's quick reply.

The verbal dispute between Alex Judge and Robert Wallace had ascended to the point of violence as others looked on. Wallace turned toward Judge and put his hand in his pocket—an action Judge apparently interpreted as reaching for a knife. The latter speedily dodged five or six steps to his right and picked up

22

a stout club in the form of a wagon standard. Thus armed, Judge attacked Wallace, felling him with four blows to arm, shoulder, and head. Wallace jumped up immediately as two of the bystanders restrained Judge. While Wallace stood still, Judge broke free and, grabbing his club with both hands, struck Wallace on the head with all his might. Downed by the terrific blow, Wallace got up "looking foolish" (that is, appearing addled by the hit), picked up a closed knife from the ground, opened it, and started toward Judge. Someone warned him, "Shut up your knife, you can't get to that man while he has got that stick in his hand; he will kill you." Although he heeded the warning, pocketed the knife, and walked away, Wallace had already been fatally injured. Later that day he died in Locke's home, the victim of a fractured skull inflicted by Alex Judge's last powerful stroke.

In case after case, the main thrust of George Washington Stone's judicial opinions was to narrow the grounds and efficacy of the self-defense argument as a means to legitimate a killing. Stone and his supreme court colleagues rigorously upheld the duty to retreat. Thus, in his opinion rejecting Alexander Judge's plea of self-defense in the killing of Robert Wallace, Stone invoked the avoidance factor in the duty to retreat. Judge, Stone noted, could easily have escaped from the scene of his cotton-field quarrel with Wallace. Judge gained no sympathy from Stone, who in his opinion spoke strongly in favor of "the old, sound, and"—in America—"much disregarded doctrine, that no man stands excused for taking human life, if, with safety to his own person, he could have"—as Judge could have—"avoided or retired from the combat."[62]

At the heart of George Washington Stone's enthusiasm for the duty-to-retreat principle was his belief that "its observance would exert a wholesome restraint on unbridled passion and lawlessness, and would, in the end, preserve to the commonwealth many valuable lives."[63] Yet the "tendency of the American mind" was in another direction—one favoring violent self-defense by the "true man." Support of the duty to retreat such as Stone's was decidedly on the wane. The standing-one's-ground doctrine would become the rule in the majority of southern states and would also dominate the central and western United States. The pure, traditional duty-to-retreat provision would shrink to a minority of states to be found, mainly, in some northeastern states and South Carolina, Florida, and Alabama in the South.[64] These duty-to-retreat states were too few in number to form a critical mass that might significantly affect general American attitudes and, as Judge Stone had hoped, "exert a wholesome restraint on unbridled passion and lawlessness."

Among legal scholars there was one, however, who raised a passionate voice against the demise of the duty to retreat: Joseph H. Beale, Jr., of the Harvard Law School. Beale served briefly as the dean of the University of Chicago Law School, but almost all of his long and distinguished career as a professor of law was spent at Harvard.[65] Like Stone—whose opinions he had read—Beale was concerned with the broad, long-term social implications of the abolition of the duty to retreat in favor of standing one's ground. Beale had also read, with disapproval, the "true man" opinion of Ohio and the "American mind" thesis of Indiana. In a state of outrage, Beale presented his views in two articles in 1903. One—in the *Columbia Law Review*—was a sober, systematic discussion of case law in which he controlled his anger and held the statement of his own views to a minimum.[66] The other—in the *Harvard Law Review*—was a blast against the Americanization of the common law of homicide to exclude the duty to retreat.[67] With cold fury Beale denounced standing one's ground as a "brutal doctrine," for his perspective was a humanitarian as well a legal one. First he scored Sir Michael Foster for having distorted the previous authorities, Coke and Hale, to produce his doctrine of no duty to retreat, but the main onslaught was directed against the American judges (in Ohio, Indiana, and elsewhere) who implemented Foster and against their surrender to a social climate in which murder was taken so lightly and even widely approved. The outspoken Beale minced no words when he wrote that "the ethics of the duelist" were enshrined in the courts of the West and South where judges

24

found it "abhorrent" to "require one who is assailed to seek dishonor in flight." Instead, Beale applauded the pronouncement of Judge William S. Thorington, an Alabama colleague of Stone, who wrote in an 1891 case that the law of self-defense based on the duty to retreat provided no "balm or protection" for "wounded pride or honor in declining combat, or sense of shame in being denounced as cowardly"; "such thoughts" of wounded pride or honor "are trash," fumed Thorington, "as compared with the inestimable right to live.[68]

In regard to the conflict in the law between the duty to retreat and standing one's ground, Beale himself found that "there should be no theoretical doubt. No killing can be justified, upon any ground" unless absolutely necessary to gain a result permitted by the law. Focusing on the crucial issue, the humanitarian Beale was firm in his insistence that "it is not necessary to kill in self-defense when the assailed can"—"distasteful" as flight might be—"defend himself by the peaceful method" of "withdrawing to a place of safety." "The problem," said Beale, "is the same now as it was three centuries ago in England": the superior claim of human life versus a spurious concept of honor. Yet Beale was well aware that the violent conditions of America exerted powerful social pressure against self-defense through retreat or flight: "It is, of course, true that to retreat from an assailant with a revolver in his hand is dangerous, and one whose revolver is in his hip pocket is not to be despised." Unfortunately, this bred a "hip-pocket ethics" in which questions of cowardice and honor supplanted reverence for life. Beale correctly sensed that he spoke for a minority when he wrote "it is undoubtedly distasteful to retreat, but it is ten times more distasteful to kill." Beale conceded that "a really honorable man" would "perhaps always regret the apparent cowardice of a retreat," but in "the case of a killing to avoid a stain on one's honor," he would "regret ten times more, after the excitement of the contest was past, the thought that he had the blood of a fellow-being on his hands."[69]

In writing of "hip-pocket ethics" Joseph H. Beale was thinking especially of the Southwest, and it was in Texas—of all American states—where the no-duty-to-retreat doctrine of standing one's ground became so deeply entrenched as to be referred to by legal scholars generically as the "Texas rule." Eventually the United States Supreme Court would speak approvingly of the Texas rule. In striking contrast to the unbending attitude of George Washington Stone and his rigorous application of the duty to retreat in his courtroom crusade against homicide in Alabama was the permissive legal attitude represented by the extremely violent state of Texas, a state with an explosive mixture of deep-Southern and frontier-Western characteristics.[70] In Texas the Americanization of the common law of homicide reached its apogee. More than any other state, Texas altered the old English common-law tradition of the duty to retreat.

Comprising a web of statutes, penal codes, and state supreme court decisions, the Texas system changed little after the adoption of the first penal code in 1856. As the foreword to a recent version of the penal code of Texas candidly admitted, the code "retains too much of the frontier in its treatment of firearms [and] still permits too much force on too many occasions."[71] Thus the Texas penal code, with remarkable continuity since antebellum times, provided "private citizens with wide discretionary powers to kill their fellow citizens legally and with impunity."[72] Far from being restricted, the rights of killers were explicitly favored. A comparative study found that the Texas penal code significantly widened the common-law doctrine of justifiable homicide.[73] Nor was the permissive penal code the end of the expansive trend in Texas law, for the study also noted that the interpretations of the Texas supreme court further liberalized what the already tolerant penal code allowed.[74]

True to pattern, the duty-to-retreat doctrine fared badly in the common law of the Lone Star state. In his 1885 opinion in *Bell v. State*,[75] Judge Samuel A. Willson of the highest court of Texas forthrightly acknowledged that, although the old tradition of "the common law required the assailed party to 'retreat to the wall,' " the Texas penal code's abolition of the duty to retreat was "a statutory innovation upon the common law. . . ."[76] The facts of the *Bell* case reveal in human terms the impact of this Texas innovation in the law of self-defense. Shortly after midnight in Waco, Texas, on March 28, 1883, Bill Bell, driver of a horse-drawn cab, and his drunken passenger, A. T. Moreland, entered into a dispute over the scanty sum of twenty-five cents—Moreland's fare. Moreland was both the larger man and the aggressor in the quarrel, but he had the misfortune to insult the honor of the smaller man, Bell. The altercation turned physical when Moreland attacked Bell with his fists. In defending himself with a knife, Bell fatally wounded Moreland.[77] The trial court convicted Bell of second-degree murder, but this verdict was reversed upon appeal to the state's highest court. Speaking for that court, Judge Willson held that the lower court had erred by failing to instruct the jury that, according to Texas law, Bell had no duty to retreat before killing in self-defense. Thus the court held that Bell's act was a "justifiable homicide."[78] In one of the diminishing number of duty-to-retreat states, such as Alabama, Bell's conviction for murder would not have been reversed.

Sociologist Henry P. Lundsgaarde has revealed that the duty-to-retreat issue is directly relevant to the high incidence of homicide in recent Texas history. In a searching study of 268 Houston homicides, Lundsgaarde noted that the absence of a retreat provision in Texas law added significantly to the carnage in the Space City, since in case after case "both killers and victims could easily have de-escalated the seriousness of the situation by retreat."[79] Reflecting the tolerant Texas legal attitude to taking life in defense of self, probably no state exceeded Texas in allowing a person to kill in defense of property, including a possession of "slight value" that "could ordinarily be given up momentarily with only little, if any, loss of face."[80] This is in stark contrast to the attitude in late nineteenth-century Alabama, where the supreme court held that it "would be shocking to . . . have it proclaimed . . . that one may, in the broad daylight, commit a willful homicide in order to prevent the larceny of an ear of corn."[81] With so many legal provisions for justifiable homicide in Texas, Lundsgaarde found that a majority of the 268 killers he studied qualified for consideration by the courts as persons who had justifiably committed homicide. Consequently, although 90 percent of the 1969 Houston killers were apprehended, less than half of them suffered any penalty at law.[82] Both Lundsgaarde and legal scholar G. W. Stumberg found an implicit system of legalized violent self-redress: so permissive were the Texas laws "pertaining to justifiable homicide," wrote Lundsgaarde, that the need "for police, judges, juries, and any form of third party authority [is practically eliminated] as long as one can convincingly establish that the killing was a response to a threat against person or property."[83]

Carried to its extreme in Texas, the Americanization of the common law of homicidal self-defense ultimately gained the blessing of the United States Supreme Court, which in effect adopted the "Texas rule" of no duty to retreat in the 1921 case of *Brown v. United States*.[84] Before this resolution of the issue of the duty to retreat in federal court case law, however, the Supreme Court waffled on the matter. Prior to 1895 this highest of all American courts had not ruled on duty to retreat, but in that year a case from the violence-prone Indian Territory came before it. Now eastern Oklahoma, the Indian Territory had been established by the federal government to include the lands of the Cherokees, Chickasaws, Choctaws, Creeks, and Seminoles. By the late nineteenth century, the Indian Territory, although still the bailiwick of these "Five Civilized Tribes," had a large contingent of white settlers and some blacks, and the case of *Beard v. United States* involved a homicide among whites.[85] While the majority of the Indian, white, and black residents of the Indian Territory were law abiding, there was in their midst a large unruly element including fugitives from the law in the states.[86] The turbulent Indian Territory was in the jurisdiction of the federal district judge for western Arkansas, whose seat was in Fort Smith, a town in Arkansas just over the line from the Indian Territory. The powerful judge in question was Isaac C. Parker, whose frequent imposition of the death penalty on Indian-Territory miscreants earned him the feared sobriquet of "the hanging judge."[87] Parker resembled George Washington Stone in his hatred of homicide.

The *Beard* case grew out of a typical Indian Territory—indeed, typical American—episode: a dispute over a cow and a calf resulted in the killing of Will Jones by one Babe Beard. It may have been this case that inspired Joseph H. Beale's term "hip-pocket ethics," for it was fear of a revolver in Will Jones's hip pocket that caused Beard to stand his ground and fatally crush Jones's skull with the stock of his own shotgun. Found guilty of manslaughter, Beard appealed all the way to the top of the American judicial pyramid where, for his colleagues on the Supreme Court, Justice John M. Harlan—best known now for his ringing dissent in *Plessy v. Ferguson,* the 1896 case supporting the school segregation of blacks and whites—upheld Beard's appeal.[88] Realizing the importance of the issues involved, Harlan wrote a lengthy opinion in which he closely analyzed the judge's instructions to the jury in Beard's trial. A major factor in Harlan's opinion nullifying Beard's conviction was the judge's instruction to the jury that Beard had had a duty to retreat. Harlan could find no justification for the instruction. He cited Foster, East, Bishop, and Wharton and approvingly quoted the "true man" passage in the *Erwin* case to support his contention that there was, contrary to the trial judge and the old English common law, no duty to retreat. Harlan prefaced his list of the states that had abandoned the duty to retreat with a long quotation from the "American mind" section of *Runyan v. State.*[89] In effect, Harlan and his Supreme Court colleagues held that their mind and the "American mind" were as one in rejecting the duty to retreat.

The imprimatur of Harlan and the Supreme Court should have been the crowning glory in the American reign of the legal rule in behalf of standing one's ground, but a year later the matter was cast in doubt by the decision of the Supreme Court in *Allen v. United States,* another case of homicide in the Indian Territory being heard on appeal.[90] To Joseph H. Beale, Justice Henry Billings Brown's opinion in the *Allen* case seemed to revert to the old English endorsement of the duty to retreat.[91] It was partly to resolve what was to Beale, and no doubt to others, an apparent discrepancy between the Supreme Court's positions in the *Beard* and *Allen* cases that led Justice Oliver Wendell Holmes to write such a strong and colorful opinion twenty-five years later in the case of *Brown v. United States*.[92]

Appropriately enough, the *Brown* case originated in Texas. Since a 1917 killing in the town of Beeville took place on federal property, the resulting trial was held in the federal district court rather than in a state or local court. The killer, Robert B. Brown, was convicted of second-degree murder. He appealed unsuccessfully to the federal circuit court.[93] Thus rebuffed, he appealed to the United States Supreme Court, which agreed to hear the case and rendered its decision in 1921. The issue was whether Brown had been under a duty to retreat before killing in self-defense. The lower courts held that Brown was under such an obligation and, failing to meet it, was guilty of murder. Speaking for a seven to two majority of the Supreme Court, Justice Oliver Wendell Holmes took a contrary view.

The greatest legal philosopher ever to serve on the Supreme Court, Oliver Wendell Holmes also had a gift for words that "pierced the mind."[94] Best known for his enduring judicial opinions upholding civil liberties, Holmes could hardly have been more different in background than William E. Niblack, but both were united by their belief in no duty to retreat. Niblack, a Democrat, was a product of the grass roots of pioneer America, out of which grew his opposition to the duty to retreat. With only a smattering of collegiate education, Niblack learned his law in the office of a frontier attorney in southern Indiana. Holmes, a Republican, was, on the other hand, an elite Easterner separated by many generations from the frontier. His father, the senior Oliver Wendell Holmes, was a distinguished physician and one of the nation's leading authors. On both sides of his family, the son, Oliver Wendell Holmes, Jr.,[†] came from the Brahmin aristocracy

---

[†]In later years Holmes dropped the "junior" from his name, as will be the practice here.

of Boston. Like many of his ancestors and his father, Holmes was a graduate of Harvard, where he also obtained his law degree.

From his youth the temperament of Justice Oliver Wendell Holmes inclined him away from a doctrine favoring retreat when life and honor were at stake, and this tendency was deepened by his experience as a Civil War soldier. Holmes went straight from his role as class poet of the Harvard graduating class of 1861 to a three-year term in the Twentieth Massachusetts Volunteer Infantry Regiment.[95] All authorities agree that Holmes's battle-scarred wartime career was the key formative phase in the life of the future Supreme-Court justice.[96] As a junior officer Holmes fought in four major campaigns and in at least ten battles, of which five—Antietam, Chancellorsville, the Wilderness, Spotsylvania Court House, and Cold Harbor—were among the greatest in the entire war. Seriously wounded three times and nearly killed more than once, Holmes was fortunate to get through his three-year term of duty with his life. Many of his closest comrades did not.[97]

Strongly motivated by the ideals of courage and honor, Holmes truly earned the reputation of being an uncommonly brave and gallant young officer—a reputation in which he took great pride.[98] Even as a justice of the Supreme Court many decades later, Holmes's thoughts were never far from the battles of his youth.[99] His searing wartime experiences had, as he said, touched his heart with fire. There was in him always "the nerve, never far from the surface, of the old soldier."[100] Within the month that he wrote the no-duty-to-retreat opinion in *Brown v. United States*, Holmes, as on many occasions, took a friend to a site not far from Washington that was scene of one of his many wartime exploits[101] and the subject of his one of his favorite military reminiscences.[102] Philosophically, spiritually, and emotionally, Holmes was a product of the Civil War, and like so much of his intellectual life, his opinion in *Brown v. United States* was strongly influenced by his Civil War ordeal.

Oliver Wendell Holmes was a major contributor to the growth of the American mind—a national mentality characterized by, among other strands, pragmatism and utilitarianism.[103] Aside from the wit, wisdom, and philosophy of his judicial opinions and his role in the development of the doctrine of legal realism, Holmes's greatest intellectual contribution was his classic study, *The Common Law* (1881), whose keynote declaration was that "the life of the law has not been logic: it has been experience."[104] Meanwhile, Holmes practiced law and taught it briefly at Harvard, served as associate and chief justice of the Massachusetts supreme court, and in 1902 was appointed to the United States Supreme Court by his fellow aristocrat, Theodore Roosevelt, with whom he shared many beliefs about life and war.

As the author of a brilliant and influential work on the common law, it was fitting that Holmes crafted the Supreme Court's doctrine in a crucial case on the common law of homicide and self-defense: *Brown v. United States.* In private correspondence with a close friend, the eminent English political scientist Harold J. Laski, Holmes told how he prepared himself to write his opinion in the *Brown* case and what attitudes and thought went into the decision, which was read to the litigants and the public in the presence of his Supreme Court colleagues on May 16, 1921.[105] To Laski he wrote of his pride in the opinion and how he approached the case as one focusing "on the business of retreating to the wall when defending one's life."[106] It was an issue for which, going back to his Civil War battles, Holmes was emotionally as well as philosophically primed, but he dutifully consulted legal authorities and prior cases as he bent to the task of writing his court's opinion in a case he found to be interesting as well as significant. One of the authorities he read was Joseph H. Beale. Holmes wrote to Laski of his respect for Beale's 1903 article in the *Harvard Law Review* strongly favoring the duty to retreat,[107] but in his opinion Holmes forthrightly rejected the view so ardently espoused by Beale.

Holmes's opinion in *Brown v. United States* was typically incisive and to the point. First he reviewed the facts of the case. There had long been bad blood between Robert B. Brown and his victim, James P. Hermes. Twice before, Hermes had attacked

Brown with a knife, and Hermes had recently made threats—passed on to Brown—that "the next time, one of them would go off in a black box." On the fatal day, May 7, 1917, both men were at work on a U.S. post-office construction project. Brown was supervising the excavation of the building site. Because of Hermes's threats Brown brought a pistol to work that day and placed it on his coat about twenty or twenty-five feet from where he was in charge of the work. Hermes came up to him, and the two had angry words over whether a certain patch of earth should be moved. Brown, the superintendent, said it should not, whereupon Hermes advanced on him with a knife. Brown made for his coat, grabbed the pistol, and, standing his ground as Hermes struck at him with the knife, fired four shots at his opponent and killed him.[108]

With his summation of the facts of the case completed, Holmes noted that the judge in the district court trial had instructed the jury that "the party assaulted is always under the obligation to retreat, so long as retreat is open to him, provided he can do so without subjecting himself to the danger of death or great bodily harm." (Although Holmes did not specifically say so, this would have meant Brown's flight from the scene.) Accordingly, continued Holmes, the trial judge refused to instruct the jury "that if the defendant [Brown] had reasonable grounds of apprehension that he was in danger of losing his life or of suffering serious bodily harm from Hermes he was not bound to retreat"—that is, not bound to flee. "So," concluded Holmes, "the question is brought out with sufficient clearness whether the formula laid down" in the district court—the duty to retreat, amounting in this case to a responsibility to run from the scene—"and often repeated by the ancient law is adequate to the protection of the defendant's rights."[109]

The issue clearly joined, Holmes quickly and decisively resolved the legal question in favor of Brown, who had killed to save his life against the knife-wielding Hermes.[110] Holmes's approach to the case echoed the theme of his book on the common law: that the law is a living, growing organism, to be molded by

33

the needs of a changing society.[111] Holmes now applied this principle in his critique of the duty to retreat: "Concrete cases or illustrations stated in the early [English] law in conditions very different from the present, like the reference to retreat in Coke, Third Inst. 55, and elsewhere have a tendency to ossify into specific rules without much regard for reason."[112] Rejecting such obsolescence, Holmes maintained that "rationally the failure to retreat is" only one "circumstance to be considered with all the others in order to determine whether the defendant [Brown] went farther than he was justified in doing; not a categorical proof of guilt. The law has grown, and even if historical mistakes have contributed to its growth it has tended in the direction of rules consistent with human nature. Many respectable writers"—and here Holmes probably had in mind certain authorities cited by Brown's attorneys: Foster, East, Wharton, McIlvaine in *Erwin v. State,* and Niblack in *Runyan v. State*[113]—"agree that if a man reasonably believes that he is in immediate danger of death or grievous bodily harm from his assailant he may stand his ground and that if he kills him he has not exceeded the bounds of lawful self-defense."[114] To this learning on the subject, Holmes added his own memorable thrust to the heart of the matter: "*Detached reflection cannot be demanded in the presence of an uplifted knife.*" "Therefore in this Court, at least," Holmes went on, "it is not a condition of immunity that one in that situation should pause to consider whether a reasonable man might not think it possible to fly with safety or to disable his assailant rather than to kill him."[115] Well aware that the killing took place in the Lone Star State, Holmes approvingly added that "the law of Texas very strongly adopts these views."[116]

In a letter to Laski on May 12, 1921, Holmes revealed even more of his thought on the *Brown* case, remarking that "I don't say all I think in the opinion." His full view of the matter was even more emotional and hostile to the notion of retreat than his opinion indicated. Thus Holmes—in notable and conscious contrast to Beale—wrote favorably of Texas, in which "it is well settled" that "a man is not born to run away." More generally, Holmes informed his distinguished correspondent that on the subject of retreat the law "must consider human nature and make some allowances for the fighting instinct at critical moments."[117]

Holmes's reference to "the fighting instinct at critical moments" stemmed from his experience in the Civil War, in which his own fighting instinct had been tested in many, many moments critical to his survival. As a Civil War soldier Holmes abhorred retreat. He was extremely proud that his regiment—with one of the half-dozen highest casualty rates in the Union army—"never ran": that is, never broke and ran in the crisis of battle as many other regiments did.[118] Holmes was also proud of being "out in front" of the men of his company, encouraging them on the attack.[119] On one especially perilous occasion (discussed below) in which he served as a courier, Holmes took pride that he was able "to get the order through & not knock under or turn back."[120]

In reading the case of *Brown v. United States,* one readily senses Holmes's sympathy for Robert B. Brown.[121] The confrontation between Brown and James P. Hermes with the former killing in self-defense had much in common with a remarkable experience of Holmes's own during the Civil War. On May 29, 1864, he was astride his horse bearing an important dispatch across the eastern Virginia countryside. Suddenly Holmes and a few others were confronted and heavily outnumbered by a score of Confederate soldiers who blocked the road. Gunfire erupted, and Holmes was ordered to surrender, but, as he tersely recounted, his would-be captor "hadn't quite got his carbine unslung & I put my pistol to his breast and pulled [the] trigger" but "missed fire." Holmes and two of his men got through as Holmes dodged rebel gunfire by "lying along side of [my] horse Comanche fashion."[122] Holmes had tried to kill in a wartime case of man-to-man combat and would have done so had not his weapon misfired: he meant to slay another in self-defense just as Brown did kill Hermes.

Holmes's Civil War fight of May 29, 1864, was one of the peak emotional events of his life. Twenty years later he drew on it in a Memorial Day address to veterans of the Grand Army of the Republic.[123] There are striking analogies between the passages of battle remembrance in Holmes's 1884 oration and the ordeal of Brown upon which, much later, Holmes passed judgment for the Supreme Court. For himself and his audience of fellow soldiers, Holmes in 1884 recalled the heat of battle—the combat situation in which one's "life or freedom" (like Brown's) while "nearly surrounded by the enemy" (much like Brown as Hermes came at him with a knife) depended upon "swift and cunning" thought (not "detached reflection"): "Shall I stand the best chance if I try the pistol or the sabre on that man who means to stop me? Will he get his carbine free before I reach him, or can I kill him first?"[124] In a like situation, Brown, his life in jeopardy, knew similar questions: Could he get to his pistol in time, and could he use it to save himself from Hermes who had threatened to put him in "a black box"? Brown was obliged to react with "swift and cunning" thought (as Holmes had in a military fight) with no time for the "detached reflection" demanded, as Holmes saw it, by the legal duty to retreat of which Holmes, for the Supreme Court, absolved him.

For Justice Oliver Wendell Holmes the idea of no duty to retreat was far more than a principle of federal and state common law—important as that was. Transcending the legal maxim, it was a deeply felt philosophy of behavior with the authority of a moral value—one that, as Niblack, Holmes, and many others agreed, grew out of American conditions and lodged in the American mind. Although Holmes's apothegm, "detached reflection cannot be demanded in the presence of an uplifted knife," is sometimes quoted, Holmes scholars have generally ignored the case of *Brown v. United States*. Holmes's opinion in *Brown v. United States* strongly upholds the bellicose doctrine of no duty to retreat—a bellicosity that apparently contradicts the values of civility and tolerance seen as the hallmarks of Holmes's classic opinions upholding the widely admired liberal doctrine of civil liberties. Of course, to Holmes there was no contradiction between his opinion in *Brown v. United States* and his supposedly more enlightened opinions in the famous civil liberties cases, since to Holmes—as to so many other Americans—the right to stand one's ground and kill in self-defense was as great a civil liberty as, for example, freedom of speech. Middle—and late— twentieth-century devotees of civil liberties (especially among the liberal cognoscenti) have tended to impute their own idealistic liberal political ideology to Holmes, in whom, however, it did not exist. Holmes was a strong civil libertarian but, as Sheldon M. Novick shows in his biography, *Honorable Justice,* Holmes was not a liberal in the middle—and late—twentieth-century political meaning of the term.

No one more directly stated the social philosophy of standing one's ground than President Dwight D. Eisenhower in a nationally televised speech of 1953. President Eisenhower, the leader of the "Free World" in a time of cold war and the commander of the victorious Allies in western Europe during World War II, expressed the ethos of no duty to retreat when he informed his nationwide audience that as a boy in Abilene, Kansas, he had been reared to "prize" the code of Abilene and "our Marshal," the renowned gunfighter Wild Bill Hickok. The President still believed in that code, which, he proudly declared, was "meet anyone face to face with whom you disagree"; "if you met him face to face and took the same risk he did, you could get away with almost anything as long as the bullet was in the front."[125]

2

The Gunfighter: The Reality Behind the Myth

"Will you give me even chances?"
∧ Western gunfighter to his opponent (1878).*

President Eisenhower is no isolated example, for Americans have always been fascinated by fiction and film purveying the image of Western gunfighters like Wild Bill Hickok. (In an aside to his audience in the 1953 speech, Ike chided those who might have been unfamiliar with Wild Bill: "If you don't know about him, read your Westerns more.")[1] Yet historians and critics have tended to denigrate the significance of Western gunfighters, contending that there were relatively few of them and that they were unimportant in real historical terms.[2] This chapter departs from the common wisdom of scholars and holds instead that there were a great many gunfighters—not just a few famous ones like Hickok—and that the noted (as well as other) gunfighters were important in objective terms, not merely for their powerful impact on the American imagination.

There were two types of Western gunfighters: grassroots gunfighters and glorified gunfighters.[3] The glorified gunfighters were those who became regionally and nationally famous: Wild Bill Hickok, Wyatt Earp, John Wesley Hardin, Billy the Kid, and

39

many others.⁴ It is the glorified gunfighters around whom the mythology of gunfighting centers, for these are the legendary figures of the subject.⁵ Despite the exaggerations of myth and legend, the glorified gunfighters were not phonies. They were historically significant figures. In general they were violent protagonists in the great social, economic, and cultural conflicts that rocked the West in the late nineteenth century. Such conflicts were often highly politicized, and the glorified gunfighters were frequently strongly partisan as either Republicans or Democrats. Many of them were also key players in a social drama in which conservative forces consolidated authority in the West in the interest of property, order, and law. Both Wild Bill Hickok and Wyatt Earp, as well as many others, were glorified gunfighters who represented this trend of the conservative, consolidating authority of capital—a trend general in late nineteenth-century America, not just the West. The historical process of myth building has, however, converted the images of such glorified gunfighters from the reality of men who were politically partisan and ideologically conservative to the apolitical, nonideological gunfighting heroes of myth and romance.

The grassroots gunfighters of the West were kith and kin to the glorified ones, and they were also socially significant but in a different way. I refer to them as "grassroots gunfighters" because their exploits became little known beyond their own localities; they lived and made their reputations only at the grass roots. Also, the term "grassroots gunfighters" suggests one of the most important facts about Western gunfighting: its pervasiveness. There were thousands of gunfighters and thousands of gunfights. The social institution of gunfighting was not at all restricted to the famous gunfighters but was all too often a feature of daily life in the West. Both the grassroots and glorified gunfighters adhered to the Code of the West:⁶ a cluster of social values that mentally programmed typical Westerners to use their guns, often in allegiance to the ideal of no duty to retreat. Grassroots gunfighters were the most numerous examples of the

Western proclivity to violence. As such they were exemplars of the ubiquitous gun culture of the West.[7]

While grassroots gunfighters frequently shot their victims in the course of narrow personal disputes in isolated local situations, they were also often mobilized at the grass roots to fight on the front lines of the great social, economic, and cultural conflicts of the West. Not famous themselves, grassroots gunfighters were much enrolled as rank-and-file participants (often deadly ones, as in the case of the bitter Mussel Slough conflict in California[†]) in the famed wars of the truly wild West—conflicts in which the stakes of power and property were huge.[8] These grassroots gunfighters were, then, relatively anonymous participants in heralded conflicts whose gunshooting laurels were usually monopolized by the glorified gunfighters. Whatever the division of fame, both the glorified and the grassroots gunfighters were crucial figures, because their gunplay was so often the decisive factor in resolving deeply conflicted situations.

Although not the entirety of the matter, a political and ideological interpretation is necessary before one can penetrate the fog of mythology in order to understand, truly, both the glorified and grassroots gunfighters of the West. Certain factors were basic to the politics and ideology of a multitude of Western gunfighters—factors that will be illustrated in this chapter and the next one:

- America was a strongly politicized nation after 1860, and Western gunfighters were no exception to the pattern in which most men were loyal Democrats or loyal Republicans.[9]
- The Civil War was of enormous importance. Numerous adult Western white males of the 1860s–1890s had lived through the Civil War, and many had fought for the North or South. Many gunfighters—including those who, like Wyatt Earp and John Wesley Hardin, had been too young to fight in the war—strongly identified with either the Union or the Confederacy.[10]

†On the Mussel Slough conflict, see Chapter 3.

41

- The gunfighters, like most Westerners, were immigrants to the region, usually from the North or the South. Their origins were proudly maintained in personal identities as Northerner or Southerner, which in turn coincided or conveged with and reinforced Civil War allegiances.

- Membership in political parties often paralleled and interacted with regional origins and Civil War loyalties. Westerners, including the gunfighters, who haled from the North and were Unionminded were often Democrats, as was a leading Tombstone deputy, William M. Breakenridge,[11] but a more common pattern was for Northerners and Unionists to be Republicans and for Southerners and ex– or pro-Confederates to be Democrats.

- Along with the cultural proclivities (Northern or Southern) and political preferences (Unionist or Confederate; Republican or Democratic) of Western gunfighters were ideological predispositions to be either conservative or dissident. Most Republican gunfighters reflected the conservative stance of their political party. Gunfighters of dissident persuasion tended to be Democrats, as was the hotly partisan John Wesley Hardin. Yet not a few of the Democratic gunfighters, like their Republican counterparts, aligned themselves with or served conservative men of power, as did Sheriff Pat Garrett, the slayer of Billy the Kid. Most dissident Democratic gunfighters of Southern origin or sympathy were, however, strongly conservative in the realm of racial relations—a notable example being John Wesley Hardin, who relished his many killings of African-Americans.[12]

Packing the most weight in the power struggles of the highly conflicted West of the middle and late nineteenth century were those gunfighters who were ideologically conservative, as were Wild Bill Hickok and Wyatt Earp, whose careers will be explored in this chapter, and Walter J. Crow, whose role will be emphasized in the next. Shorn of their ideological and political identities by the process of myth making, Hickok and Earp became part of the legend of the West while Crow, because of the nature of the conflict in which he was a gunfighting champion of one side, did not.

Typical of the politically conservative gunfighters was an enthusiastic Republican of Arizona, Tom Graham, who in reaction to the presidential election of 1888 condemned the Democratic party as the representative of the lazy and improvident. Declaring "I hate the sight of a Democrat" and asserting that he was a Republican for "1000 different reasons," he did, however, focus on his view that the GOP was the conservative, entrepreneurially oriented political party. Famed in Arizona of the 1880s for his deadly role in a bloody feud, this highly partisan gunfighter hotly, if ungrammatically, objected that "the Democrats never done anything only sit back in some old cabin with sunflowers growing all round the house." Graham further derided the Democratic party as one of "corn bread" and "cheap living" while applauding his own Republican party as that of "work" and the much more preferable (to Graham) "wheat bread." "The Democrats," Graham went on, "never have anything doing or going on in the country"—they "just wait on the cloud to roll by and it never rolls." Concluded this gunfighting Arizona Republican, "We want business in the country" not Democratic "talk."[13]

If gunfighters were partisan and ideological, what were the issues that drew on their politics and ideology and energized their gunplay? The answer lies, of course, in the variety of conflict and violence in the West that was so enormous in the nineteenth century. Within this immense diversity of violence one major conflict stands out. At its core was the conservative consolidating authority of capital—the urban, industrial, often corporate forces that were, in Alan Trachtenberg's conception, "incorporating" America during the late nineteenth century.[14] (In the West this process of incorporation extended well into the twentieth century.) Yet there were opposing factions and individuals who fought the incorporating trend politically and sometimes violently. The violent resistance to incorporation has recently been traced by scholars: by David Thelen, who has followed the "paths of resistance" in industrializing and urbanizing Missouri in the post–Civil War period;[15] by Altina Waller, who has depicted insurgent feudists of West Virginia and Kentucky following their own violent pathways of resistance to the forces of incorporation;[16] and by Robert McMath, who has similarly found the violently resisting small ranchers and farmers cutting the fences of the would-be incorpo-rators of the central Texas countryside in "the age of capitalist transformation."[17]

In the West the incorporation trend resulted in what should at last be recognized as a civil war across the entire expanse of the West—one fought in many places and on many fronts in almost all the Western territories and states from the 1860s and beyond 1900 into the 1910s. In the broadest terms, this Western Civil War of Incorporation pitted insurgent Indians against the squeeze play of political pressure and military force that concentrated them in reservations stippling the great West. It also bred cultural and economic factors that impinged on the traditional lifeways and livelihoods of the Hispanos of the Southwest, who fought back, for example, in northern New Mexico with resisting *gorras blancas* and in south Texas with the *bandidos*.[18] In the mines, mills, and logging camps on the "wageworkers' frontier" of the West, workers resisted corporate industrialists with strikes that fre-quently ended in violence between labor unionists and the para-military and military forces who joined in an alliance of capitalism and government.[19]

As farmers and ranchers moved into the prairies, plains, and mountain country of the West, dramatic local conflicts often brought grassroots and glorified gunfighters to the fore in such rabid vendettas as those embodied in the Johnson County War in Wyoming, the Cochise County War in Arizona, and the Mussel Slough conflict in California.[20] In these and many other strug-gles in the Western Civil War of Incorporation, gunfighters—both grassroots and glorified—played crucial roles. On one side were the conservative *incorporation gunfighters* whose ranks in-cluded glorified gunfighters such as Wild Bill Hickok of Kansas, Wyatt Earp of Arizona, and Frank Canton of Wyoming and grassroots gunfighters such as Walter J. Crow of California.[21] On the other side were the dissident *resister gunfighters,* some of whom were themselves mythologized as the "social bandits" of the West[22]—and one of whom Robert M. Utley has treated in his definitvely demythologizing study of Billy the Kid.[23] It is these

conceptual categories of *incorporation gunfighters* and *resister gunfighters* and not the mythical categories of hero and villain that
are the keys to unlocking the reality behind the myth of the
American as gunfighter.

Also crucial to the incorporation of the American West was the
region's emerging, solidifying top-to-bottom social structure.
This social structure was hierarchically organized and, as elsewhere in the United States, featured a relatively narrow elite
atop a widely varied middle class of business and professional
men, farmers, ranchers, and skilled craftsmen. Below the middle
class was a largely amorphous base of the unskilled and the poor.
Diffused through this hierarchical but loose social structure were
many who resisted the authority of the law and the claims of the
aggressive men of capital. This large, unruly element of the
alienated was at times thrown into alliance with true outlaws,
forming a coalition that resisted those who both dominated and
sought to increase the scope of property-oriented law and authority.[24] The recalcitrant ones often displayed a tenacious allegiance to what were essentially highly traditional, even premod-
ern, social values: law and order *per se* were much less prized
than personal and family relationships.

Whether outlawed or not, those who resisted the dominant
trend of society were often, in line with their traditional values,
strongly prone to combat and violence. They were not offended
by disorder, for in the accepted reality of their lives tumult was as
likely as not to be the norm and was easily squared with their
social values, which the more cosmopolitan citizenry in the growing towns and cities saw as antiquated and harmful. Comfortable
with turbulence, the recalcitrant had little interest in or sympathy for the incorporating process stressing the aggregation of
wealth, the consolidation of capital, and the centralizing of authority at the local, the state (or the territory), and the national
levels. Ambitious men of property, however, saw necessity in the
task of suppressing—especially in the local realm—those who
resisted and exerted a frustrating inertia against what were
viewed as the rightful forces of economic and cultural progress:

the modernizing of society and the incorporation of power and authority. In consequence, the incorrigible disorder and violence of the outlawed and the alienated was met with the ultimately successful violence of vigilantes[25] and local officers of the law. Thus in the realm of law enforcement, two prototypical gunfighting paragons—Wild Bill Hickok and Wyatt Earp—were, contrary to the mythology that has usually made invisible the true reality of their lives and social roles, in the van of the Western Civil War of Incorporation that in time saw the rout of the outlaw and the disorderly by the materially ambitious incorporators of authority and modernizers of society.

The mythology of the West and its gunfighting is entangled with the real lives of the glorified and grassroots gunfighters and the exemplary careers of Hickok and Earp as incorporation gunfighters. In American intellectual history the strangling vines of myth have all but choked away recognition of the reality of the social significance of the American as gunfighter. The seductions of entertainment and escape, heightened by the voracious popular appetite for myth and legend, have left the reality of the subject of Western gunfighters buried beneath a mass of "fakelore." However, for all of its enormous distortions, the culturally powerful myth of the gunfighter by its very existence suggests that there was indeed a highly significant reality behind the myth. Wild Bill Hickok and Wyatt Earp, as well as their thousands of colleagues among the glorified and the grassroots gunfighters, illustrate both the distortions of myth and the home truths of the reality of the American as gunfighter. The myth of the gunfighter is, then, the highly selective, almost abstractly stylized representation of an important reality. At the core of both the myth and reality of the American as gunfighter is the theme of no duty to retreat as an energizer of violent behavior.

The archetypal expression of the myth of the gunfighter was provided by Owen Wister in his immensely popular and highly influential novel of 1902, *The Virginian*.[26] In one respect, *The Virginian* was a literary episode in the Western Civil War of Incorporation. As a wealthy Harvard graduate, Owen Wister was an ultraconservative member of America's elite of the elite: its Northeastern aristocracy into which Wister was born and among whom he hobnobbed with close friends Oliver Wendell Holmes (whose United States Supreme Court decision nineteen years after the publication of *The Virginian* federally legitimated the no-duty-to-retreat ethos of the hero in Wister's novel) and President Theodore Roosevelt, the man to whom Wister dedicated *The Virginian* (a dedication greatly appreciated by Roosevelt, who liked the novel very much).[27] A key episode in the Western Civil War of Incorporation occurred in Wister's favorite Western state, Wyoming. In that state the forces of incorporation were led by a faction of arrogant, range-hungry Eastern and British aristocrats who headed the Wyoming cattle industry and who in 1892 sponsored a vigilante campaign against resisting rustlers, cowboys, and small-townsmen, most of whom were Democrats or Populists and who had a bastion in the central Wyoming county of Johnson. This conflict and its climax in the vigilante campaign became known as the Johnson County War.[28]

Owen Wister was strongly sympathetic to the cattle kings who made Wyoming one of the major battlegrounds in the Western Civil War of Incorporation. Wister, who loved outdoor life in the state and spent much time in it, was personally close to the Wyoming cattle kings who, backed by four key Republican politicos (the president of the United States, the governor of Wyoming, and its two U.S. senators), employed incorporation gunfighters like Frank Canton in their drive to incorporate Wyoming.[29] In crucial respects *The Virginian* is a fictionalized version of the Johnson County War. The hero, the Virginian, is in effect an incorporation gunfighter—a cowboy protagonist who represents the conservative social values so highly prized by Owen Wister. The villain, Trampas, whom the Virginian slays in the novel's climactic walkdown, is an evil, odious member of the story's faction of bad men. In Wister's novel Trampas and the bad men are modeled on the real-life targets of Wister's good friends among Wyoming's cattle-holding elite.[30]

What enthralled the readers of Wister's *The Virginian* much more than its ideological content, however, was the individual rivalry between hero and villain and the hero's love affair with the heroine—a plot that became the model for almost countless stories, novels, and films comprising the formula "Western": hero meets heroine, villain threatens hero, hero kills villain, hero weds heroine.[31] Thus the climactic episode in *The Virginian* was the walkdown between the hero and the villain—the patterned, mythic face-to-face gunfight of the type to which Dwight Eisenhower referred to in his 1953 speech.† As Wister etched the scene for his avid readership, the sun is setting over a little Wyoming cattle town. With the light still glowing above the mountains to the west, the Virginian—with no thought of retreat—paces down the dusty main street of the frontier settlement. Waiting chastely and anxiously in her upstairs room in the local hotel is the Virginian's affianced sweetheart, a schoolteacher. In the street below, the villain confronts the Virginian, matches him stride for stride, shoots first, misses, and falls dead before the unerring, fatal fire of the Virginian. Next day the Virginian and the schoolteacher marry, and the episode concludes with the triumphant hero and his bride riding into the west for their honeymoon in the mountains.[32]

Owen Wister's fictional walkdown could have been based on a very real walkdown that occurred not long after the end of the Civil War[33] and, more than any other, represents the emergence of the gunfighter tradition in American history. Man-to-man gunfights in the manner of the walkdown may have occurred before the Civil War, but they were too few and too obscure to catch the public fancy or create a tradition. This was partly because a key ingredient in the prototypical walkdown—the repeating revolver—had been too recently perfected (in the late 1830s and in the 1840s)[34] to be used generally in personal disputes. More familiar to antebellum America was the duel—a face-to-face gunfight, to be sure, but one mainly connected with the archaic "gentlemen's code" of the stratified society of the Old

†On Eisenhower's speech, see the conclusion of Chapter 1.

South; a social institution that predated the Western Civil War of Incorporation.[35] As the society of the Old South waned after the Civil War, the Code of the West—with the associated role of the gunfighter and the practice of the walkdown—rose to supplant it in the West of reality and in the popular mind of America.[36]

The particular no-duty-to-retreat walkdown that occurred in the public square of the remote southwest Missouri town of Springfield in July 1865 received national publicity, and in its aftermath the duty to retreat became a legal issue. Whether or not it was actually the first walkdown, the gunfight in Springfield was the effective beginning of the walkdown tradition, for it was the first to receive wide public recognition as such.[37] In this case, the victorious gunfighter was Eisenhower's fondly remembered hero, Wild Bill Hickok.

No stranger to gunplay in 1865 was Wild Bill. Born James Butler Hickok in 1837, he had been reared in a strongly abolitionist family in northern Illinois;[38] his father aided fugitive slaves by operating a stop on the underground railroad.[39] Hickok's deeply rooted Northern background and viewpoint were to have a profound effect on his career as the first famous gunfighter of the West. Hickok received his first pistol when only a boy and soon reveled in target practice.[40] As a schoolboy, he may have imbibed his own version of the Western myth through some of the increasingly popular but spurious biographies and novels focusing on the frontier.[41] In 1855, at the age of eighteen, Hickok headed west to Kansas from which, after a time, he roamed on to New Mexico and back to Nebraska. Often working as a driver of stagecoaches and freight wagons, the young man had various adventures and contacts. As a twenty-year-old in 1857, he befriended a lad of eleven (later to be renowned as Buffalo Bill) who immediately idolized him, and two years later Hickok seems to have met his own idol, Kit Carson.[42]

By 1861 Hickok was a hardy, experienced frontiersman of twenty-four in the employ of the local stage station in Rock Creek, Nebraska, where his blond locks gained him the nickname of "Dutch Bill." At this time, Hickok's career as a gun-

fighter began. His supervisor, the local stagecoach superintendent, Horace Wellman, was drawn into a dispute with David C.
McCanles, a prominent man and bully of Rock Creek. Loyal to
his boss, Hickok was point man on the Wellman side when a
battle erupted with McCanles and his band. When the guns fell
silent, Hickok had slain the local champion, McCanles, and was
also widely but incorrectly credited with the lives of two of
McCanles's henchmen who succumbed in the general melee. At
a subsequent hearing the self-defense plea of Hickok and his
cohorts was accepted.[43] Even in this early year of 1861 there
were war-of-incorporation aspects of Hickok's first gunfight, for
he fought as the hireling of the company that would ultimately
dominate the stagecoach routes of the West, while his victim was
a local man typical of the more parochial interests to be eroded
and tamed by the incorporating trend.

Meanwhile, the Civil War had broken out in nearby Missouri,
and there was no doubt on which side the strongly antislavery,
pro-union Hickok would fight. There followed several years of
service as scout, detective, and spy for the federal armies in Missouri and Arkansas.[44] In a classic work historians Charles and
Mary Beard interpreted the Civil War as, in effect, a war of incorporation: in the Beards' phrase a "second American Revolution"
in which the aggressive incorporating forces of Northern industry and finance overthrew the agrarian South's long-standing
domination of the nation.[45] Early in this period, an impetuous
Hickok saved a bartender from a lynching in Independence, Missouri. To a female admirer of this exploit, "Wild Bill" was the only
proper designation for its protagonist,[46] and so it has been ever
since. As the relentless war bloodied the border country of Missouri and Arkansas, Hickok began to get a reputation to match his
new nickname. Many of the stories were tall tales, but there is little
doubt that, as Union spy and scout, Wild Bill participated in some
hot gunfights.[47]

During the war Hickok crossed the path of Dave Tutt, who, as
scout and guerrilla, was something like a Confederate version of
Wild Bill. Tutt was a scion of a redoubtable family that had been a

principal in a sanguinary feud in the Ozark country of northern Arkansas. Rumor said that Hickok and Tutt had one or two near-fatal encounters during the Civil War.[48] There was bad blood between the two in the first postwar summer as each emerged in Springfield as the leading exemplar of his respective political and wartime faiths. Tutt was Springfield's local Confederate-minded paragon of gunplay, while Hickok had the identical status for those of Union loyalty. To this ideological rivalry was added a simmering resentment between the two over a gambling debt and over the affections of a woman, Susannah Moore.[49] The climax came toward sundown on July 21. Shadows from the massive courthouse and the surrounding elms lengthened over the huge three-acre public square. Hogs seeking relief from the heat wallowed in mud holes. Ox teams slowly dragged wagons in and out of the square. Loungers about the hitching racks and the stores were alert—they had heard tales of threats exchanged by Tutt and Hickok.[50]

What these witnesses to the West's precedent-setting walk-down saw was the following. Having left the Lyon House, a hotel a block away, Wild Bill Hickok entered the square and strode from its southeast corner toward Dave Tutt, who came out of a livery stable and headed straight for his rival. "Don't come any closer, Dave!" was Wild Bill's warning. Heedless, Tutt drew his gun. At about fifty to seventy-five yards, both fired almost at once, although Hickok may have gotten off his shot an instant sooner. As Tutt's bullet whistled overhead, Hickok's surely aimed shot pierced his opponent's heart.[51]

As the prototypical social exemplar of the new American concept of standing one's ground, the Western gunfighter was both defined by Wild Bill Hickok in his besting of Dave Tutt and vindicated by a jury which upheld the notion of no duty to retreat: Arrested and charged with murder, on August 5–6, 1865, Wild Bill was tried on the reduced charge of manslaughter. Hickok's plea of self-defense was resisted by the trial judge, who invoked the duty to retreat against Wild Bill (Hickok certainly had not retreated nor attempted to escape the gunfight): the judge, reported a local newspaper, "instructed the jury to the . . . effect" that Hickok "was not entitled to an acquital [*sic*] on the ground of self-defense unless he was anxious to *avoid the fight*,[†] and used all reasonable means to do so." The jury, however, must have seen Hickok as a "true man"[††] who rightfully stood his ground, for, continued the newpaper, "the jury seems to have thought differently" and in rejecting the doctrine of the duty to retreat found Wild Bill not guilty.[52]

Wild Bill Hickok's triumph over Dave Tutt gained him national fame and made him America's first well-known gunfighter.[53] Later exploits added to his initial notoriety. Like virtually all of the prominent Western gunfighters, Hickok was not a free-lancer but, rather, a protagonist in a situation of social conflict. As such, Wild Bill was the prototypical peace officer who, in behalf of the local captains of commerce, brought an incorporating order to the wild new boom towns of the Great Plains cattle industry. This was Hickok's most historically significant role, but he also earned fame as a scout in the warfare between the U.S. Army and the plains Indians, and in the course of that activity he became known as the "plainsman" *par excellence.*

Wild Bill's spectacular career as an incorporation gunfighter, peace officer, and plainsman coincided chronologically with the equally vivid careers of the renowned gun handlers Jesse and Frank James and the Younger brothers. As bank and train robbers the Jameses and the Youngers were, unlike Hickok, outlaws and resister gunfighters. Hickok had been a Unionist during the Civil War, while the Jameses and Youngers had been Confederate guerrillas. Hickok had been aligned with the Unionist military and paramilitary Republican-party Jayhawkers and Red Legs of Kansas,[54] while the Jameses and Youngers had bitterly fought them.[55] In the post–Civil War era, the Jameses and Youngers were heroes to many of the Democrats and the Confederate-minded who in deed or spirit resisted corporate incorporation in

†Emphasis added.
††See Chapter 1, on the "true man" doctrine.

Missouri,[56] while Wild Bill Hickok was a hero to the Union-minded of the North and those who were much more sympathetic to the national incorporating trend.[57]

From 1866 on, Hickok reestablished himself as a fixture in the Great Plains region. First, he served for three years as a deputy U.S. marshal, actively collaring horse thieves and deserters from the U.S. Army.[58] It was while serving as deputy U.S. marshal that Wild Bill acted as a guide for General William Tecumseh Sherman when the latter visited Kansas in 1866 to inspect the army's theater of operations against the plains Indians.[59] During these years Hickok also from time to time rendered valuable duty as a scout for George A. Custer's Seventh Cavalry Regiment.[60] In his spare time Wild Bill, a Radical Republican in politics, frequented the Leavenworth, Kansas, gambling rooms of another Radical Republican, Colonel Charles R. (Doc) Jennison.[61] As the Civil War commander of the infamous Jayhawkers (Seventh Kansas Volunteer Cavalry regiment) and as a leading Red Leg, Doc Jennison had a bad reputation among all but the ideologically minded like Hickok who gloried in the cause of the triumphant Union.[62] A stream of articles in nationally read magazines and newspapers cemented in the American mind Hickok's well-earned standing as the most expert pistol shot in the West.[63]

Playing a key role in Wild Bill's success as an incorporation gunfighter and peace officer was his gift for self-dramatization and his technique of intimidation. Tall, with long, flowing, blondish hair, a dandy in dress—characteristically accoutered in fancy buckskins and later a Prince Albert coat—James Butler Hickok might have been derided as a fop and a fraud by the hard-bitten, not easily impressed denizens of the plains, but instead he was taken with the utmost seriousness. All knew that his twin ivory-handled Colt revolvers were worn not merely for show but could and would be used with deadly effect in the twinkling of an eye. With a more than full quota of his own vanity, General Custer (for whom Hickok rode as a scout) was almost in awe of Hickok. Wild Bill, Custer said in 1872, "was a Plainsman in every sense of the word. . . . Whether on foot or on horseback, he was one of the most perfect types of physical manhood I ever saw. Of his courage there could be no question," and "his skill in the use of the rifle and pistol was unerring," but he was "entirely free from all bluster and bravado." Yet, continued Custer, "his influence among the frontiersmen was unbounded; his word was law, and many are the personal quarrels and disturbances which he has checked . . . [by his simple declaration] that 'this has gone far enough' . . . if need be followed by the ominous warning that . . . [the disturber of the peace] 'must settle it with me.' "[64]

Custer's description may be read as an epigraph to the climax of Wild Bill Hickok's career as gunfighter: his service as an officer of the law in Hays and Abilene, Kansas, during which he killed four persons. His success in keeping order in Hays in 1869 was purchased with the lives of two culprits who fell before his peerless shooting. Two years later, Abilene—the boyhood home of President Eisenhower[†]—called on Hickok to restore order after its marshal, Tom Smith, had been killed by a homesteader.[65]

Sodbusters were, however, hardly the biggest problem for Wild Bill or for any of those who sought to keep the peace in such turbulent Kansas cow towns as Abilene, Caldwell, Ellsworth, Hays, Newton, Wichita, and Dodge City. Order in such localities hung in the balance between two rival groups who needed each other but whose ultimate objectives placed them in stormy conflict. As the railheads or shipping points linking the cattle ranges of Texas with the stockyards of the Midwest and, eventually, the American consumer's appetite for beef, the Kansas cattle towns were dominated by the their merchants.[66] This mercantile elite wanted the patronage of the drovers and the cowboys of Texas who moved the longhorns up the Chisholm and other trails to the brokers and packing-house purchasers who awaited them in Abilene and all the other railroad towns. After months on the trail northward, the cowboys and their bosses were in need of the supplies the merchants were glad to

†See Chapter 1, and this chapter.

purvey to them for bonanza profits. The cowboys also craved untrammeled entertainment. Hundreds of miles of tiresome as well as dangerous trail driving without the amenities of a single town along the way were finally behind them, and they hit the likes of Abilene with pockets full of pay and an avid desire for whiskey, gambling, and women. With herds left on the outskirts, the custom was for the cowboys to ride into town shouting and firing celebratory shots into the air. Next came hot baths and the purchase of new, clean clothing to replace the ragged garments of the trail. A hearty meal in one of the many obliging restaurants was quickly followed by a tour of the local saloons for drink and gaming. For many, the night of carousing was topped off (or begun) by a visit to one of the local houses of prostitution where love could be bought for money. Generally favored behavior included the wearing of guns, kept handy for high-spirited shooting or worse. This end-of-trail ritual of wild play was what most cowboys looked forward to as they headed toward the urban oases of Kansas. The unrestrained cow-town carousing was kept up by most as long as their money lasted.[67]

The town merchants wanted the profits of the cowboy trade, which could yield a fortune, but not the violence and disorder that was a constant threat from the cowboy way of life in the cattle towns. Thus the cowboys needed the supplies and the comforts offered by the town businessmen, which the latter were eager to supply for as high a price as possible. The cowboys and merchants needed each other, but neither would tolerate the demand of the other: from the merchants a demand for nonviolent behavior, and from the cowboys a demand for pleasure without restraint.[68] To this rivalry of ends and means between the two groups was added a hostility—always latent and often overt—that was in effect a replay of the Civil War animosities so recently aired on the battlefield. In all of this were overtones of the Western Civil War of Incorporation. That is, the merchants, the residents, and the peace officers of the Kansas cow towns were generally Northerners, Kansans, Unionists, and Republicans, while the cowboys were overwhelmingly Southern, Texan, rebel, and Democratic in their backgrounds. The cowboys deeply resented the Yankees who dominated the business of the towns at which they arrived avid for excitement.[69] Thus the Kansas cow towns were being incorporated into an America dominated by new forces of commerce, industry, and finance. The Texas cowboys in their own rugged ways and with little comprehension of the overall social trend resisted such incorporation.

For the Kansas mercantile elite, which abetted the incorporating trend, the problem was to keep the cowboys under control: to restrain their violence while retaining their business. The solution hit upon was the two-fisted, fast-firing, straight-shooting peace officer whose prototype was James Butler Hickok.[70] He— and those who emulated him—provided a countervailing force of gun power sufficient to awe the cowboys: skilled with their six-guns though they were, they were outclassed by officers of the law with the talents of a Wild Bill Hickok or, later, a Wyatt Earp.

The climax of Hickok's career came amidst murderous cross-currents of this sort in Abilene during the summer and fall of 1871. True to his skill and reputation, Hickok as marshal controlled the restive, violence-prone Texas cowboys off the trail.[71] Meanwhile, a feud developed with Hickok, as incorporation gunfighter and Northern Unionist peace officer and Republican, on one side and a faction of ex-Confederate, Texan saloon keepers, gamblers, and resister gunfighters (all Democrats) on the other side. In the background were still-smoldering Civil War animosities. At the head of Hickok's enemies were Ben Thompson and Phil Coe, Texas partners in the Bull's Head saloon.[72]

Thompson was a Confederate veteran and a rabid Southern loyalist as well as an acclaimed gunfighter. Known as a "gentleman gambler," Coe shared the ultra-Southern values of his crony and partner.[73] There were, then, in the cultural climate of this typical Kansas cow town all the usual reasons why Thompson and Coe hated Hickok and vice versa, but what sparked the chain reaction of conflict was an episode that was bawdily comical in all but its total and tragic finale. Wild Bill had been hired by the Abilene town council to preserve order in what was expected to be an unusually rowdy and violent summer.[74] Not long after Hickok put on the marshal's badge, Thompson and Coe installed a new sign above the entrance of the Bull's Head saloon. The sign graphically portrayed a big longhorn bull physically aroused to the maximum of his masculinity. Morally proper Abileneans objected to the uninhibited display, whereupon the town council ordered Hickok to take care of the matter. This the marshal did by ordering Thompson and Coe either to take down the sign or to change it. Thompson angrily refused, so Hickok sent painters aloft to alter the sign. When the workmen were done, they had "materially changed" the "offending" animal from a bull to a steer.[75]

Ben Thompson seethed over the outcome of the sign dispute, and the anger of Thompson and his partner, Phil Coe, may have grown when Hickok supposedly put an end to a shady gambling setup in their saloon.[76] John Wesley Hardin, a cowboy and rancher as well as the star gunfighter of Texas, was soon on the scene. Thompson tried to maneuver his fellow Texan and Democrat (who shared all of Thompson's anti-Northern prejudices) into killing Hickok, but both Hardin and Hickok were far too wary of each other for such a gunfight to occur.[77] Yet the mutually bad feeling of Hickok versus Thompson and Coe festered in much the same manner as had that between Tutt and Hickok six years before. In 1871 as in 1865, Kent Ladd Steckmesser notes, "the classic elements of the Hickok saga—politics, poker, and women"[78]—were involved. To the ill will of politics (the Unionist and Republican Hickok against the Confederate and Democratic Thompson and Coe) and gambling (the crookedness in the Bull's Head saloon allegedly scotched by Wild Bill) was added, according to tradition, a rivalry between Coe and Hickok over a beautiful whore, Jessie Hazell.[79] With Thompson out of town, the individual conflict came down to one that pitted the incorporation gunfighter, Hickok, against the resister gunfighter, Coe.

The trouble came to a head on Thursday, October 5. At dusk of that day, Phil Coe and a large crowd of fifty or so turned rowdy, carousing and roaring in the street. Clearly a challenge to

Wild Bill Hickok's role as keeper of the peace in Abilene, the noise and disorder of Coe and company was met by the marshal with a mixture of strictness and conciliation: he treated them to drinks before warning them to quiet down. After Hickok departed, Coe and his group gathered in front of Abilene's largest saloon—one whose name, the Alamo, was calculated to attract the patronage of Texans. Coe fired a shot, probably with the intention of luring Hickok back to the scene where Coe could surprise and shoot him.[80] If so, the ruse was partly successful. Hickok came charging up, and the result was, as the local newspaper described it, an instant walkdown with Wild Bill being "confronted by Coe, who said that he had fired a shot at a dog. Coe had his revolver in his hand, as had also other parties in the crowd. As quick as thought the Marshal drew two revolvers and both men fired almost simultaneously." Coe and Hickok "were not over eight feet apart" and, since both were "large, stout men," made good targets. Wild Bill took one shot harmlessly through his coat, and another "passed between his legs." As usual, Hickok's aim was true. Shot in the stomach, Phil Coe died in agony three days later.[81]

Wild Bill Hickok himself had only five years of life left. After the gun victories over Tutt, Coe, and others Hickok's last years were an anticlimax concluded by an ignominious death. As a "living legend,"[82] life was not smooth for Wild Bill. An 1873–74 foray into the East as a featured performer in a Wild West stage show was not a success. Hickok could not stand the gimmickry of it all and pined for the frontier.[83] Back west, nothing quite worked out for him. In the last year of his life, Wild Bill married Agnes Lake Thatcher, a noted circus manager and performer of the era.[84] It was a love match,[85] and Hickok was at last ready for matrimony after decades of philandering. No longer having a role in the incorporating West, Wild Bill was restless and ill at ease: his career was on the wane while that of his wife was still on the rise.

In early 1876, the last year of his life, Hickok was seemingly the same as ever: tall, handsome, and dominating. In fact Wild

Bill, without a job and supported by his wife, was floundering.[86] Close friends of Hickok knew that he was in quite bad shape. Worst of all for a gunfighter, his eyesight was failing him.[87] His eye trouble was apparently the result of trachoma, a frequent frontier affliction.[88] Whatever inner doubts plagued him, Wild Bill made plans to join the gold rush to the Black Hills of Dakota Territory. When he arrived in Deadwood in mid-July 1876, Hickok had less than a month to live. His objective of making a strike through gambling and prospecting eluded him. Neither desultory work on a mining claim nor gambling came to much.[89] The news of the late-June death of his friend and patron, Custer, on the Little Big Horn accentuated Wild Bill's low spirits.[90] With those to whom he was close, the famous plainsman shared a premonition of impending death.[91]

On the hot, sleepy afternoon of August 2, 1876, Hickok drifted into one of his Deadwood haunts, the Number Ten saloon. As he sat at a table playing cards, Wild Bill faced the front door but did not have, as was his custom, his back to the wall. The aging gunfighter—now nearly forty years old—grumbled about the omission, but chums in the card game joshed Hickok away from his preferred back-to-the-wall chair. Thus James Butler Hickok was fatally vulnerable when, from behind him, Jack McCall, an obscure, alcoholic frontiersman, made his fame and ended Hickok's with a shot to the latter's head.[92] After the shooting, four cards in Wild Bill's last poker hand were noted: the ace of spades, the ace of clubs, the eight of clubs, and the eight of spades—two aces and two eights. Ever after, in the legend of the West, aces and eights were known as "the dead man's hand."[93]

The perfidious manner of Wild Bill Hickok's death enhanced the popular view of the heroic character of his life. Hickok would be enshrined in what became a Valhalla of heroic gunfighters who met their deaths by betrayal: Billy the Kid (shot in a midnight ambush by his erstwhile friend, Pat Garrett),[94] Jesse James (shot in the back by a henchman who sold out Jesse for the reward),[95] and John Wesley Hardin (shot in the back by a gunfighting peer jealous of John Wesley's fame).[96] Whether peacekeeper (Hickok) or outlaw (the others), these Western gunfighters met a timeless test of the hero: tragic death by treachery. Yet mythic concepts of heroism and villainy blurred the social significance of an incorporation gunfighter like James Butler Hickok, a prototypical and key belligerent on the Great Plains front of the Western Civil War of Incorporation where he and others whose weaponry was on the side of the law established order in the interest of the commercial and financial conquest of the cattle-studded prairies.

While Wild Bill Hickok was gaining notoriety as America's first famous gunfighter, the phenomenon of no-duty-to-retreat gunplay proliferated from the Great Plains to the Pacific Coast. By about the end of the nineteenth century there had been, according to an authoritative tabulation, 255 professional gunfighters who were involved in 587 gunfights resulting in 181 deaths.[97] This is, however, a drastic undercount of gunfighting, for it includes only the glorified gunfighters: Hickok, the Earps, Billy the Kid, Hardin, and the rest.

By the 1860s, man-to-man gunfighting was an established practice in the West. Down to 1900, there were thousands of Western gunfighters. As grassroots gunfighters, the vast majority of them earned neither national nor regional fame and were ignored by myth makers. Though very skilled gun handlers, these grassroots gunfighters usually took part in fewer affrays, individually, than the glorified gunfighters nor were they ordinarily touted as crack shots. Yet one of these unheralded grassroots gunfighters claimed five dead or dying victims on a single occasion—an exploit unmatched by Hickok, Hardin, or any of the notables.[98]

Although they will probably never be fully tabulated, thousands of Western deaths—not just a scanty 181—resulted from the shooting of the grassroots as well as the glorified gunfighters.[99] Heavily armed Westerners in the grip of no-duty-to-retreat notions of honor and bravery were prone to resolve differences with a gunfight. To a considerable extent the typical Western man of the rural areas and the cattle and mining towns was,

given cause and opportunity, a gunfighter. Grassroots Westerners easily became grassroots gunfighters.

Texas was an early and continuous theater of the gunfighting
custom. Cattle-industry entrepreneur and incorporating capitalist Joseph G. McCoy knew Texas cowboys and ranchers well. Of
them he wrote: they make "habitual use of the pistol," are "fair
to good shots," and have "the habit of settling their disputes,
often very trifling, with the revolver," which, "with some, is considered the first and only legitimate law, argument, or reason"
for the conclusion of a quarrel.[100]

Just as Wild Bill Hickok was the prototypical glorified gunfighter, the following two-versus-two walkdown in central Texas,
1867, was a prototype of the deadly grassroots gunfights, which
acquired little or no renown beyond their own localities. As in so
many conflicts throughout Texas and the West, this fight grew
out of a wrangle over range rights. Here was the essence of no-
duty-to-retreat gunplay, whose motif was, in the words of an old
ballad, "I'll die before I'll run."[101] Truly a duel to the last man,
there was no flight or retreat on either side. Not until three of
the four participants were dead or mortally wounded did the
shooting stop. What happened was described in the central
Texas dialect by the pseudonymous "Lunar Caustic," a local
schoolteacher whose report appeared in a Galveston newspaper:

> Hit seems John Bell and Walt Edwards had words up on the
> Sandies, and Bell sent Edwards word not to come stock hunting on
> his range. Well, they met out on Lower Hog Eye, hit's a branch of
> the Cabasas over in the edge of Karnes [County], and who begun
> and shot first he [Lunar Caustic] couldn't ondertake to say, but hit
> was a very good fight and only four men in it. There was old man
> Edwards and Walt agin John Bell and Charley Thee, two and two a
> side and a very good fight. Walt Edwards and Charley Thee was
> shot down directly, but Charley kept a shootin' at old man Edwards
> long as he could raise his weepin—it was a very good fight and
> John Bell emptied his six-shooter and never missed only one shot.
> Walt Edwards and Charley Thee fell in their tracks and was killed
> on the ground, and old Man Edwards is dead since, of a wound

> through his shoulder, and John Bell was the only one not hurted, and hit was a very good fight.[102]

John Bell, the only survivor of this appalling episode, is not a glorified gunfighter of the West, but his expert marksmanship (only one of six shots went astray) entitled him to far more recognition than the near anonymity of his participation in an obscure but murderous backland battle. Bell is typical of the long-forgotten gunfighters whose activities are buried in local sources and histories. The violence of John Bell and thousands like him was a significant social reality of the American West.

Far from Karnes County, Texas, there was another remarkable (but not untypical) example of the gunfighter culture of the West. The mining town of Bodie, California, became one of the West's best known boom towns in the late 1870s and early 1880s after the gold and silver strike of 1876 produced a rush to Bodie resulting in a peak population of over 5,000. By 1885 mine production had plummeted, however, and all but a remnant of the Bodie boomers moved on to newer bonanzas in Arizona, Colorado, Alaska, and elsewhere. By the post–World War II housing surge of the 1940s and 1950s the distant ghost town of Bodie was attracting to its high, bleak site not prospectors but urban Southern Californians who, in pickup trucks or trailers, took back to their dream houses and patios rich loads of valuable bricks lifted from the crumbling buildings of old Bodie. No doubt few of these city-dwelling brick foragers had ever heard the phrase that made Bodie famous in the history and folklore of the late nineteenth-century West: "a Bad Man from Bodie." That phrase became in the Western idiom a generic term for any gunfight-prone tough, whether from Bodie or not.

Yet, as Roger D. McGrath has shown in his compelling study of Bodie, the myth of the Bad Man from Bodie was based on a horrendous reality. "The 'Bad Man from Bodie' was not a fictitious character," declared an eyewitness, John Hays Hammond, one of the greatest mining engineers and capitalistic incorporators of the West, who started out with a job in violent Bodie.[103] By the standards of both its time and ours, Bodie was a highly homicidal place. At the center of the violence was the Bad Man from Bodie—the Bodie gunfighter.

Bodie gunfighters included men from a wide variety of the occupations of the mining town: miner, teamster, carpenter, businessman, attorney, bartender, and lawman.[104] They also represented the geographical diversity of the West, for most of them were seasoned veterans of one or more of the raucous mining camps of the region. There were, however, no famous gunfighters among them. Like the foursome who shot it out in Karnes County, Texas, the Bodieites were grassroots gunfighters. It is important to note, also, that a great many residents who never actually engaged in a Bodie gunfight habitually went about armed and were experienced gun handlers, ready to use their weapons under provocation. They too were part of Bodie's gunfighter culture.

In bare statistical terms, there were about seventy shootings or shootouts in Bodie's boom years with thirty men killed and another two dozen or more wounded.[105] "Without a doubt," declares McGrath, "Bodie was a shooter's town. It was the home of the badman. It was also the home of many average workingmen who used guns to resolve their differences.[106] Yet at the core of the carnage were nineteen man-to-man gunfights engaged in by the Bodie badmen referred to by McGrath. Numbering two dozen, these gunfighting badmen were not outlaws. Ordinarily law-abiding citizens, they were, however, always ready for a fight. The Bodie badman, as sketched by McGrath, was

> proud and confident, brave to the point of recklessness, and willing to fight to the death. He was usually young and single, and well travelled. He moved from one mining town to the next as each experienced its boom times. When he worked, if it was not as a professional gambler, it was usually as a gunman for a mining company, a police officer, a bartender, or a miner. He spent much of his time in saloons drinking or gambling, and there occurred most of his gunfights. He was always "heeled" or armed with a

revolver. The piece was often a Colt—the Lightning, or "self-cocker," as it was commonly called, was the preferred model. The badman normally carried his gun not in a holster but in a coat or *hip pocket,*[107] or simply tucked into his waistband. He was always ready to use the weapon and he frequently did. His targets were mostly other badmen.[108]

The twenty-four Bodie gunfighters did use their guns for what they saw as good and sufficient reasons. Alcohol consumed in the many, many saloons, barrooms, and dance halls of Bodie often inflamed emotions to the point of gunplay.[109] More than any other thing, however, McGrath found Bodie gunfighters to be characterized by *"reckless bravado:* a willingness to exchange gunfire over a careless remark, an insult, or a challenge to fighting ability."[110]

Reckless bravado was general throughout the boom towns of the West and was, of course, another manifestation of the no-duty-to-retreat syndrome. Hot-firing six-shooters backing up the passions of reckless bravado in a no-duty-to-retreat mood often escalated personal disputes—feuds, grudges, and quarrels—into Bodie gunfights,[111] which usually occurred on open streets or in saloons. There were at least two classic walkdowns; in one, each gunfighter hit the other, and both died. The other kind of walk-down, whose firing began at very long range, produced neither casualties nor hits.[112] The great majority of Bodie gunfights were at short range, whether they were street fights or saloon shoot-outs. Typical of these close-quarters gunfights was that between Frank Viles and Ed Loose on April 8, 1882. On the outs for some time, Viles and Loose, upon encountering each other in a Bodie dance hall, instantaneously drew their guns. Shots were exchanged, and Loose was wounded.[113]

One of the most shocking gunfights featured Alex Nixon, the youthful, strapping president of the Bodie Miners' Union. A trivial dispute with one Tom McDonald in the Shamrock saloon led to angry words between Nixon and McDonald, and then Nixon felled McDonald with a powerful blow. McDonald was game and not about to retreat or flee. Rising to his feet, he stepped back from Nixon, drew a six-shooter, and challenged him: "Will you give me even chances?" "Yes, by God," Nixon agreed. Drawing his own weapon, Nixon fired away, as did Mc-Donald. McDonald's first shot mortally wounded Nixon.[114]

The legal outcome of the killing of Alex Nixon by Tom Mc-Donald was typical of Bodie gunfights (and of such encounters elsewhere), fatal or not: the grand jury declined to indict Mc-Donald for the murder of Nixon. Thus in Bodie, a typical West-ern community imbued with no-duty-to-retreat thinking, gun-fighting had a high degree of legitimacy as a way of resolving differences. The striking lack of legal action against Bodie gun-fighters is a telling instance of the pervasive reach of the gun-fight culture of Bodie—and the West. Public opinion in Bodie (and elsewhere in the West) held that a gunfight was an emi-nently proper and honorable way of settling personal disputes—disputes whose contestants, it was thought, should not be tou-ched by the law even if the outcome was death or injury.

The most famous of all the thousands of Western gunfights took place on October 26, 1881, near the O.K. Corral in Tomb-stone, Arizona. In it Wyatt, Virgil, and Morgan Earp and John Henry (Doc) Holliday faced Ike and Billy Clanton and Tom and Frank McLaury. The resulting exchange of bullets was fatal to Billy Clanton and the McLaury brothers, while their opponents all survived in what was a remarkable triumph for the Earps and Holliday. A month-long inquest after the event produced a find-ing by magistrate Wells Spicer that the Earps and Holliday were innocent of murder in the three deaths but had acted in self-defense in their capacity as peace officers. The decision was a controversial one, but Spicer's ruling was squarely in the context of the new American legal tradition of no duty to retreat that allowed one to stand one's ground and kill in self-defense.[115]

More than any of the others it was Wyatt Earp who emerged as the hero of the famous gunfight near the O.K. Corral. The powerful pressure of the Western myth to reduce complex his-torical figures to the attractive simplicities of such categories as hero and villain is nowhere better exemplified than in his case.

The reality of Wyatt Earp has long been deeply obscured by the powerful, omnipresent myth of Wyatt Earp as a heroic gun-fighting antagonist of Western badmen. The legendary Wyatt Earp was virtually codified in the popular mind by the impact of two appealing myth-making books of the early twentieth century: *Tombstone: An Iliad of the Southwest* (1927) by Walter Noble Burns and *Wyatt Earp: Frontier Marshal* (1931) by Stuart N. Lake.

Turning from myth to reality, the key to understanding Wyatt Earp is to see his Tombstone triumph in the context of Arizona's 1881–82 Cochise County conflict—one of many such struggles in the decades-long Western Civil War of Incorporation. In Cochise County the incorporating trend was spearheaded by a Tombstone faction of mining industry entrepreneurs and engineers and their allies among the town's business and professional elite. Resisting them were the "cowboys" of rural Cochise County. Among the members of the incorporating faction was Wyatt Earp, who used his gunfighting skill to break the resistance of the cowboys.

One must also turn from the spurious heroism of the Wyatt Earp myth to the realistic view that there were two often contradictory sides to the man: Wyatt Earp the *rounder* and Wyatt Earp the *Republican*. According to the traditional meaning of the word, a rounder is "one who makes the rounds of dissolute resorts"—a term that in a bygone America was often applied to those like Wyatt Earp who, in saloons and elsewhere, indulged a fondness for drink, gambling, and women. The legend of Wyatt Earp folds in aspects of the rounder but wholly ignores the other Wyatt Earp—who as a conservative member of the Republican Party was an incorporation gunfighter with natural affinities to society's rich and powerful.

As a Northerner reared in a Unionist family, Wyatt Earp—who himself became a lifelong, loyal Republican—reflected and adhered to the social ideal of the Republican party in Gilded-Age America: an allegiance to conservative values and enterprising capitalism. Yet the rounder and the Republican in Earp represented contrasting polarities in American life. The prototypical conservative, property-oriented Republican usually had no time for the pleasure-loving hedonism of the rounder. The conflict of rounder versus Republican was an enduring tension in Wyatt Earp's life until, beginning in his Tombstone period, it was eventually resolved. In his younger days in the Great Plains country of Kansas, Dakota, Texas, and present Oklahoma, the rounder Wyatt Earp was in the ascendant. As he grew older, his Republican identity became stronger. It was hard for Earp to surmount the rounder aspect of his career. Gambling and saloon life had strong appeal for him, and he was too habituated to his rounder haunts ever to forsake·them completely. After Tombstone, however, he found a way to reconcile his rounder self with his urge for Republican respectability, although at best he could only soften, not erase, his rounder tendencies. Many of his cronies were fellow rounders, and some of them such as Doc Holliday and Luke Short were, like Earp, famous gunfighters. As a Republican in Tombstone, however, Wyatt Earp began to move in quite another world where his GOP compatriots were not rounders but highly respectable men of property.

If the rounder and the Republican personas vied for supremacy in the character of Wyatt Earp, one thing united them: his status as a gunfighter. Earp was easy and comfortable with gunfighting peers like rounders Holliday and Short as they stood at the bars and sat around the card tables of the West, while the use of his gunfighting skill in the interest of lawfully gained wealth and property gained him the admiration and the patronage of his monied Republican friends in Tombstone. They eagerly turned to Wyatt Earp in their quest to consolidate a Western and an American society based on the power of expanding capitalism.

The victory of Wyatt Earp and his colleagues in the gunfight near the O.K. Corral was an outgrowth of the highly conflicted social, economic, and political situation in Cochise County and its county seat, Tombstone. A matrix of specifically local but typically Western factors made the county and its seat a seething cauldron of strife and no-duty-to-retreat gunplay. Social, economic, and political tensions produced alignments and a clash in value systems leading to a remarkable series of violent events.

Cochise County, Arizona, was an arena of sharp political conflict in which Democrats were arrayed against Republicans in a way that was quite typical of late nineteenth-century politics in America. The closing decades of the nineteenth century comprised the period in our nation's political history when the spirit of partisanship was liveliest, the Republican and Democratic parties were strongest, and the percentage of voting by the enfranchised was highest.[†] Arizona reflected the national pattern: there was hot competition between the Democrats and Republicans at all three levels of government—the territorial, the county, and the municipal. Far-flung Cochise County was characterized by a front of Republican-dominated Tombstone against the Democratically inclined interior of the county.

The mine and mill managers and supervisors of Tombstone and its three satellite towns of Charleston, Contention, and Fairbank, as well as the business and professional men of these communities, tended to be Republicans. The Republican party in Cochise County was thus an urban group whose members were often Northern in background, as exemplified by mayor and newspaper editor John P. Clum; mine owner and manager E. B. Gage; mine partner, banker, and diarist George W. Parsons; magistrate and attorney Wells Spicer; and Wyatt Earp and his brother Virgil, who served twice as Tombstone's chief of police.

The split between rural Democrats and urban Republicans in Cochise County was sharpened by the economic dichotomy of the county, which found the Republican party clustering around the mining and ore-processing industry that dominated Tombstone and the smaller mill towns, while the strength of the Democratic Party was to be found in the pastoral realm of cattle ranching. The value system of mining-oriented Tombstone placed a heavy emphasis on law and order as the basis for social stability

[†]On these three features of late nineteenth-century American politics, see, among many authorities, Robert D. Marcus, *Grand Old Party: Political Structure in the Gilded Age* (New York: Oxford University Press, 1971).

and economic progress. Business and professional men in Tombstone were entirely dependent upon the vigor of the mining industry for their prosperity, and the mining industry was in turn heavily dependent upon the investments of outside capitalists, especially those of the eastern United States and California. Such investors were repelled by the violence and lawlessness verging on anarchy which threatened their outlays of capital. Driven by the profit motive, the Tombstone elite wished to incorporate Tombstone into the corporation-dominated industrializing and urbanizing structure of America.

The value system that was predominant in the rural reaches of vast Cochise County was far different from that to be found in incorporation-minded Tombstone. Out in the county there was an emphasis on highly traditional, not modern, values. Loyalty to family, individual self-reliance, and self-redress of wrongs were among the values most highly regarded. In reflection of a free-and-easy attitude toward rustling and outlaws often found throughout the rural West, there was little esteem for law and order as such. Although horse theft was strongly condemned, the rustling of cattle did not result in social stigma provided it was not directed against closely neighboring herds. There was general recognition that many respectable ranching estates had, in their early days, been built up with the assistance of rustling. Outlaw activity was widely tolerated as long as the culprits observed the universal customs of personal courtesy and respect for others.

As cowboys, many of the young men of Cochise County often took part in both legitimate ranching and the illicit activity of rustling. A host of the cowboys were from Texas or the South, and more law-abiding fellow Texans and Southerners tended to excuse their brash young compatriots. Around the northern margins of Cochise County, the cattle king, Henry Clay Hooker, a New Englander in origin, was an indignant victim of rustling. Most of the rustlers of Cochise County concentrated their cattle thefts across the border in Mexico or against more distant neighbors like Hooker.

As exemplified by Newman H. (Old Man) Clanton, not all of the rustlers were youngsters, but so many were that the term "cowboy" became a generic one for the rural outlaw faction of Cochise County, which ran in a spectrum from full-time ranchers like the Clantons and the McLaurys, who actively dealt on the side in stolen cattle, to the professional outlaws and gunfighters like John Ringo and Curly Bill Brocius, both of whom had Texas cowboy backgrounds.

Yet the alignment of the rural cowboy faction of outlaws against the urbanites from Tombstone was embedded in a deeper antagonism than even that of the lawless against the law-abiding. The two factions represented, respectively, the cowboy pastoral culture and the urban capitalistic culture, making their hostility an incident in the Western Civil War of Incorporation. For the cowboys out in Cochise County who periodically made trips to Tombstone, the object was often a good time through drinking, gambling, and fornication. The tendency of the cowboys to enshrine Tombstone as a place of wild pleasure contrasted with the austere goal of the economically ascendant mine managers of Tombstone. The mining executives and their allies among the business and professional men saw young, booming Tombstone as a big-time mining center of the West that employed capital-intensive industry and technologically advanced hard-rock deep mining in the interest of steady capitalistic profit. In this image of the economic development of Tombstone there was hardly a place for violence-prone cowboys attracted, after weeks of dusty life out on the range, to Tombstone's faro layouts, dance halls, saloons, and loose women.

Headed by Wyatt and Virgil, the five Earp brothers formed a crucial bloc among the contending forces. Wyatt, Virgil, and James Earp had served as rounder lawmen in Dodge City, Kansas, but in Tombstone Wyatt and his brothers wished to forsake the Dodge City model and reverse the pattern of their lives. Now the Earps were small-time capitalists on the make attracted to the possibilities of gain in fast-growing Tombstone and the flourishing mines of Cochise County. The Earps desired to be respected as successful businessmen and property holders, and they went in heavily for speculative investments in mineral properties and real estate. As good Republicans, they stood in well with such members of the social, economic, and political elite of Tombstone as E. B. Gage and John P. Clum, men who, as noted, were also the leaders of the Republican party in the boom town.

Yet Wyatt Earp could not completely transcend the rounder pattern of Dodge City, for the habits of saloon life, gambling, and enforcing the law against cowboys were what he knew best. Moreover, there was an interest in the gunhandling talents of all the "fighting Earps." Tombstone mining and milling executives and business and professional men organized themselves in a vigilante movement known as the Citizens' Safety Committee. In so doing they wished to exorcise disorder, stabilize life in Tombstone, and convince actual and potential Eastern and California investors that Tombstone was an orderly city into which capital could be poured with a heady expectation of profit. The vigilante movement was, however, unwieldy and lay dormant. Instead, for day-to-day preservation of order, the Tombstone elite needed the skills of Virgil and Wyatt Earp, who had a knack for knocking cowboys on their heads and were never afraid to draw their guns against the outlaws or the unruly. As staunch Republicans, the Earps were more than acceptable to the establishment of Tombstone.

During 1881 a feud developed between the Earps and Doc Holliday on one side and the cowboy faction on the other. In effect the Earps and Holliday were violent point-men for the incorporating social and economic values represented by urban, industrial, Northern, capitalistic Tombstone, while the Clantons and the McLaurys (supported by their criminal allies John Ringo, Curly Bill Brocius, and others) were equally violent protagonists of the resistant rural, pastoral, Southern cowboy coalition of Cochise County.

The festering conflict erupted in violence on October 26, 1881, in the prototypical Western shootout of all time: the deadly encounter near the O.K. Corral. As noted earlier, the

Earps and Doc Holliday were found to have slain their opponents, Billy Clanton and Tom and Frank McLaury, justifiably in the enforcement of law and in self-defense. Yet the anti-Earp historian, Ed Bartholomew, joined by other but by no means all authorities, branded the episode in retrospect as simply one of barefaced murder on the part of the Earps and Holliday.

The controversy is now more than a century old, and it will probably never be definitively settled. Whether the Clantons and the McLaurys presented a mortal threat to the Earps and Holliday as the Earps successfully claimed at law, or whether the Earps provoked their rivals and then, with Holliday, murdered them as others have claimed, the fact is that on the afternoon of the battle, Wyatt and Virgil Earp and Doc Holliday were older, much more experienced gunfighters and were more determined and better prepared for a showdown than were the Clantons and the McLaurys. The Earp party also had an edge in that the first shots were fired, as the Earp family tradition maintained (without ever disclosing in public), by Doc Holliday and Morgan Earp. With the circumstances in favor of the Earps and Holliday, it is not surprising that the shootout ended with their triumph.

The central and most controversial figure in the Cochise County conflict was Wyatt Berry Stapp Earp—the fourth-born son of Nicholas Porter Earp, who with his wife, Virginia Ann, moved his growing brood ever west. Thus Wyatt, with a background similar to that of Wild Bill Hickok, was born in 1848 in northern Illinois of a father who would later be a Unionist and a Republican.[116] Wyatt's three older brothers, Newton, James, and Virgil, all served in the Northern army during the Civil War,[117] but Wyatt was too young to take part. While the war raged in 1864, the patriarch, Nicholas, moved the family (including Wyatt) to southern California from Iowa, to which the clan had moved from Illinois in 1850. Yet none of the Earps took root in California at this time, and in 1866 Nicholas led the family back to the Midwest. Wyatt and Virgil eventually joined the Earp family in their new home of Lamar, Missouri, a town on the southern stretch of Missouri's border with Kansas.[118]

In Lamar in 1870, Wyatt Earp married Urilla Sutherland and was first attracted to law enforcement. Elected to the office of constable in 1870 at the age of twenty-two,[119] Earp did well as a youthful law officer, but in that same year he suffered a demoralizing blow in the death of his beloved young wife, who succumbed to typhoid fever. Perhaps unable to overcome his grief over the loss of Urilla, Wyatt vacated his Lamar constableship and lapsed fully into the life of a rounder.[120] Soon he was in the Indian Territory (present eastern Oklahoma) where in 1871 he jumped bail after being arrested for horse theft.[121] A hardened Wyatt Earp put this ignominy behind him as he emerged several years later in Wichita, the metropolis of southeastern Kansas.[122] Like Abilene, Wichita was an end-of-cattle-trail boom town and was typical of such towns, with wild cowboys from Texas threatening persistently to take it over.[123] Helping to control the cowboys was Wyatt Earp, who served as a policeman in Wichita in 1875 and 1876. Once again he ably enforced the law. But an ill-advised fist fight and the typical Earpian wanderlust soon had him on his way to Dodge City.[124] This early, pre–Dodge City phase was for rounder Wyatt Earp and his brothers the most unsavory period in their lives. In addition to Wyatt's arrest for horse theft in the Indian Territory, women of the Earp name were fined for prostitution in Wichita.[125]

The peripatetic Wyatt Earp was in and out of Dodge City between 1876 and 1879, a confirmed rounder but one who served as an active, tough, and respected enforcer of the law against cattle-trail Texas cowboys and all other violators.[126] Wyatt held the positions of policeman and assistant marshal in Dodge, and it was there that he, along with others, took part in what may have been his first gunfight—one with fatal results for a young cowboy.[127] Very early in his wanderings, Earp became an adept gambler[128]—a skill pursued long after, either as a pastime or an occupation. During the 1870s when not in Dodge City, Wyatt ranged widely over the Great Plains, often gambling assiduously: from the Black Hills far north in Dakota Territory[129] to Mobeetie down in the Texas panhandle[130] and on to turbulent Las Vegas,

New Mexico.[131] In these travels, Wyatt sometimes reverted to shady practices as a bunco artist or confidence man, activities which were apparently sidelines to his persistent card playing and gambling.[132]

Finally, in December 1879, Wyatt, James, and Virgil Earp (later joined by Morgan and Warren) moved into the wondrous new mining town of Tombstone.[133] Up to this time, Wyatt had shown two faces to the world. One was a tough but respected lawman. The other was a thorough rounder: gambler, accused horse thief, prostitute's companion, saloon habitué, bunco artist, and confidence man. Late in his Kansas period there had been, however, a glimmering of Wyatt Earp the respectable Republican, for in Dodge City he took a wife and was commended for his "many Christian virtues." In Tombstone, Wyatt strove to subordinate his rounder identity to that of his upright Republicanism. Although he worked variously as a stagecoach guard and a law officer, the new Wyatt Earp was not content with a such a career but, along with his brothers, established himself as an aggressive small capitalist with shrewd investments in mining properties and real estate in the speculative, frenzied ambience of the booming town of Tombstone and its environs. As the oldest of the five brothers, Wyatt, Virgil, and James proved to have "good business judgment" and "a sense of acquisitiveness."[134] The Earp family image in Tombstone was enhanced, too, by the stern, determined Virgil Earp, who served in two key law-enforcement positions: federal deputy marshal and Tombstone chief of police (or city marshal).[135] However, according to the Tucson *Arizona Daily Star* it was Wyatt who, with a "more refined appearance" than the other Earps, was also "cold and calculating" and the "brains" of the outfit.[136]

Yet all of this was not quite enough, for Wyatt employed his old rounder talent of gambling to fill out his livelihood as gaming manager in the popular Oriental saloon.[137] Meanwhile, in his law-enforcement role the Republican Wyatt Earp gained firm allies among the GOP industrial, business, and professional elite of Tombstone. First among these compatriots was the incisive

John P. Clum, who would be Wyatt's good friend ever after: from Tombstone to Alaska to, finally, their last years in Los Angeles. Clum was a colorful frontier character in his own right. A former football player at Rutgers College, Clum went west to Arizona where he set up and headed the San Carlos Apache Indian Reservation. He then joined the rush to Tombstone and became editor of the aptly named newspaper, the *Tombstone Epitaph*, to which he gave a strong identity as the staunch Republican mouthpiece of Tombstone and the editorial-page opponent of the outlaw depredations of the Cochise County cowboys. A natural, magnetic leader, Clum also occupied the mayor's chair in Tombstone.[138]

Idolizing Wyatt Earp was another Easterner—a young member of America's aristocracy, Endicott Peabody. Although his was an elite Massachusetts banking family of Brahmin lineage, the idealistic young Endicott Peabody turned his back on banking and business to forge in religion and education one of the most eminent careers of his era in America. Becoming a minister in the Episcopal Church, Peabody founded Groton—the most exclusive of all New England private schools for boys. It was to Groton that Franklin D. Roosevelt went for schooling, and it was his much revered Groton mentor, the Reverend Endicott Peabody, whom Roosevelt invited to Washington, D.C., to conduct family religious services on the days of his first and second inaugurations as president of the United States.[139] All of this was far in the future, and now—in the early 1880s—the rugged, athletic young aristocrat, Peabody, had interrupted his ministerial studies to bring religion to Tombstone and provide the boom town a personal example of muscular Christianity.[140] He was successful as the founder of St. Paul's Episcopal Church in Tombstone,[141] and he was strong in his admiration of Wyatt Earp[142] as the brave guardian of the values of law, order, property, and the Republican party.

Another one of Wyatt Earp's Tombstone devotees was an ambitious member of the banking fraternity, George W. Parsons. In private hours Parsons kept a remarkable diary that not only provided a detailed record of Tombstone events but recorded the viewpoint of the Republican party faction to which both Parsons and Wyatt Earp belonged.[143] Notable also was E. B. Gage, one of the industrial kings of Tombstone. An Easterner and a graduate of Dartmouth, Gage was president and superintendent of one of Tombstone's greatest mines, the Grand Central. In economic terms Gage was the most glittering member of the prestigious Wyatt Earp fan club in Tombstone. Another admiring acquaintance of Wyatt Earp was the youthful Yale alumnus John Hays Hammond, who, in the earliest phase of his incomparable career in Western mining, came to town to inspect the fabulous mines of Tombstone.[144] A crony of Wyatt's among Tombstone's lawyers was Wells Spicer, who, before coming to Tombstone, had been a prominent attorney in Utah.[145] Possibly related to Wyatt by marriage, Spicer was "generally regarded as a friend of the Earps,"[146] and later, as a Tombstone magistrate, he would uphold the spirit of no duty to retreat in rendering a crucial legal decision in favor of Wyatt, his brothers, and Doc Holliday.[147]

Consorting at times with the Republican establishment of Tombstone, busy with his investments in city and county property and enterprises, serving as the Oriental saloon's top gambler, Wyatt Earp was, however, a controversial figure, involved in political and personal disputes and feuds during most of his Tombstone years. One such episode was his longtime competition with John Behan. Having first served as deputy sheriff of Pima County (in which Tombstone was located before Cochise County was carved out of Pima County in early 1881), Wyatt, as a firm Republican in a territory—Arizona—whose government was controlled by the Republican party, felt he was entitled to be appointed sheriff of the newly created Cochise County, whose seat was Tombstone. But Wyatt lost out to, of all people, a Democrat: John Behan. The latter was an old Arizona hand whose indirect personal connection to James G. Blaine—the famed "Plumed Knight" of Maine who, as a member of the U.S. Senate, was one of the most powerful GOP politicos of his time—got him the position of county sheriff. The irony, then, was that for personal reasons a Republican grandee, Blaine, threw the weight of his decisive influence to the side of the Democrat, Behan, rather than the Republican Earp in their keen rivalry for the job of Cochise sheriff, a most lucrative and coveted position. Thus Behan and not Wyatt Earp became sheriff of Cochise County. Feeling that his skill as a lawman, his talent as a gun handler, and his politics rightfully entitled him, not Behan, to be sheriff, Wyatt was bitterly and lastingly aggrieved.[148] Earp's contest with Behan for the post of sheriff was one of high stakes in power and money. The loss of this key law-enforcement job was a damaging blow to Wyatt's "sense of acquisitiveness" as well as his self-esteem.

Meanwhile, John Behan remained the leader of Cochise's dominant Democratic clique, which some called the "County Ring."[149] Leading local Democratic colleagues of Behan were Harry M. Woods, Artemus E. Fay, and two brothers, Thomas and John Dunbar.[150] The political power base of the Behan Democratic organization was anchored firmly, among other places, in the criminous cowboys of the county.[151] Behan, Woods, Fay, and the Dunbars headed the anti-Earp alignment in Cochise County, but more and more vigorous in it were two sets of brothers: the Clantons and the McLaurys.

Both the Clantons and the McLaurys were, as working ranchers, truly cowboys as well as being among the leaders of what all—including the president of the United States—referred to as the "cowboy" faction of Cochise County. Joined to the legitimate ranching operations of the Clantons and McLaurys was heavy, illicit dealing in cattle stolen by themselves or others.[152] It was against the rustling and the depredations of cowboys like the Clantons and the McLaurys that John P. Clum thundered in *Epitaph* editorials. The enmity that developed between the Clantons and McLaurys on one side and the Earps and Holliday on the other grew out of a tangled thicket of charges and countercharges[153] but even more significantly was tightly tied to the opposing social forces each side represented: the incorporating urban, capitalistic culture of Tombstone in the case of the Earps and the resistant, rural, pastoral culture of outlying Cochise County for the Clantons and McLaurys.

The feud of the Earps versus the Clantons and McLaurys festered during 1881 and came to a climax on October 25–26 of that year. This explosive two-day span came during Virgil Earp's second term as Tombstone chief of police. Aroused by the threats of the Clantons and McLaurys, Virgil deputized his brothers Wyatt and Morgan and Wyatt's close friend, Doc Holliday, to serve as police officers. Wearing official badges of authority, the Earps and Holliday clashed several times with the Clantons and McLaurys on the 25th and 26th. Once, Wyatt Earp pistol-whipped Tom McLaury with his six-shooter. Trumped and frustrated by the legal authority of the Earps and Holliday, Ike and Billy Clanton and Frank and Tom McLaury struck back with threats against them.[154]

By early afternoon on October 26, 1881, Tombstone was seething with stories of the skirmishes between the two sides. Word of the threats of the Clantons and the McLaurys against the Earps as officers of the law sped around the town. As Wyatt Earp, the rock-ribbed Republican, remembered, the defiance by the Clantons and McLaurys "was something not to be ignored. The merchants and bankers, and men of business everywhere" in Tombstone "suddenly realized that the foundations of the law were threatened; this was a challenge to the State; anarchy would be next. The thing must be stamped out, and now was the time to begin, and the leading lights"—a dozen heavily armed prominent men of Tombstone—came forward to the Earps, pledging to join them in facing the Clantons and McLaurys. "Men, you can't do this," said Wyatt to the volunteer gunfighters, "some of you will be killed." He explained that "the danger would be greatly increased with men who were inexperienced and that it would be better" for the Earps "to make the fight alone." It took five minutes of impassioned argument for Wyatt to convince these would-be gunfighters to stay out of the impending confrontation.[155] Rumors of a coming gunfight between the antagonistic parties were rife.[156] Tombstone was waiting, and it did not have long to wait.

One of Tombstone's main streets was Fremont. Leading into it was an alley from the O.K. Corral, owned by John Dunbar, a strong Democratic opponent of the Earps and all of the Republicans of Tombstone. The corral was a haunt of the Clantons and the McLaurys, who were friends of its owner. Two lots away from the alley was a vacant space between one-story frame buildings. It was in this vacant lot, near to but not at the O.K. Corral, that the opposing sides came face to face with each other.[157] As Ike and Billy Clanton, Frank and Tom McLaury, and their friend Billy Claiborne lingered in the lot (either waiting to shoot it out or waiting to leave town peaceably, according to which side is believed), four resolute, well-armed men—Wyatt, Virgil, and Morgan Earp and Doc Holliday—marched up to them.[158] Police chief Virgil Earp commanded the cowboys to put up their hands.[159] Almost immediately thereafter came the first shots; they were fired by Morgan Earp and Doc Holliday.[160] It was a bright, crisp fall day and at an elevation of 4,539 feet a chilly one. Accordingly the members of the Earp party were accoutered in long, dark coats to keep out the cold.[161] These spacious outer garments did not, however, hamper their marksmanship, which was deadly. Because they were unarmed, Ike Clanton and Billy Claiborne were allowed to flee the scene unscathed.[162] That left four in the Earp group against three on the cowboy side. When the thirty seconds of shooting were over, all three of the cowboys were dead or dying. The cowboys were wiped out, but before succumbing to the superior gun handling of their rivals they nonetheless exacted a heavy toll on the Earp side, for Virgil and Morgan Earp and Doc Holliday were all wounded. Of the seven men in the gunfight, only Wyatt Earp was untouched by lead.[163] Although he would kill again within months, this was Wyatt Earp's supreme moment as a gunfighter.

The public reaction in Tombstone to the outcome of the gunfight was both jubilant and apprehensive. As its head, Mayor

John P. Clum called out the strongly pro-Earp Citizens' Safety Committee, a vigilante band of leading citizens, to stand by, for there were fears that outraged cowboys would raid Tombstone in anger over the deaths of their Clanton and McLaury colleagues. The fear of a cowboy raid (which never came) was surmounted by joy over the all-out triumph of the Earp side. The victors heard excited voices: "I knew you'd win, Wyatt!"—"I knew it!"—"all of you." All four of the victorious gunfighters were pounded with congratulations. Mayor Clum was the first to salute Wyatt, with the eminent E. B. Gage close behind.[164] The elation was not just for the winning gunfighters but also for the conservative cosmopolitan, capitalistic, incorporating, and partisan Republican social values vindicated by their gunfire.

The postgunfight celebration of October 26, 1881, was timely because the triumph of the Earps marked the high point of the Republican party in Tombstone and the social forces it exemplified.[165] Within a few years, uncontrollable flooding deep down in the shafts closed the bonanza mines of Tombstone.[166] E. B. Gage, erstwhile Earp supporter and magnate of the Grand Central Mine, stayed on, but others left by the thousands, and Tombstone fell into a long, dreary existence as a faded boom town.[167]

Meanwhile, the October 26 gunfight was, contrary to the Tombstone myth, not the conclusion of the Earp-cowboy conflict but the initiation of months of violence in the climactic phase of the feud. Soon after the October shootout, one Will McLaury came to town to mastermind a cowboy campaign of vengeance. Will McLaury, who practiced law in Fort Worth, Texas, was the brother of Frank and Tom.[168] The Texas attorney organized both a legal and an extralegal, violent effort against the Earps.[169] The legal drive was thwarted by magistrate Wells Spicer in his decision absolving the Earps and Holliday of fault in the gunfight near the O.K. Corral.

Inspired and directed by Will McLaury, the vengeful violence against the Earps was at first a great success. On December 28, 1881, Virgil Earp was shot from ambush; he survived but for the rest of his life could not easily use his injured left arm.[170] Next, on

March 18, 1882, Morgan Earp was fatally shot by unseen parties as he played pool in a Tombstone recreation hall.[171] Following these blows, it was the mission of an enraged Wyatt Earp to exact revenge. This he did in early 1882 in his capacity as a deputy U.S. marshal, an office he obtained through his Republican political connections.[172] Earp led a posse through Cochise County in pursuit of cowboy culprits. In his lust for blood retribution, Wyatt killed Florentino Cruz and, later, Frank Stilwell—men whom the coroner's jury had accused of killing Morgan Earp.[173] Wyatt claimed also to have slain gunfighter Curly Bill Brocius, one of the notable bravos of the cowboy faction.[174] Curly Bill's body was never found, leading some to doubt Earp's story of having killed him. Yet Curly Bill disappears from the historical record after the time that Wyatt assigned to his death,[175] and it is likely that Wyatt did indeed do away with him.

Wyatt Earp's threefold mortal revenge for the death of one brother and the drastic wounding of another was about as much as he could possibly do under the circumstances. Wyatt then left Arizona, for by this time an irate Sheriff John Behan was on his trail, bent on arresting him for the Cruz and Stilwell homicides.[176] With Wyatt's exit, all of the Earps (and Holliday, too) were gone from Cochise County and Arizona. The eventual exodus was a planned one, for in the bloody aftermath of the October 26 gunfight at the lot on Fremont Street, the Earps realized that Tombstone and the county were becoming too hot for them. Accordingly they began selling off their mining and real-estate properties.[177] Thus the triumph of October 26, 1881, and its aftermath was a Pyrrhic victory for Wyatt Earp and his clan.

By the end of the violence in late March 1882, the atonement-minded cowboys had badly hurt the Earps but were ultimately the losers. Although Virgil Earp was sorely wounded and Morgan Earp dead, the cowboys' prime target, Wyatt Earp, was unscathed, while the cowboy loss of six lives was so heavy that by midsummer 1882 the power of the cowboy faction in Cochise County was, even with the Earps gone, forever broken.[178] Promisingly begun with the shootings of Virgil and Morgan Earp, Will

McLaury's vendetta against the Earps was eventually a failure despite the searing casualties in the Earp family. The victory of the Earps was, as noted, dearly bought—paid for with the injury to Virgil and the death of Morgan, the forced sale of the Earp properties (although apparently at a good profit, especially for Wyatt) in Tombstone and vicinity, and the necessary withdrawal from Arizona. Still, the shattering of the cowboy combine of Cochise County by Wyatt Earp and his entourage had been a great triumph in behalf of the incorporating values of authority, order, and capitalistic enterprise upheld by Clum, Gage, and the Republican elite of Tombstone. Yet the fruits of this stunning victory were not to be enjoyed by the elite, whose economic ambitions would be defeated, not by the cowboy resister gunfighters, but by the waters that flooded the mines of Tombstone.

Emotionally stricken by the wounding of one brother and the death of another, Wyatt Earp was, however, a much greater success when he left Arizona in 1882 than when he entered it three years earlier. Now Wyatt Earp was nationally acclaimed as one of the great gunfighters of the West. The making of the legend of Wyatt Earp was under way. Dollar figures are not ascertainable, but in material terms (increasingly important to the ambitious Wyatt Earp) it appears that Wyatt emerged from his Tombstone period much more well to do than when it began. Moreover, the identity of rounder Wyatt Earp was diminished by his new role in Tombstone as a staunch Republican and man of property. As an incorporation gunfighter, the Republican Wyatt Earp had proven himself to Tombstone's "true men" of social, economic, and political power. In return, he gained their lasting regard. The Republican Wyatt Earp was, however, more and more forgotten by Americans at large as the growing myth of Wyatt Earp the gunfighter erased knowledge of the conservative values for which he had actually fought the cowboys in the Cochise County War of 1881–82.

Thus Wyatt Earp left Cochise County, Arizona, to spend the remaining forty-seven years of his life moving around the West.[179] He continued to seek higher social standing and respectability. A major gain came when, not long after he left Tombstone, he took for his third and last wife a lovely young Jewish woman who was far above him in the social scale. This was Josephine Sarah Marcus, of a wealthy San Francisco mercantile family.[180] Yet Wyatt Earp's third wife was not without her own social stigma. Her profession was acting, but being an actress on the Western circuit at that time was, to many, a barely respectable occupation for a female if even that. Moreover, the young woman's standing among the proper was lowered by her time spent in Tombstone (before she met Wyatt Earp) as John Behan's mistress. Rivalry between Behan and Wyatt Earp for the affections of this stunningly beautiful young stage player was another key factor in the ill will between the two men. In time, the youthful indiscretions of Josephine in Tombstone would be forgotten as she settled into what became almost half a century of respectable married life with Wyatt Earp. Capturing the love of Josephine Sarah Marcus was one of Wyatt's notable triumphs in Tombstone, and marrying above himself was a key factor in this upward social mobility, which saw him rise from being an obscure Great Plains rounder in the 1870s to lasting fame and membership in the Western upper middle class of the late nineteenth century.

From the 1880s on, Wyatt and his new wife (whom he and all the Earps called Sadie)[181] roamed about the West: to Colorado; to Idaho; a long stretch in California; into the Alaska Gold Rush; to the Nevada boom town of Tonopah; until, finally, they settled down in southern California.[182] In this peripatetic life, Wyatt Earp did well in a variety of business and sporting endeavors: real-estate investing, a stable of race horses, saloon ownership and management, and gambling.[183] The Earps, true to Wyatt's growing Republican respectability, associated with the wealthy and prominent: mining titan Horace A. Tabor and his glamorous wife, Baby Doe, in Colorado;[184] the California land-owning, hotel-keeping millionaire and sportsman, Elias Jackson (Lucky) Baldwin;[185] John H. McGraw, ex-governor of Washington, and Seattle booster and banker Erastus Brainerd, both of whom Wyatt knew in Alaska;[186] and Nevada corporation lawyer and later governor and senator, Tasker L. Oddie.[187] By 1888 Wyatt was worth $30,000[188]—an amount that would be equal to many times more in today's dollars. Earp hit his economic peak in Alaska where he sold the co-share of his Nome saloon for such a profit that he was ballyhooed as "Colonel Wyatt 'Mazuma' Earp."[189] The Alaska profits were, according to Sadie, the nest egg for Wyatt's Tonopah ventures and for the easy semiretirement of Wyatt and Sadie in the 1910s and 1920s.[190] There is a 1900 picture of Wyatt Earp in Nome that as Glenn Boyer has noted, reveals not a pistol-packing gunfighter but the prosperous suit and ample waistline of a successful businessman.[191] Sadie probably had much to do with Wyatt's material success, for her beauty and San Francisco sophistication very likely helped him gain entry to fashionable and affluent business circles. Bright and sharp, Sadie may well have had a significant advisory role in Wyatt's profitable economic endeavors.

Yet the rounder in Wyatt Earp was not gone but significantly transformed, for the post-Tombstone Wyatt had become what he remained to the end of his days: a *high-toned* rounder as well as a successful Republican businessman of the incorporated West. Indeed, rounder merged into Republican, and tension between the two contrasting identities dissolved. As a high-toned rounder, Wyatt Earp was in the headlines for refereeing the famous 1896 boxing match in San Francisco between Bob Fitzsimmons and Tom Sharkey.[192] More broadly, Wyatt formed firm friendships with members of a turn-of-the-century Western glitterati: writer Rex Beach,[193] gambler Tex Rickard,[194] and promoter Wilson Mizner.[195] High-toned rounders Rickard and Mizner went east to gain national fame,[196] but they never forgot Wyatt Earp, whom Mizner, for example, visited in the last days of the old gunfighter's life.[197]

Unlike Rickard (who became world famous for building the great indoor arena Madison Square Garden in New York City)[198] and Mizner, Wyatt did not go east. He and Sadie were dyed-in-the-wool Westerners. They spent their last decade (the 1920s) together, wintering near their favorite small mine on the California desert[199] and spending the rest of the year in Los Angeles,[200] where Wyatt became a friend of noted Western movies stars William S. Hart and Tom Mix.[201] Hart and Mix, along with Wilson Mizner, would be pallbearers at Wyatt's funeral.[202] In his final years Earp frequently attended Los Angeles's prestigious Wilshire Congregational Church.[203] The end came on January 13, 1929.[204] Wyatt Earp's last weeks were spent in comfort and calm with loyal Sadie by his side and their affectionate cat dozing the hours away in her favorite spot, Wyatt Earp's capacious lap.[205]

Five decades before his peaceful death in Los Angeles, Wyatt Earp had been an incorporation gunfighter—and a brilliantly successful one—while his opponents in the Cochise County War (the Clantons, McLaurys, John Ringo, Curly Bill, and others) were among the dead and defeated resister gunfighters in the Western Civil War of Incorporation. As ardent Republican, Wyatt Earp believed sincerely in the process of incorporation, and in effect he struck a bargain with the conservative incorporators of the West: to their side he would bring his gunfighting skill, and in return he would gain rising prosperity in a society which he, with his gunfire, helped create and incorporate.

The legend of Wyatt Earp is correct, at least, in that the gunfight near the O.K. Corral was the pivotal moment in his life, although the legend ignores the political, economic, and ideological factors that brought about the gunfight and the role Earp played in it and in Cochise County, Arizona. A socially significant episode in the Westen Civil War of Incorporation, the gunfight near the O.K. Corral has in mythic terms been established in the popular mind as the apotheosis of the no-duty-to-retreat gunfighting tradition whose prototype Wild Bill Hickok had established in Springfield, Missouri, in 1865. The battle of the Earps and Holliday with the Clantons and McLaurys thus stands as the most famous shootout in Western history. Yet it was far from being the deadliest.

In Holbrook, Arizona, on September 4, 1887, Sheriff Commodore Perry Owens alone equaled the toll of human life achieved by Wyatt Earp and his party in the Tombstone gunfight near the O.K. Corral.[206] Well-known in its day, Owens's exploit is now forgotten by all but specialists. Even more ignored in the annals of Western gunfighting is another no-duty-to-retreat shootout that resulted in more deaths than any other gunfight in the region's history—a gunfight long buried in obscurity, because it did not conform to the demands of the Western myth. This was the gun battle in a California wheat field on May 11, 1880, whose shocking outcome was seven dead[207]—more than twice the number of fatalities in the Earpian gunfight near the O.K. Corral.

3

California Conflict and
the American Dream

"We founded an American community, in which peace and order, honesty and decency, industry and economy, plenty and comfort prevailed."
Petition of California settlers to the President of the United States (1880).*

On May 11, 1880, a long-simmering conflict came to a violent climax in the Central Valley of California. Before the day was over, seven were dead or dying in the outcome of a deadly gunfight in a wheat field six miles northwest of Hanford, the small-town metropolis of the Mussel Slough area. The gunfight was savage. All those who exchanged shots would lose their lives.

By the 1870s and 1880s the spirit of no duty to retreat—sanctified by major state supreme court decisions in Ohio and Indiana and epitomized by the exploits of grassroots and glorified gunfighters—had become a key cultural institution of California and the West. In countless instances the no-duty-to-retreat attitude mentally programmed Californians and others to stand their ground and kill in defense of themselves, their property, and their values. In the Golden State the doctrine of no duty to retreat inspired the intransigence of the two opposing sides in a great struggle for the control of land in the agriculturally rich Mussel Slough district located thirty miles south of Fresno.

The Mussel Slough gunfight was a no-duty-to-retreat high

point in a vast trend of land consolidation that afflicted California and the West with pervasive violence in the late nineteenth century and produced a tragic legacy of lethal gunfighting.

Those slain in the Mussel Slough gunfight of May 11, 1880, represented two sides that had for years bitterly contested the ownership of thousands of acres of rich Mussel Slough farmland. Five of those slain in the gunfight were members of and represented the faction of settlers who were willing to defend their homes and farms with their lives. Behind this resolution not to retreat in the face of danger was the settlers' version of the American dream: a cooperatively built community of thriving farmers inspired by allegiance to a deeply rooted homestead ethic.[1] Two of those who died were from the other side, supporters of a mighty railroad claiming ownership of the land, their opponents, the settlers, had converted through years of struggle and sacrifice from a barren desert to an agricultural conucopia. The supporters of the railroad (and the railroad owners, too) had their version of the American dream conflicting with but just as idealistic as that of the settlers: success to be gained, not by cooperative community effort, but through individual enterprise in a market economy.[2]

The railroad involved was the Southern Pacific. In 1880 it was owned and led by a remarkable triumvirate of Leland Stanford, Charles Crocker, and Collis P. Huntington. These three Californians—Yankees orginally from the northeastern United States—along with their now-deceased partner, Mark Hopkins (another Yankee), had gained fame in 1869 by completing the western leg of the first rail connection between California and the East. This was the Overland Route, and the corporate entity of the undertaking was the Central Pacific Railroad, the recipient of a huge federal land grant to subsidize construction. Despite the lavish federal subsidy in land (and credit), the challenge in completing the Overland Route was daunting, and the accomplishment of the "Big Four" (Stanford, Huntington, Crocker, and Hopkins) in so doing was an enormous personal triumph for them. Successful but obscure Sacramento merchants in the 1850s, these four crafty Yankee businessmen had emerged in the 1860s and 1870s as California's most noted and powerful industrialists; their impact ramified through the full range of the social, economic, and political system of the state.

They carved out distinct roles for themselves. Hopkins, the treasurer and efficient bureaucrat, was the most retiring of the four; he died in 1878, reducing the Big Four to the Big Three. Huntington—financier and logistical genius—was the most creative and powerful of the Big Four, but because he was their congressional lobbyist and eastern financial representative and purchasing agent with an office in New York City, he was not usually as visible in California as the others. As a lobbyist, Huntington's remarkable powers of persuasion were frequently clinched with hard cash (delivered through intermediaries) or other illicit material rewards. To Californians the name of Huntington became, in time, a byword for corruption. Later to serve for a time as president of the Southern Pacific, Crocker had been the hard-driving construction boss of the Central Pacific project. Stanford, as a stalwart of the Republican Party who had served as governor of California early in the Civil War, relished his role as public-relations front man and politico for the railroad; he also served as president of the Central Pacific and later, like Crocker (but much longer), president of the Southern Pacific. Although Stanford was the only one of the Big Four to gain high office, all four were founders of the Republican party in California, and in the 1850s they had been idealistically opposed to the expansion of slavery into the territories. Much later in his life— and while the odium of corruption was imperishably connected to his name—Huntington had been a major contributor to the support of African-American education in Virginia, where he built a large shipbuilding yard and drydock. To their dying days Stanford, Huntington, Crocker, and Hopkins were proud pillars of the Republican party and, as entrepreneurial industrialists, solid members of its conservative wing on economic matters.

Chartered some years after the Central Pacific, the Southern Pacific drew on its own huge federal land grant along a line bisecting California from San Francisco through the Central Valley to its terminus on the Colorado River boundary of Arizona.[3] In charge of this railroad empire, the Central Pacific and the Southern Pacific, the Big Three of Stanford, Crocker, and Huntington were in 1880 unequaled in their power in the state of California. Because of the immense clout they unhesitatingly wielded in political and economic affairs, neither the Big Three nor their railroads were loved in the Golden State. While they sincerely viewed themselves as great entrepreneurial benefactors of California,[4] many citizens saw Stanford, Crocker, and Huntington as oppressive monopolizers of the state's land and wealth.[5]

The roots of the challenge to the Big Three and the Southern Pacific mounted by the Mussel Slough settlers went deep. In the middle and late eighteenth century, America endured a crisis of land, population, and wealth in which the increasing concentration of property in the rural and urban elite, as a result of a narrowing land base in the face of steeply growing population, spread discontent far and wide. From 1740 to 1799, there were nine rural rebellions in the back country of America stretching from Massachusetts and Vermont to South Carolina. Inspiring the rural rebels was their ardent, shared belief in the homestead ethic, an enduring body of values centered on the belief in the right of rural Americans to have and to hold a family-size farm. After the Revolution, the crisis of land, population, and wealth faded (although the homestead ethic did not) owing to the rapid expansion of frontier settlement west of the Appalachians, which relieved the population pressure on the land in the original thirteen states and diluted the concentration of wealth in the hands of the few.[6]

Following the Civil War, Americans began to perceive a new version of the earlier land-population-wealth crisis as an alarming trend of land consolidation and enclosure threatened the small landholders of the West. Henry George of San Francisco, later to be famous as the author of *Progress and Poverty,* articulated the new perception. George's social philosophy was moored in a deep belief in the homestead ethic. As he expressed it, the health of

American society rested on "the cultivator of a small farm"[7]—
"owning his own acres, using his own capital, and working with
his own hands."[8] Yet Henry George feared for the continued
existence of the independent small farmer on whom the homestead ethic centered. *Progress and Poverty* did not appear until
1880, but in publications during the 1870s George, writing in San
Francisco, spelled out his view of the new land-population-wealth
crisis facing California, the West, and the nation in an era of land
consolidation.

In a book entitled *Our Land and Land Policy* (1871), Henry
George noted that the American population was rising steeply
while the availability of land was narrowing just as swiftly. Although the Western wide-open spaces of the federal public domain were huge, only about one-third of that expanse was then fit
for cultivation. With the total supply of unoccupied land thus
restricted, there was a further problem of the increasing monopolization of the best land, due especially to the imperial land grants
to great railroads such as the Southern Pacific and the Central
Pacific. More than anything else, said George, the gigantic railroad land grants were causing "the monopolization of land" and
making "the many poorer, and a few richer." And George saw that
of all states, the problem of land monopoly was greatest at home,
in California.[9] By 1877 Henry George saw "all wealth and power
tending more and more to be concentrated in a few hands."
"What sort of a republic will this be in a few years," asked George,
"if these things go on?"[10] With the Southern Pacific Railroad heading the land monopolists of California, George denounced the
trend by which "large bodies of our new lands" were being concentrated "in the hands of the few" with the consequent "absorption
of small farms into large estates."[11]

What Henry George observed was a gigantic American movement of consolidation in the form of land enclosure. This process
of consolidation resulted in frequent episodes in the Western Civil
War of Incorporation. One such episode was the Central Valley
conflict between the settlers and the Southern Pacific Railroad.

The settlers, as noted, had their own ideology based on the

homestead ethic upon which they aspired to the American dream of success through cooperative community effort. The railroad exemplified the drive to incorporate the West in the interest of the conservative, consolidating authority of capital in a market economy dominated by corporate enterprise. One dimension of the incorporating trend was land monopolization and enclosure through giant land grants such as that made to the Southern Pacific.

Dissident Westerners reacted to the trend of incorporation and the land-population-wealth crisis with resistance that was often violent. Thus the process of incorporation, often aggressive and violent, provoked resistance that resulted in many a battle in the Western Civil War of Incorporation—a war that repeatedly flared up in surpassingly bitter local struggles for power. Often referred to locally and by later historians as "wars," these conflicts were indeed local civil wars remarkable for their casualties and unremitting character. Social, economic, and political factors fostered alignments that bred antagonists prone to resolve an irrepressible conflict with no-duty-to-retreat violence. Sometimes these examples of the Western Civil War of Incorporation pitted intransigent mining magnates and their lieutenants against the nascent labor-union movement of the West. Especially violent conflict of this sort broke out, for example, in the Coeur d'Alene mining region of northern Idaho in the 1890s[12] and was broadly perpetuated into the early twentieth century in great outbreaks of industrial conflict in mine and mill, field and forest in such widely dispersed spots as Cripple Creek and Ludlow, Colorado,[13] Wheatland, California,[14] and Everett and Centralia, Washington,[15] as well as in such metropolitan centers as Los Angeles and San Francisco.[16] Again and again, however, the Western Civil War of Incorporation hinged on opposed land claims resulting in brush-fire conflicts, charring the land and its people from the prairies of Texas to the plains and mountains of Wyoming and on to the valleys of Arizona and California.

As the nineteenth century wore on the grim analysis of Henry

George was borne out by a series of struggles that emerged from the land-enclosing trend he deplored. Throughout the West range wars stemmed from the land-enclosing tactics of large-scale ranchers exercised at the expense of the small ranchers and homesteading farmers. Among numerous examples of these land-oriented conflicts in the Western Civil War of Incorporation was the 1877–78 outbreak in Custer County, Nebraska, in which homesteaders were locked in violent combat with big cattlemen.[17] In Johnson County, Wyoming, aggressive cattle kings waged war in 1892 against violently resisting small ranchers and homesteaders.[18] The Great Plains region of Texas smoldered with long-term conflict in the 1880s and 1890s, peaking in the "Fence Cutters' War" of 1883–84, during which small farmers and ranchers used the guerrilla tactics of fence-cutting violence against the larger ranchers and farmers who were enclosing the open range for themselves.[19] Northern New Mexico in the early 1890s was the locale of the White Cap movement—a violent campaign by poor Hispanic villagers to fight off the takeover of the communally held sheep ranges that were the basis of their livelihoods.[20]

In California itself there unfolded before the horrified eyes of Henry George[21] and others the Mussel Slough conflict in Tulare County, 1878–80. No episode could have better illustrated the warnings and admonitions of George in regard to the evil consequences of the land-monopoly trend of the late nineteenth century. The settlers of the Mussel Slough region employed the tactics of vigilantism to resist the land-enclosure campaign carried on by the Southern Pacific Railroad and its clients.

Before 1870 the Mussel Slough area, about thirty miles south of the present city of Fresno in the southern Central Valley of California, was virtually a desert.[22] The Mussel Slough, which gave its name to the area, was only a long arm of the Kings River. The latter, draining the heavy snows of the Sierra Nevada, was the key to the development of the Mussel Slough district. The vast irrigation potential of the Kings River would be aggressively implemented during the 1870s.[23] The Mussel

Slough district was about eight to ten miles wide and nearly twenty miles long.[24] Lured by promotional pamphlets of the Southern Pacific Railroad distributed not only in California but east of the Mississippi, settlers began to pour into the region. By 1880 the population was pushing four thousand.[25] Three new town sprang up: Hanford, Grangeville, and Lemoore. Laid out by the Southern Pacific Railroad in 1877 along its branch line from Goshen to Huron, Hanford became the small urban center of the Mussel Slough vicinity.[26] Irrigation improvements were made by the cooperative efforts of hundreds of families and came to include a large, complex system of seven main canals with their branches.[27] Some of the irrigation canals (or ditches) were very wide.[28] Thousands of acres were watered by these ditches, and a thriving people prospered as a result of them. The principal product of the Mussel Slough area was wheat, and from its former barren status the district became a deep breadbasket of California, which was then one of the great wheat growing states in America.[29]

Hanford was not large in 1880—fewer than a thousand folks lived there— but it was a bustling little town, the third biggest in far-flung Tulare County. In Hanford were four churches, good schools, a city water works, twelve retail establishments, four hotels, a flour mill, and six grain-storage warehouses with a capacity of ten thousand tons.[30] For the busy farmers and townspeople who took time out from their daily tasks, there was also inspiring mountain scenery. The lofty, snow-capped Sierra Nevadas loomed in the east.[31] To the west were lower but closer ranges. Despite the unattractive place name of "Mussel Slough," life in the area was good. From Hanford, well-tilled and well-irrigated fields were seen in every direction.[32] Living in a broad vale between two great mountain ranges of California, the citizens of Mussel Slough were proudly conscious of their existence in one of the finest garden spots of the state.[33]

While the cultivation of the land went well, the people in their social and economic relations were beset almost from the beginning by dire troubles. Hanford and its Mussel Slough environs did not escape the plague of crime and lowlife that so often afflicted American frontier communities. Outlaws made periodic forays from haunts in the wilds of the western ranges, and gamblers and prostitutes descended on Hanford. Drawing on the deeply imbedded tradition of frontier vigilantism of which California was a stronghold, the settlers from Modesto to Hanford took things into their own hands with at least five vigilante movements from 1872 to 1884.[34]

The violence between vigilantes and the criminous did not, however, exhaust the factor of conflict in the troubled region, for an even greater vendetta was that between the settlers and the Southern Pacific Railroad in the latter's triple role as rail monopoly, land-owning giant, and behind-the-scenes political power in California. This bitter episode in the Western Civil War of Incorporation turned on the twin issues of land titles and land prices. In the Mussel Slough region, the even-numbered 640-acre land sections were held by the federal government for disposal to the pioneers, but one-half of the entire land of the district was held (or claimed) by the railroad in the form of the odd-numbered 640-acre sections, which had been granted to it in 1866 by the United States government as a subsidy to be eventually used for the construction of rail lines southward through California.[35]

In controversy were at least twenty-five thousand acres claimed by the railroad under the federal land grant,[36] while settlers claimed that the failure of the railroad to complete a line all the way from Tres Pinos, far to the north, to Huron, west of Hanford, meant that the railroad had violated the terms of the land grant and should therefore forfeit the land back to the government.[37] In great number, settlers occupied these disputed lands, intending to establish their own claims under the federal preemption land law. The question of who rightfully had title to the land was in litigation, but meanwhile settlers disputed the prices at which the railroad sought to market its land should it triumph in the legal wrangle over the land grant. The crux of the settlers' position was their contention that the railroad in its promotional pamphlets had promised to sell most of its agricultural acreage for only $2.50–5 (or little more) per acre without any additional charge for the value of the improvements (irrigation ditches, buildings, soil development, etc.) the settlers might have made on the property.[38] In contrast to this, the railroad by 1877–78 was determined to charge settlers the market value of the land, including the improvements made by the settlers themselves. The rates the railroad intended to charge for the land varied but were from $20 to over $30 per acre—many times the $2.50–5 price emphasized in the railroad promotional pamphlets.[39]

The economic stakes on both sides were enormous. For example, at the $20 per acre rate, the railroad stood to realize as much as $500,000 from sales of the disputed acreage in the Mussel Slough area[40]—a huge sum in the deflated dollars of the 1870s and 1880s. For the individual settler, the rate of $20 per acre would amount to a total cost of $1,600 for a relatively small one-eighth section of 80 acres. For a quarter-section the bill would be $3,200; for a half-section the charge would $6,400. For the great majority of the landholders settled on the railroad-claimed sections, these were prices that were impossibly beyond their means.

The irony is that the agricultural policy of the Southern Pacific Railroad in California was, on the whole, quite enlightened. Administered by its astute, forceful land director, Jerome T. Madden, the railroad's policy in general was to encourage farmer and rancher settlement along its lines in the interest of building up the railroad's freight traffic through the development of the country. At the core of the policy was the sale of acreage from the railroad's huge land grant. The Southern Pacific shaped its sales policy in favor of true settlers rather than land speculators. The prices it charged settlers were reasonable, because the railroad did not wish to discourage settlement by demanding excessive rates for the land.[41] In the Mussel Slough region, however, the railroad took a hard line in order to repel a direct threat to its claimed ownership of the grant lands (about the legality of which it felt there was not the least shadow of doubt) and to defeat the settlers' attempt to undercut the railroad's complete freedom to set its own prices for its own property.

The incorporating thrust of the Southern Pacific's relentless land policy was a direct affront to the homestead ethic of the Mussel Slough settlers. In particular, the railroad's land-enclosing threat violated the keystone of the homestead ethic: the belief in the right to have and hold a family-size farm, especially in the case where the settler, by bestowing his labor on the homestead, had gained what was seen as the natural right to hold it without legal challenge. To the Mussel Slough pioneer as to the American farmer going back to the mid-eighteenth century, the land of the homestead improved by the labor of the settler could not "be taken" away from him, so New Jerseymen asserted in opposing a powerful proprietary elite in 1746, "without breaking thro' the Rule of Natural Justice; for thereby he would be actually deprived of the Fruits of his Industry."[42] Allegiance to the homestead ethic thus inspired the settlers to resist incorporation in a landed society dominated by the Southern Pacific Railroad and its Big Three owners.

In defense of their occupancy of the land, the Mussel Slough settlers drew heavily on the homestead ethic as they took their case to the highest level—to President Rutherford B. Hayes. When Hayes visited San Francisco in 1880 he received an impassioned, eloquent petition from settler representatives. In their petition the settlers described how they had added their labor to the land to establish the rightfulness of their claims. We organized irrigation companies, said the petitioners,

> and saturated the sterile plain to the extent of . . . thousands of acres. . . . We accomplished this work in the face of great natural obstacles, with very little means, and under extreme conditions of hardship, toil and endurance. . . . In brief, through sheer energy and perseverance by the investment of our means . . . continued through the best years of of our lives, and relying firmly upon the rights we had acquired as American citizens, and upon the pledges of the Southern Pacific Railroad Company [in regard to low land prices], we converted a desert into one of the garden spots of the

> State. . . . We . . . acted like men . . . [who believed] that they were securing, fairly and honorably, permanent homes for themselves and their families.

In the course of their improvements and unremitting industry, the settlers were building, also, a community for themselves and their neighbors.

> We erected fences, houses, barns, school houses, and churches, after the manner of a permanent and well-ordered community. We laid out and established roads, which are now in many places shaded by thrifty trees. We cultivated fields and orchards, and produced . . . cereals, vegetables and fruits. . . . We raised stock of all kinds and of choice breeds. We beautified our homes with gardens and vines. We supported thriving villages and one considerable town [Hanford].

[In short, the plea concluded,]

> We founded an American community, in which peace and order, honesty and decency, industry and economy, plenty and comfort prevailed.[43]

Typical of those who participated in this process of founding an American community to realize the American dream were a husband and wife, Frank and Mary E. Chambers, who in the 1870s sought an unincorporated life on Mussel Slough land claimed by the railroad. "I shall never forget my first impression of the country," Mrs. Chambers later reminisced, "I was so discouraged with the looks of it that I did not want to look out [of] the wagon. Nothing but cattle and horses" were to be seen "until it looked like one vast corral, with no more appearance of vegetation than a well swept floor." Although the Chamberses had no experience with farming, they were determined to stick it out. The cattlemen told them that they would "starve to death, as it was impossible to raise anything on the dry plains." But Frank and Mary Chambers did not believe the stockmen, whom they looked on "as an indolent people who had never made an effort to cultivate the soil; but we, with our energy and perseverance, would make the wilderness to blossom and bear."

The stockmen were right, however, and the Chamberses led a hand-to-mouth existence their first year and soon found that there was no hope without irrigation. With others they banded together to dig the seven-or-eight-mile-long Lower Kings River Ditch. Women and children happily ran out to see the first water flow into the ditch from the river, but the joy was premature, for the parched land too swiftly absorbed the water. Three tough years followed, and then the twenty-seven-mile-long Peoples Ditch was dug by settlers "without a dollar and a living to make the while." But not until a third irrigation canal, the aptly named Last Chance Ditch, was completed did the Chamberses finally begin to succeed as farmers.[44]

Having been assured in written communications from the railroad that they would have to pay no more than $2.50 per acre for their land should the railroad's claim to it be upheld, Frank and Mary Chambers were starkly disillusioned by what happened in 1877. At this time, the Southern Pacific sent in its land appraiser and, with evaluation of the Chambers-occupied land, "up went our land from $2.50 to $22 per acre. And why? Because we had a house, barn, orchard, alfalfa pasture, flower garden, ditches, and a well cultivated farm. Our ditch interests cost us about $1,500, and now, just as we wer getting our heads above water, here comes the demand, $22 per acre or leave the land."

"Are we to walk out of our houses and leave them to strangers without even a murmur?" Mary Chambers asked in behalf of all the settlers. Contrary to the railroad's denunciation of the settlers as lawless squatters, "we have," she declared in 1880, "made a country, built towns, churches, and school houses" and, at last, gained the respect and sympathy of the stockmen.[45]

Hundreds of Mussel Slough pioneers like Frank and Mary Chambers joined the Settlers' League to defend their home places against the claims of the Southern Pacific Railroad. Court records show that the Mussel Slough settlers who contested the railroad's claim occupied an average of 128 acres.[46] One of these struggling settlers was Robert B. Huey, born in Pennsylvania but a Californian since 1856, who married in 1865, took a hand at school-teaching, and then moved on to a Mussel Slough quarter-section in 1869. With a growing family, Huey built a house, dug a well, planted shade trees, and put in a garden but did not do well as a farmer on the arid land until in 1872 he began irrigating his acreage with Kings River water from a big ditch dug and maintained by the cooperative efforts and money of Huey and his neighbors. With the precious irrigation waters, Huey planted almost all his land in grain and soon was prosperous enough to build a barn, put in an orchard and vineyards, and make an addition to his house.[47] Then in 1878 the blow fell: attorneys for the Southern Pacific Railroad sued Huey for possession of the 160-acre lot, which he had improved with $3,500 worth of labor and capital investment.[48] Like many other Mussel Slough settlers, Huey claimed the quarter section under the federal preemption land law, which allowed a settler to purchase at a minimal rate land already occupied by the settler. The railroad denied Huey's claim, holding that Huey's tract was legally part of the giant checkerboard federal grant of land made to the railroad in 1866.

The social philosopher of the settlers' movement in which the Chamberses, Huey, and others enlisted was J. W. A. Wright of Hanford, who had pursued the agrarian ideal from Alabama to California and been high in the councils of the state and national Grange.[49] To Wright the Mussel Slough area was, in line with the homestead ethic, a realization of the "ideal of a mixed husbandry on the land, systematically" cultivated "by independent and enterprising ranchers on small farms." It was this unincorporated, group-created society based on the affirmation of the homestead ethic that attracted Wright to Mussel Slough and caused him to lend his enthusiastic suppport to the settlers' movement against the railroad.[50] Another leader of the settlers' movement sounded the note of no-duty-to-retreat resistance to incorporation in a railroad-dominated society: the settlers were, he declared, "fighting" for their "homes," defending what they believed "to be right," standing by the houses and tracts which they "had made comfortable with years of toil and privation."[51]

Initially, the defense was nonviolent, beginning in 1874 with petitions to Congress. A lobbyist was sent to Washington, D.C., in 1876 and 1878 while a legal defense of the settlers' land claims was underway.[52] Soon the settlers organized a vigilante movement to defend their land occupancy violently against the railroad and the well-to-do who were eager to buy the land tracts out from under them at the railroad's high rates. After railroad land appraiser W. H. Clark moved into the Mussel Slough area in 1877 to begin assessing the value of land tracts prior to the railroad's placing them on the market, six hundred of the pioneers met at Hanford on April 12, 1878, to found the Settlers' League.[53] With an elaborate organization of a grand league, six subordinate neighborhood leagues, officers, a constitution, and a schedule of dues to raise funds for the legal campaign, the Settlers' League was at first a nonviolent organization and one that was in part modeled on the insurgent militancy of the Irish Land League.[54] Such were the mounting tensions inflamed by the settlers' fears of being made homeless by the railroad, however, that in less than a year the daytime, legal activities of the Settlers' League were eclipsed by the night-riding of league members garbed in masks and gowns to hide their identities.[55]

The specific action of the railroad that brought the violent vigilante response of the settlers came in the fall of 1878 when the railroad began to bring suit against those occupying the odd-numbered sections claimed by the Southern Pacific.[56] The settlers struck back in November 1878 with their first acts of violence. In that month the night-riding vigilantes burned down the house of a tenant of a well-to-do farmer who aligned himself with the railroad.[57] In March 1879 the settlers organized military companies that openly paraded the streets of Hanford, Grangeville, and Lemoore in following months,[58] and from November 1878 until the fatal climax on May 11, 1880, the night-riding, violence, and intimidation continued.[59]

Underlying the violence was the bitterness of a dispute that split the Mussel Slough domain into two hostile, violence-prone factions, each imbued with the social doctrine of no duty to retreat.

On one side was a minority faction that supported the railroad and was entirely comfortable with the trend of incorporation. Some of its members were in process of paying the high railroad rates for land in order to oust the original settlers. Heading this prorailroad, land-enclosing faction were Walter J. Crow, a young, well-to-do farmer with roots in the Modesto area,[60] and Mills Hartt, a tough-talking, chip-on-his-shoulder former Southern Pacific station agent.[61] Members of the prorailroad faction were significantly better off than the rank-and-file of the Settlers' League. Hartt, for example, had the ample means to purchase for the hefty price of $6,288 a half-section of railroad-claimed land cultivated by two members of the Settlers' League.[62]

Locally spearheading the resistance to the Southern Pacific's incorporating process were five men who headed the antirailroad Settlers' League movement: John J. Doyle, Major Thomas J. McQuiddy, Luther J. Hawley, J. W. A. Wright, and James N. Patterson. Each had a distinctive role in the movement. Doyle was the initiator, the activist, the strategist, and the organizer.[63] McQuiddy was a charismatic leader and radical grassroots politician who would soon become the Greenback party's candidate for governor of California.[64] Hawley was the secretary.[65] Wright was the intellectual and penman.[66] Patterson was always at the center of the most critical action.[67] They were a formidable group of men; this is shown not only by their actions but by the surviving portraits of the full-bearded Doyle, McQuiddy, Hawley, and Patterson. McQuiddy and Patterson were steely-eyed individuals, and it is easy to imagine them at the head of night-riding activities. Doyle and Hawley, too, gaze steadily out of their portraits, and one senses an implacability of purpose on their part as well.[68]

Perhaps none exceeded the violence-prone McQuiddy in the power of his personality and in his defiance of the railroad. A fiery California opponent of the Western trend of incorporation, McQuiddy, as a result of his role in the Mussel Slough resistance, was indicted but became noted for his ability to evade arrest. Finally arrested, he was never brought to trial.[69] When a Sacramento man, one Jackson, purchased title from the railroad for the tract of land occupied by McQuiddy, the latter left a belligerent note on his gatepost that so unnerved Jackson that he hurried back to the capital city, never to return, while McQuiddy and his family calmly reoccupied their place.[70] The Civil War service of McQuiddy and Hawley[71] (along with that of other war veterans in the Settlers' League) enhanced their effectiveness as League leaders, and the military temper learned in wartime may well have been put to use in night-riding activities.

Firmly and deeply oriented to the homestead ethic, these Settlers' League leaders were set apart from the Hartt and Crow group in a number of ways. Somewhat older, the League leaders ranged in age from the middle thirties to the early fifties. These leaders were from both the North and the South.[72] Hawley, for example, was from Ohio by way of Oregon, to which he had come in 1851.[73] Two had served as majors in the Confederate army,[74] while one had been a captain in the Northern army during the Civil War.[75] Common allegiance to the homestead ethic transcended the divided Civil Way loyalties of these chieftains of the Settlers' League. Yet the Civil War military service of these men (and others in the League) may well have reinforced, as it did for Justice Oliver Wendell Holmes, belief in no duty to retreat (on Holmes, see Chapter 1).

Still, sectional animus may have been a factor in the Mussel Slough dispute. There was a strong contingent of settlers with Southern backgrounds, and one authority has contended that they were well aware that the Southern Pacific Railroad headed by the Big Three was dominated by persons of Yankee origin. According to this view, the settlers tended to see the railroad magnates and their policies in the same light in which most white Southerners viewed the Northern Radical Reconstruction leaders in the South: odious outsiders bent on bringing their victims low.[76] In the Mussel Slough vicinity, there were also deep-seated feelings of class consciousness and animosity. Mills Hartt was especially contemptuous of the antirailroad settlers, whom he derisively referred to as "sandlappers"[77]—a California 1870s–80s equivalent of our term "redneck." Walter J. Crow expressed the murderous emotions of hatred welling up in his clique when telling friends that he would either have a certain piece of land or kill its occupant.[78] In general, the prorailroad group viewed the "sandlappers" as being led "by a set of demagogues" who were generally "poor" and consequently "very anxious to get something for nothing" by their "agitation" against the Southern Pacific land claim.[79]

Indeed, the town of Hanford, located in the cockpit of the Mussel Slough troubles, had become a radical center in California. It was a California stronghold of the national Anti-Monopoly League,[80] and the Settlers' League's most radical leader, John J. Doyle, had ties to the militant labor movement of San Francisco led by Denis Kearney,[81] while the homestead-oriented agrarianism of J. W. A. Wright was in contrast to the social conservatism of the members of the prorailroad faction. The latter relished their own values, which were characteristic of the self-aggrandizing propertyholders and enterprisers of the incorporating West.[82]

With the settlers increasingly resorting to night-riding vigilante tactics and the Hartt-Crow faction airing reckless threats, the situation during 1879 and 1880 neared the flash point. Despite the searing emotions involved, both sides were, in the spirit of no duty to retreat, pursuing rational policies based on force and violence calculated to gain their respective ends.

While the Settlers' League followed its deliberate pace of resistance to the railroad through a legal route leading eventually (and fruitlessly) to the United States Supreme Court, it was also pursuing a vigilante campaign of violence and intimidation that had two objectives. First, the Settlers' League vigilantes sought to use their might and violence to take entire control of the Mussel Slough area. Second, and more specifically, they hoped to stop the execution of prorailroad legal judgments in the Mussel Slough district.[83] This aspect of their strategy became crucial after Judge Lorenzo Sawyer of the Federal circuit court in San Francisco rendered a definitive judgment in favor of the Southern Pacific land claims on December 15, 1879.[84]

To the misfortune of the Mussel Slough settlers the federal circuit court in San Francisco was under the sway of Lorenzo Sawyer, who willingly made his courtroom a citadel of capitalistic consolidation and expasion in the Western trend of incorporation. An ever-grateful Sawyer owed the inception of his long judicial career in California to an 1862 appointment by Leland Stanford, then governor of California.[85] A Gold Rush veteran, Sawyer was a close personal friend of both Stanford[86] and Charles Crocker[87] of the Southern Pacific. Sawyer was proud of the judicial assistance he had given as a California state supreme court judge in the 1860s to the railraod-building achievements of Stanford, Crocker, Huntington, and Hopkins.[88] Forty-niners all and self-made successes in the California Gold Rush, Sawyer and the Big Four shared the same American dream of success through untrammeled individual effort. Thus Sawyer brought to his tenure on the United States circuit court a social and economic philosophy favoring individual and corporate enterprise, which he and his colleagues in the federal court system of the late nineteenth century were solidifying into a judicial doctrine that was of immense benefit to monopolistic corporations such as the Southern Pacific.[89]

Judge Sawyer's judicial ruling of December 15, 1879, hit the Mussel Slough area like a bombshell and was the basis for the Southern Pacific's launching of twenty-three suits of ejectment against Settlers' League members in the spring of 1880.[90] In the view of Settlers' League militants this increasingly successful legal campaign of the railroad dictated the intimidation of persons inclined to make land purchases from the railroad that would result in the dispossession of the original settlers. Hartt and Crow were too determined and violence-prone themselves to be vulnerable to this tactic, but the strategy of violent intimidation was successful against others, including employees of the railroad. The zealots of the Settlers' League, said a Hanford resident, imposed a "reign of terror" on the Mussel Slough area. Warnings were posted against the purchase of railroad-claimed land. Behaving like vigilantes, the armed and masked "military branch" of the Settlers' League paraded nightly in the streets of Hanford to intimidate its opponents. Certain staunch supporters of the legal cause of the Southern Pacific were ordered to leave the community and lost no time in doing so.[91]

Meanwhile, as both grassroots and incorporation gunfighters, Mills Hartt and Walter J. Crow armed themselves to the teeth and let it be known far and wide that they would use gunplay to back up their purchases of land claimed by the railroad.[92]

With implacable attitudes on both sides, the Mussel Slough conflict in the spring of 1880 moved swiftly toward its violent climax of May 11. The crisis was precipitated by what seemed to be duplicity on the part of the railroad and its allies. Politically the situation did not look good for the Settlers' League. Its protest against the Southern Pacific attracted many words of sympathy but no action. The state legislature supported the settlers and had sent a resolution to Congress in behalf of the Mussel Slough people.[93] Sympathetic also were two U. S. senators and one congressman from California,[94] but the settlers were losing in the courts, and the executive branch in both state and nation had not been very helpful. The administration of President Rutherford B. Hayes stood aloof. Yet in spring 1880 the settlers took hope from a surprisingly conciliatory attitude on the part of one of the Big Three, Leland Stanford, who visited the Mussel Slough country in March 1880 and then followed up the visit by appointing Doyle, McQuiddy, and Patterson to a committee to negotiate, if possible, a compromise between the settlers and the railroad.[95] The settler representatives carried on intermittent discussions with Stanford for "about a month" looking toward "an equitable arrangement" to resolve the land dispute.[96]

These hopes were dashed by what the settlers believed was an egregious double-cross when in early May 1880 the United States marshal for California, Alonzo W. Poole, suddenly appeared in the Mussel Slough vicinity. The legal writs borne by Poole obliged him to dispossess individual Settlers' League members in favor of the Southern Pacific's land claims[97] More broadly, each side—railroad and settlers—believed too strongly in its own principles and contrasting versions of the American dream to yield on critical points. Thus a true compromise was impossible, and an action by one side was misinterpreted or rejected by the other. Both factions were in a strongly no-duty-to-retreat mood. A showdown on this front of the Western Civil War of Incorporation was near.

The railroad's program of dispossession followed a significant escalation of the dispute by the Settlers' League; on April 14 Doyle, McQuiddy, and Patterson had visited railroad representative D. W. Parkhurst in Hanford to demand that he leave the area. That night masked and armed men confronted Parkhurst with the same command, resulting in his departure the next day. The league met sometime in the week before May 11 and prepared itself for violent resistance to the railroad's power play, legally enforced dispossession of settlers.[98] For the morning of Tuesday, May 11, the Settlers' League had scheduled a great picnic, an occasion for which they had engaged as a speaker the stormy petrel of California politics, Judge David S. Terry, to whom they were looking for inspiration and encouragement.[99]

Although Terry was unable to appear at the picnic, his involvement (or near involvement) in the Mussel Slough conflict is symbolically appropriate. Militantly opposed to the railroad and strongly in favor of the settlers, Judge Terry was a hot-tempered, violence-prone individual who while serving on the California state supreme court in 1859 killed United States Senator David C. Broderick in a duel.[100] In California, David S. Terry personified the violent spirit of no duty to retreat, and on the morning of May 11, 1880, that spirit was running high on both sides of the Mussel Slough conflict.†

---

†The sensational killing of Judge Terry on August 14, 1889, by David Neagle both typified and was another dramatic example of the ambience of no-duty-to-retreat violence that so remarkably characterized California in the middle and late nineteenth century. This was because the slaying of Terry—one of the most prominent Californians of his time—hinged on the killer Neagle's role as the bodyguard of one of the most prominent Americans (and Californians) of the era: Stephen J. Field, associate justice of the United States Supreme Court, 1863–96. The controversial homicide was, according to Neagle and Field, provoked by an assault on Field by Terry on August 14. The Terry-Neagle-Field imbroglio

Despite Terry's inability to appear, the Settlers' League went on with its picnic plans, and the railroad faction used the settlers' preoccupation with the festivities to pull off what would have been a crucial land grab. Early in the morning of May 11, a heavily armed party of four persons set out to dispossess the Settlers' League partners, Henry D. Brewer and J. O. Storer, from the north half of an odd-numbered section northwest of Hanford, which Mills Hartt had purchased from the railroad. In addition to Hartt, the party of four was composed of Walter J. Crow; William H. Clark, the hated Southern Pacific land appraiser; and the federal marshal, Alonzo W. Poole, who had the responsibility of enforcing the United States court's writ of ejectment against Brewer and Storer.[103] Moving among the wheat fields in a route taking them steadily toward the disputed half-section, the party was halted near Brewer's house by the appearance of a mounted group of Settlers' League members

---

also illustrates the volatile, violence-prone nature of nineteenth-century California social history and was indirectly connected to the Mussel Slough episode. Although never chief justice of the U.S. Supreme Court, Field dominated it philosophically during his long term on the Court and, according to constitutional historian Leonard W. Levy, was one of the half-dozen most influential figures in American judicial history.[101] David S. Terry and Stephen J. Field were political enemies, but it was Terry's threats against Field—growing out of a heated personal and legal dispute—that resulted in the employment of Neagle (who had been a tough Tombstone lawman in the era of Wyatt Earp) as Field's bodyguard. The killing of Terry by Neagle was indirectly related to the Mussel Slough conflict: Field, a Californian, was a judicial ally of Lorenzo Sawyer (see note 89) and, like Sawyer, was a jurisprudential protagonist of the Southern Pacific and a personal friend of Stanford and other railroad leaders. Terry, on the other hand, was a leader of the dominant antimonopoly, anticorporation, anti–Southern Pacific wing of the California Democratic party, which struck a hard blow against the 1884 national presidential ambitions of Field, a strongly conservative Democrat. From first to last in the 1888–89 feud between them, both Terry and Field had behaved in a spirit of no duty to retreat. Field's attitude—very much shared by his surrogate, Neagle—was a reversion to his days in the California Gold Rush era when, as a volatile, dynamic, and much threatened young politico and state-court judge, Field had unmistakably let it be known that he, in an implacably stand-one's ground temper, would if need be defend himself to the death with the firearm he ostentatiously carried. Much later in life Field believed strongly that only his armed no-duty-to-retreat demeanor had saved his life and that such determination both preserved him from violence and made retaliatory violence by him unnecessary.[102]

and picnickers led by James N. Patterson.[104] Not many of the men in Patterson's party were armed, but the Leaguers had a heavy advantage in numbers. A parley ensued, and Patterson and his men insisted that Poole would have to stop executing his writs of ejectment—earlier in the morning William Braden had been evicted from his land and his possessions cast out of his home and on to the side of the road. Poole replied that his personal sympathies were on the side of the settlers but that, as U.S. marshal, he would have to and would enforce the court ruling against Braden, Brewer, and other settlers.[105]

Hopelessly outnumbered, Poole reluctantly allowed himself to be detained by the Leaguers.[106] A peaceful outcome was not to be, however, for long-standing personal enmity between one James Harris, who was present in the settlers' band, and Mills Hartt brought on an argument and a sudden burst of gunfire between Harris and Hartt. Hartt's gun spoke an instant before Harris's shot mortally wounded Hartt.[107] In retaliation, Walter J. Crow began to spray the settlers with bursts from his shotgun. First Harris, the potent resister gunfighter, was killed with a shot in the chest, then in rapid succession four other settlers (also resister gunfighters) were slain or fatally injured by Crow's lethal shooting. With Crow's last shot, the firing stopped, for by then the only armed settlers were dead or dying.[108] Crow escaped but later that day was caught in a wheat field just a mile and a half away by a small band of armed settlers who promptly and vengefully killed him.[109]

Because all of those who fired shots in the gunfight died as a result of it, no murder charges were filed in the wake of the gun battle. Thus, while all who took part in the gunfight bravely stood their ground and obeyed no duty to retreat, no legal issue of the duty to retreat arose in the aftermath of the gunfight.[110] As for the death of Walter J. Crow, the identity of his killer was an open secret in the Mussel Slough area. He was Caleb W. Flewelling, who was a hero for a few days (as the settlers condoned what was in effect a lynching), after which he heard that the federal authorities wanted him. Flewelling then fled the area for Spokane, Washington, where he lived an inoffensive life, unmolested by the law.[111]

Of those who took part in the Mussel Slough gunfight of May 11, 1880, the deadliest by far was the grassroots and incorporation gunfighter Walter J. Crow, who accounted for five lives before losing his own later in the day. Crow was blond and quiet—almost a mute—but he was one of the finest marksmen in all of California, a great wing shot who constantly practiced target shooting.[112] None of the glorified gunfighters of the West such as Wild Bill Hickok, Wyatt Earp, Billy the Kid, or John Wesley Hardin came anywhere close to killing as many men in a single episode as did Walter J. Crow. The only one of the acclaimed gunslingers who did come close was Commodore Perry Owens with his toll of three opponents on September 4, 1887, in Holbrook, Arizona.[113]

Yet Crow is unmentioned in the lengthy annals of famed Western gunfighters. One cannot, however, blame Crow's California comtemporary, leading American writer Ambrose Bierce, for this lack of recognition, for Bierce, writing a year later in his popular column in the San Francisco *Wasp,* sought to immortalize Crow in the context of the growing mythic tradition of the Western hero and the Western gunfight. Bierce payed homage to "the splendor" of Crow's "terrible courage," to his "amazing performance," to his "death struggle," and to the "startling terrors of his depature from this life, baptized with the blood of men, saluted with the wails of widows and orphans." Bierce concluded his paean by calling for recognition of "this bravest of Americans." "Will not God raise up," asked Bierce, "an historian to relate, a poet to celebrate," the "valor" of Walter J. Crow?[114]

Posterity's answer to Bierce has been no. Some of our finest writing in the field of Western history has dealt with the heroes and antiheroes of Western myth and legend, but none of these scholars mentions the name of Walter J. Crow.[115] Nor, by the same token, is the bloody Mussel Slough shootout of May 11, 1880, cited in the works of historians and afficionados who have written so lengthily of gunfights and gunfighters in the West.[116] Thus Ambrose Bierce failed utterly in his campaign for the glorification of Crow as a heroic Western gunfighter.

In one sense, the exclusion of Walter J. Crow and the Mussel Slough gunfight from the scope of historians who have studied the mythic tradition of Western heroes and the gunfight (and the tradition's counterpart in historical reality) is correct, for the mythic gunfight/hero tradition is too limited in its explanatory power adequately to contain the Mussel Slough shootout. The interpretive aspect of the Western mythic gunfight/hero tradition narrowly excludes the factors of ideology and social, economic, and political group conflict and wholly ignores the Western Civil War of Incorporation. Instead, abstract forces of good and evil are personified as hero versus villain in the mythic tradition of gunfighting without regard to any substantial context of reality. To the makers and perpetuators of the mythic gunfight/ hero tradition there was no room for the sort of social, economic, political, and ideological struggle represented by the opposed forces of the Southern Pacific Railroad and the Settlers' League. Just as the political and ideological factors represented by Wyatt Earp were excluded from the myth of Wyatt Earp as gunfighter, so was the politically and ideologically oriented Walter J. Crow excluded from the realm of the glorified gunfighters.

The most notable attempt to cast the Mussel Slough conflict and the May 11, 1880, gunfight into epic terms came twenty-one years later in Frank Norris's novel *The Octopus*.[117] Norris, however, ignored the gunfight/hero tradition in his fictional treatment. Instead, he portrayed a cataclysm featuring the vast impersonal forces of wheat and the railroad in which a titanic conflict between railroad colossus and wheat-growing land barons (in notable contrast to the small-farmer reality of the settlers' movement) was put to the service of Norris's doctrine of literary naturalism rather than Western mythology. Because the gunfight near the O.K. Corral in Tombstone, Arizona, a year and a half after the Mussel Slough shootout, took place in a classic Western mining boomtown and involved classic Western social types (famed gunfighters against cowboys), the Tombstone battle and its participants were enshrined in the West of myth and legend. Lacking such classic Western attributes, the gunfight of May 11, 1880, and its nonpareil (but not celebrated) gunfighter, Walter J. Crow, were denied admission to the pantheon of mythic Western heroism, Ambrose Bierce's plea notwithstanding.

As a violent climax to the Mussel Slough conflict, the non-mythologized May 11 shootout had, however, a stunning impact on contemporary state and national opinion. To many Americans in May 1880 the event seemed to represent the height of corporate heartlessness and greed. The lesson of the deaths of the five farmers who opposed the railroad seemed to be that one of the greatest of all American corporations, the Southern Pacific Railroad, headed by three of the most powerful and wealthy men in the nation—Collis P. Huntington, Leland Stanford, and Charles Crocker—would not rest content with its campaign to deprive hard-working farmers and family men of their land but would demand the ultimate sacrifice and have them shot down in cold blood.[118]

In California itself, the Mussel Slough shootout nourished the image of the Southern Pacific Railroad and its Big Three masters as an "octopus" holding the state in the stranglehold of its oppressive economic and political actions. Vividly crystalizing and expressing the antirailroad attitudes were the remarkable political cartoons done in color by G. Frederick Keller of the urbane San Francisco weekly, the *Wasp,* from 1880 to 1882. Within two months of the May 11 gunfight, the *Wasp* on July 10, 1880, unveiled the enduringly loathsome antirailroad image in Keller's huge cartoon portraying the Southern Pacific as a gigantic octopus with its eyes in the state capital, Sacramento, and its cruel tentacles overspreading all of California. G. Frederick Keller was a West Coast counterpart of New York City's famous political cartoonist, Thomas Nast. Just as Nast made Boss Tweed his target, Keller arraigned the Southern Pacific in a succession of hard-hitting cartoons using the octopus theme. Most striking of all was Keller's mural-like color cartoon of August, 19, 1882, entitled "The Curse of California." It showed the state in the grasp of the railroad octopus with the graves of the Mussel Slough martyrs visible in one corner. Also typical of these anti-railroad cartoons was "The Retribution Comet" (July 8, 1881), which depicted a death's-head comet streaking toward a guilty and terrified Leland Stanford and Charles Crocker in "retribution" for the deaths of the five Mussel Slough settlers.[119]

Paralleling Keller's antirailroad cartoons in the pages of the *Wasp* were the equally antirailroad writings of Ambrose Bierce, its editor and leading columnist from 1881 to 1886. Although Bierce had praised the individual courage of Walter J. Crow, Bierce's sympathies were strongly on the side of the settlers of Mussel Slough who opposed the railroad. Ambrose Bierce was to establish his fame as a writer in California with his courageous, mordant *Wasp* attacks on the Southern Pacific and its Big Three masters, whom he termed the "rail-rogues." A favorite target was Stanford, whom Bierce delighted to refer to as "Leland $tanford" or, in reference to the Mussel Slough episode and the railroad's huge landholdings, as "Stealand Landford."

Moving his column to William Randolph Hearst's *San Francisco Examiner* in 1887, Bierce in 1896 climaxed his two-decade-long journalistic crusade against the Southern Pacific with his most spectacular triumph, in which he dealt Collis P. Huntington his greatest national political and economic setback. It was largely Bierce's aggressive reporting that led to Congress's refusal to pass Huntington's cherished scheme to refinance the railroad's massive $75 million debt on a highly favorable long-term basis. Although Bierce did freely concede that the law was technically all on the Big Three's side in the dispute with the Mussel Slough settlers, much more important in his view was his conviction—shared, apparently, by the majority of Californians—that the moral right was entirely on the settlers' side. Bierce unhesitatingly condemned the settlers' tactics of violence and intimidation, but he mainly saluted the overall justice of their cause, scoring "the outrageous exactions of the railroad company under the forms of law."[120]

While Bierce and the *Wasp* were pummeling Stanford, Crocker, and Huntington and their railroad, and G. Frederick Keller was perfecting the octopus as the persisting symbol of monopolistic oppression by the Southern Pacific, seven Settlers' League members were undergoing a judicial ordeal in the aftermath of the May 11, 1880, gunfight. Tried in the federal circuit court in San Francisco in November and December 1880 for conspiring to resist the U.S. marshal, Alonzo W. Poole, were John J. Doyle, James N. Patterson, and five others. Amid well-justified mutterings in the Mussel Slough country that the court, presided over by settler-nemesis Judge Lorenzo Sawyer, was a "Railroad Court,"[†] the trial produced damaging evidence of Settler's League vigilantism, violence, and intimidation. The result was a prison term for Doyle, Patterson, and the others, which they began serving in the county jail in San Jose (there being no federal prison) in early 1881. Their jail time was not difficult but was rather the occasion of an unprecedented outpouring of public sympathy. All in all, it was more of a fete than a prison sentence; the wives of three of the prisoners were allowed to live with their husbands on the top floor of the jail, and the jailer's daughter became engaged to one of the prisoners, William Braden. Meanwhile, delegation after delegation visited San Jose to pay tribute to the antirailroad inmates. Finally, in autumn 1881, Doyle and his colleagues were released. They triumphantly entered Hanford where on October 5, 1881, a crowd of 3,000 turned out to celebrate their homecoming.[122]

More than a hundred years later, the Mussel Slough gunfight is virtually forgotten, but it gripped the emotions of Americans in the late nineteenth century. Over forty thousand Californians signed a petition to President Rutherford B. Hayes in support of Doyle, Patterson, and the others who would be convicted of conspiring to resist the United States marshal,[123] and one of America's greatest intellects, the young California-born-and-reared Harvard philosopher, Josiah Royce, wrote and published in 1887

[†]For Judge Sawyer's strong prorailroad bias, see at notes 85–89. Sawyer undoubtedly reciprocated the hostility of the Mussel Slough settlers and their supporters, whom it is very likely he included in his 1886 denunciation (in private correspondence) of "politicians, demagogues, Sandlotters, political and social tramps etc."[121]

a novel based on the Mussel Slough tragedy.[124] Indeed, novelists were intrigued by the human dimension and play of social, economic, and political forces in the Mussel Slough shootout, for in all five novels have been based on the bloody doings of May 11, 1880—the best and best-known of them being the aforementioned powerful American classic *The Octopus* by Frank Norris, which appeared in 1901.[125]

Nor were Americans the only ones stunned by the tragic loss of lives in the Mussel Slough gunfight. None other than Karl Marx, in distant London, knowing of the controversy over land monopoly in California and of its violent outcome on May 11, 1880, took notice. Six months after the fatal gun battle, Marx wrote to an American friend asking for more news on "economic conditions" in California. In his letter, Marx declared that California "is very important for me, because nowhere else" in the world "has the upheaval most shamelessly caused by capitalist" oppression "taken place with such speed."[126]

Karl Marx sensed that California was in the midst of a revolutionary situation, and it was. The wheat farmers who resisted the Southern Pacific Railroad's version of the Western process of incorporation with guns at the Mussel Slough battle and with the legal briefs of their attorneys in courts of law were ultimately defeated. In the federal circuit court in San Francisco, Judge Sawyer, the friend of railroad leaders Stanford and Crocker, continued to rule adversely on the settlers' land claims,[†] and by

---

[†]Judge Sawyer was certainly biased in favor of the railroad as a result of his philosophical convictions and his friendships with Stanford and Crocker,[127] but able legal scholars disagree on whether Sawyer's decision upholding the railroad's land claim and the ejection of the settlers was right as a matter of law. John A. Larimore cogently argues that, contrary to the settlers' contention, the railroad's claim to the land was, as Sawyer demonstrated in his opinion, a correct one in terms of a previous key U.S. Supreme Court decision and previous actions by the legislative (state and national) and executive (national) branches. Considering substantially the same evidence, however, David J. Bederman forcefully contends that Sawyer's decision had no proper basis in the law but was the result of his personal view that corporations "should be given full scope to carry out their functions."[128] Larimore, Bederman, and all authorities agree on the strongly conservative Sawyer's deep sympathy for corporations and the Southern Pacific and its owners.

the late 1880s the majority of these settlers were gone—dispossessed by the legal action of the railroad.[129] Yet the farmers fought the railroad not only with guns and legal briefs but through the political system as well, for many of them joined radical antirailroad third-party movements in California in the 1870s and 1880s. One of the fiercest of the Mussel Slough settler leaders, Major Thomas Jefferson McQuiddy, became the Greenback party's candidate for governor in 1883.[130] McQuiddy lost the election, but even before that many of the Mussel Slough settlers joined the first radical farmer-labor party in the West, the Workingmen's Party of California (or the WPC as it was usually called) founded in 1877 in San Francisco.[131] Thus the same turbulent city by the Golden Gate that during the 1870s had nurtured what ultimately became the radical single-tax program of Henry George,[132] ushered in the radical WPC, founded in 1877 by San Francisco's rough, dynamic blue-collar orator, the Irish-born drayman Denis Kearney, whose rousing speeches to restive crowds in the sandy vacant lots of San Francisco rallied the "sandlotters"—the urban wing of the WPC.[133] Kearney was soon joined by a second radical orator—a golden-voiced Baptist minister from the East, the Reverend Isaac S. Kalloch, whose social and reform-oriented Metropolitan Temple in San Francisco had the largest membership of any Baptist church in the country.[134]

Kearney and Kalloch eventually led the WPC[†] to a stunning political victory in San Francisco: Kalloch's 1879 election as

---

[†]Just as gunplay in the Western manner was a major aspect of the Mussel Slough story, so did gunplay provide two key episodes in the WPC scenario in San Francisco. Both events in San Francisco involved Isaac S. Kalloch. San Francisco's leading newspaper then, as now, was the *Chronicle,* still published in the late 1870s by its founders, the de Young brothers—Michael H. and Charles. Michael de Young was quiet and cautious; Charles, the dominant brother, was impulsive and outspoken. Both brothers were united in their desire to dominate San Francisco. The de Young brothers and their newspaper initially supported the WPC, but when they saw that they could not seize control of the WPC from Kearney and Kalloch they broke with the WPC and aggressively expressed their opposition in the columns of the *Chronicle.* This led to the violent Kalloch–de Young feud. The trading of personal insults by the Reverend Mr. Kalloch and Charles de Young escalated to the next event: the Aug. 23, 1879, point-blank shooting of Kalloch by Charles de Young in front of Kalloch's Metropolitan

mayor.[137] Meanwhile, with strong farmer support in such interior areas as Mussel Slough, the WPC was in the van of the 1878–79 movement that resulted in a new state constitution for California—a document with pointed taxation, anticorporation, and antirailroad provisions that gained it national fame as the most radically progressive state constitution of its time in America.[138] Nor did the WPC neglect the cause of the Mussel Slough settlers against their common enemy the Southern Pacific Railroad, whose owners incensed the plain people of San Francisco with the erection of ostentatious mansions on Nob Hill in a time of severe unemployment and urban privation.[139]

Mussel Slough settler leader John J. Doyle joined the WPC and was elected as a delegate from Tulare County to the 1879 WPC state convention in San Francisco. That convention of the WPC willingly included in its platform a plank against land monopoly, and delegate Doyle obtained the passage of a resolution against the railroad in support of the Mussel Slough settlers. Kearney, the charismatic WPC sachem, had a strong following in rural Tulare County and the Mussel Slough area and was enthusiastically received when he spoke in the Mussel Slough country as well as in the county seat, Visalia.[140] The farmer-labor link between the Mussel Slough Settlers' League and the San Francisco–based WPC was thus a combative alliance of rural "sandlappers" and urban "sandlotters" in opposition to the Southern Pacific Railroad, its Big Three owners, and the Western trend of incorporation.

Temple. Almost miraculously, Kalloch survived the shooting and, benefiting by a powerful surge of public sympathy, was within the year elected mayor of San Francisco on the WPC ticket. Yet the violence was not at an end, for Kalloch's son, the Reverend Isaac M. Kalloch, brooding over the insult and injury to his father, invaded Charles de Young's office and (in an incident much like the 1978 shootings of San Francisco Mayor George Moscone and Supervisor Harvey Milk in their city hall offices by ex-supervisor Dan White) shot de Young dead.[135] Unconnected to the Kalloch—de Young feud was a similar vendetta in which in 1884 Adolph Spreckels shot and wounded Michael de Young in retaliation for the accusation of the *Chronicle* that the Spreckels family's sugar business had defrauded stockholders.[136]

In 1878–80, with farmers literally up in arms against the Southern Pacific Railroad in the Mussel Slough country, with a radical new state constitution enacted, and with the WPC capturing the mayoralty of San Francisco (and the state chief justiceship), California was indeed in a revolutionary situation as Karl Marx had sensed, yet neither a violent nor a peaceful revolution ever occurred. Instead, by the middle 1880s Denis Kearney was in eclipse, Kalloch was no longer mayor of San Francisco, and the no-duty-to-retreat farmers were finally being evicted from their farms by the Southern Pacific Railroad. The Big Three of Huntington, Stanford, and Crocker were the victors in their phase of the Western Civil War of Incorporation and were as dominant as ever. Why?

A significant part of the answer lies in the realm of another aspect of Western U.S. and American history that, aside from conflict, needs to be emphasized: mobility. Of course, there were other factors in the demise of the overall radical farmer-labor movement in California. One was the irrepressible political power of the Southern Pacific magnates, whose lawyers and lobbyists soon found their way around the antirailroad provisions of the California constitution of 1879.[141] Important too was the return of national economic prosperity in the 1880s after the depression decade of the 1870s.[142]

Yet the most important factor, in the long run, was mobility—geographic and social mobility in California and the West. Henry George had been right in calling attention to the trend of land monopoly. The violence of May 11, 1880, proved his contention that large-scale land enclosure was a key social problem. But George underestimated the open, mobile character of Californian, Western, and American society. When Westerners encountered the likes of the hard times, land monopoly, and smothering trend of incorporation of the 1870s, they often reacted by resisting violently, as in the Mussel Slough conflict, or with political protest action based on a radical ideology, as exemplified by California's constitution of 1879 and the WPC movement. But even more Westerners reacted in a quite different way—by dropping out of the Western Civil War of Incorporation in order to exercise the option of mobility: by simply leaving the scene of their problems, by moving away, going somewhere else to start all over, to try again to achieve the American dream of success.[143]

Abundant quantitative research by social historians has strongly documented the restless mobility of Americans in the nineteenth century.[144] The key statistical index of this geographic mobility is the *turnover rate,* a calculation that shows how many inhabitants are left in residence in a given community after the elapse of ten years. In one typical Eastern city, only 40–50 percent of the population was found to persist after ten years' time[145]—a very high rate of mobility. But in the frontier communities of the Midwest and Far West[146] the turnover rate was much higher, with only about 20–25 percent of the inhabitants remaining in a particular community after the passage of a decade.[147] Thus Western settlements lacked the sort of demographic stability and continuity[148] upon which to base a long-term struggle against the kind of corporate and landed power and wealth represented by the Southern Pacific Railroad.

The high rate of geographic mobility shows that Westerners turned, in effect, from the group strategy of the Mussel Slough Settlers' League and the WPC to the individual strategy of enterprise and private gain. Such Westerners left the front lines of the Western Civil War of Incorporation and, instead, peacefully infiltrated the ranks of their conquerors in the incorporated society. To underscore this point, one may consider what became of those who, in the case of the Mussel Slough conflict and the WPC, spearheaded the fight against the power of industrial wealth and landed monopoly. In short, these men ultimately followed a policy of "if you can't beat 'em, join 'em," for eventually they moved from group political tactics and radical ideology to individual careers of enterprise. In effect, they exchanged the ideal of community cooperation for the American dream of success through individual effort.

Both Isaac S. Kalloch and Denis Kearney eventually joined the horde of restless, mobile Westerners. Each left San Francisco and forsook politics and oratory for personal economic activity. Kearney did not go as far in geographic distance as he did in mode of livelihood: although he only went across San Francisco Bay to Alameda County, he went much further in the change of his career, for this erstwhile drayman ended his days as a well-to-do commodity market speculator[149]—the very sort of thing he had so ardently attacked in speech after speech delivered to cheering working men in the sandlots of San Francisco. By the same token, Isaac S. Kalloch left both politics and the pulpit for training in law, and he moved much further away from San Francisco than Kearney—going all the way to the shores of Puget Sound where, in the rising new community of what would become Bellingham, Washington, this one-time red-hot opponent of the Southern Pacific Railroad in politics became a lawyer and town promoter in the interest of the Northern Pacific Railroad, the Southern Pacific's industrial, land-monopolizing, and incorporating counterpart in the Pacific Northwest.[150]

The flip-flopping careers of both Kearney and Kalloch show that the booming population and economic expansion of the West in the late nineteenth century provided a scope of individual opportunity that did much to counteract the overall process of incorporation and the land-monopoly trend stressed by Henry George.[151] The topsy-turvy careers of Kalloch and Kearney also suggest another theme—that the impact of land monopoly was differential, with its greatest impact being in the rural countryside where farmers and ranchers dwelled,[152] while in the swiftly urbanizing West of the 1880s and 1890s there was free play for city-and-town real-estate and economic development; this was what Isaac S. Kalloch staked his final career on in Washington Territory. In effect, geographic mobility was an enormous safety valve that relieved the social pressure built up by the constricting Western process of incorporation.

For the theme of individual enterprise after the failure of radical group action, the career of John J. Doyle, the prime leader of the Mussel Slough settlers, is the most instructive and poignant of all. Doyle was a young Union army veteran of the

Civil War who came to California from Indiana. In the Mussel Slough country, he grew wheat on a tract whose title he disputed with the Southern Pacific Railroad. Doyle did well as a farmer and, as emphasized, became the sparkplug in the farmers' legal campaign against the railroad's land claim and pricing policy. Doyle was an activist to the core—he lobbied Congress in the 1879s in behalf of the Mussel Slough settlers, and he master-minded the strategy of legal action all the way up to the last losing hearing before the United States Supreme Court.[153] More than anyone else, Doyle was the inspiration and organizer of the Settlers' League mass movement. In his Mussel Slough locality, John J. Doyle was a key commandant of no-duty-to-retreat resistance in the Western Civil War of Incorporation.

By 1885 Doyle was, however, among the vanquished in the West's civil war. A thoroughly defeated opponent of incorporation, Doyle was forced into mobility when he lost his land to the railroad and took his family up into the Sierra Nevada fifty miles southeast of the Mussel Slough country. In a twinkling, Doyle and his family were homeless, living literally in a tree: the "Hollow Log," a huge fallen redwood whose empty interior was divided into two rooms.[154] A bitter Doyle may have thought, as from time to time he gazed down into the haze of the Central Valley where he had fought and lost to the railroad: "This is what happens to a family man who fights the giant corporation—he and his end up living in a log!"

For Doyle the homestead ethic and the ideal of cooperative community building were now dead letters, but the American dream of success was not.[155] Indeed, Doyle was to gain ultimate prosperity in the incorporated but booming society that was California from 1890 to 1910. Thus Doyle made an about-face from opposing land monopolists like the railroad to becoming a land developer and speculator himself—not on any huge scale but on one large enough to gain lasting economic success for himself and his family long before his death in 1915.[156] In this new departure, Doyle diverted his boundless personal energy from the battle against the railroad into a new but private cause, for he had the foresight to see the resort potential of the mountain country where he and his family lived in a log. Cheaply and easily acquiring U.S. government land for which at the time there was little demand, Doyle held it until a vigorous market in resort property arose whereupon he sold his land—125 lots in all—at a healthy profit to those wanting to establish summer homes in the cool, clear mountain heights above the hot, dusty Central Valley.[157]

With the gains made from his imaginative and successful promotion of the mountain summer resort, Doyle returned to the Central Valley in the early 1890s. He avoided the Mussel Slough country with its sad memories of defeat in the Western Civil War of Incorporation and went instead to the lively town of Porterville, where he became a local leader in real estate sales and promotion.[158]

The switch in the careers of Doyle, Kalloch, and Kearney from radical reform to the pursuit of private gain was in phase with the trend of an incorporated American society and its values. In their radical reform periods Doyle, Kalloch, and Kearney believed in the alteration of economic structure in order to produce a society with a more equal distribution of wealth, but the trio collided with and lost to the forces of incorporation. The course of the rapidly expanding society and economy of America doomed to failure the late nineteenth-century radical reform efforts of the Grangers, Greenbackers, Anti-Monopolists, Single Taxers, and Populists, as well as the WPC and the Mussel Slough settlers' movement. Losers in their phase of the Western Civil War of Incorporation, Doyle, Kalloch, and Kearney adopted the practical choices of individual mobility and enterprise, which incorporated Westerners and other Americans came to prefer in overwhelming number in the late nineteenth century. After many trials and tribulations, Doyle, Kalloch, and Kearney had all realized the American dream of success. It was, however, success on a much lesser scale than that achieved by their conquering railroad opponents, Stanford, Crocker, and Huntington, each of whom amassed one of the greatest American fortunes of his time.

The triumph of Stanford, Crocker, and Huntington over the Mussel Slough settlers was, however, far from unalloyed. Huntington was in 1900 the last of the triumvirate to die. Neither the power of the Southern Pacific in California politics nor its ownership in the family of its last surviving founder was long maintained. The heirs of Collis P. Huntington sold his controlling interest in the railroad to E. H. Harriman.[159] Next, a brilliant reformer, Hiram Johnson, led a crusade that in 1910 finally terminated the Southern Pacific's grip on California politics.[160] Yet the names of Stanford, Crocker, and Huntington are still prominent in California. They endure in Stanford University, founded in 1891 by Leland and Jane Stanford as a memorial to their cherished only offspring, Leland, Jr., who died prematurely at the age of fifteen;[161] in the Huntington Library and Art Gallery, founded in 1919 by Henry E. Huntington, the nephew of Collis P. Huntington, with funds whose origins were in the railroad fortune amassed by and inherited from his uncle;[162] and in the giant Crocker Bank, founded in 1886 by Charles Crocker and carried on by his son, William H. Crocker.[163] By now the overtones of the three famous names of Stanford, Crocker, and Huntington are, in contrast to the era of the Mussel Slough conflict and the widely condemned railroad "octopus," strongly favorable because of the superlative academic standing of Stanford University, the magnificent intellectual and artistic resources of the Huntington Library and Art Gallery, and the active, vital Crocker Bank. University, library and art gallery, and bank—each one is not only a jewel of its state but enjoys a worldwide reputation in its own field.

It took many decades, however, for what so many Californians viewed as the misdeeds of the Big Three of Stanford, Crocker, and Huntington to be forgotten. Resentment over the farmer deaths resulting from the gunfight of May 11, 1880, and the subsequent ouster of the settler land claimants was still strong after thirty years and was no small factor in rallying voters behind Hiram Johnson's triumphant anti–Southern Pacific campaign, which won him the governor's chair and lasting honor as one of America's great progressive reformers of the early twentieth century.[164] In the Mussel Slough country, however, antirailroad sentiment was deep, bitter, and unsated even by Johnson's political conquest of the Southern Pacific in 1910. By then the Mussel Slough area had been detached from Tulare County to form the core of a new county, Kings, formed in 1893 in recognition of Mussel Slough population growth and to provide the people a county seat (Hanford) closer to home than Tulare County's seat of Visalia.[165] Halfway through the twentieth century there was still strong antirailroad feeling, going back to Mussel Slough antagonisms, in the adjacent counties of Tulare and Kings. Southern Pacific attorneys took care to avoid, if at all possible, jury trials in the two counties in civil cases involving the railroad, for local juries were apt to be prejudiced against the railroad regardless of the merits of its legal case.[166]

Thus the broader social and legal problems of the railroad endured long after its victory in the Mussel Slough conflict. Although ill will against the Southern Pacific was strongest in the Mussel Slough district, it was general through the southern Central Valley of California from Fresno to the Tehachapi Mountains. Such antipathy generated the Central Valley's own version of the social-bandit phenomenon. As conceptualized by British historian E. J. Hobsbawm, a "social bandit" is one in European and North American history whose crimes are viewed with approval by wide portions of society.[167] Thus Jesse James's robberies of banks and trains in Missouri and nearby states were favored by many citizens—especially farmers and small townsmen—who deeply resented what they saw as the artificially inflated profits of the banks and railroads of Missouri and the Midwest, profits which it was believed, came from morally indefensible economic exploitation of the hard-pressed rural middle and lower classes.[168] Such citizens were themselves entirely law abiding and never thought of robbing trains or banks on their own but secretly or openly applauded Jesse James (and his comrades) who did.

In Chris Evans and John Sontag, California's Central Valley had its own two-man version of Jesse James as social bandit. Evans and Sontag gained widespread sympathy for their repeated robberies of Southern Pacific trains in 1889–92.[169] As both glorified and resister gunfighters, the antirailroad lawbreaking of Evans and Sontag was a surrogate expressing the seething resentment against the Southern Pacific by peaceful, law-abiding residents. It was rumored that Evans had been in the Mussel Slough shootout on the side of the settlers.[170] The rumor was wrong, but there was a basis for Evans's supposed involvement in the Mussel Slough conflict: Evans's wife's uncle, said Evans, had been evicted from his Mussel Slough land by the Southern Pacific.[171] The train-robbing career of Evans and Sontag thrived, then, amidst strong antirailroad public opinion and climaxed in two gunfights with law officers and railroad detectives.[172] In the first of these, the two social bandits killed a Southern Pacific agent and a deputy sheriff, and in the second, on June 11, 1893, Sontag was killed and Evans wounded by a posse headed by the United States marshal.[173]

Following the slaying of Sontag and the imprisonment of Evans, Evans's wife and their daughter, Eva, captured the eager sympathy of the people by playing themselves in a melodrama entitled *Evans and Sontag, or the Visalia Bandits,* which attracted an audience of twenty-eight hundred to its San Francisco premiere in September 1893. Two scenes in the play portrayed embittered residents of the Mussel Slough country lamenting wrongs done them by the railroad and, later, vengefully holding up a Southern Pacific train. With Eva and her mother starring, the play successfully toured California and Oregon in 1893–94.[174] The melodrama accentuated popular hostility to the Southern Pacific and strengthened the image of Evans and Sontag as heroic opponents of the Western trend of incorporation. The positive reaction to the play glorifying Evans and Sontag shows that the losers in the Western Civil War of Incorporation were often the winners in the contest for favorable public opinion.

Although bested by the legal power and economic might of the

Southern Pacific Railroad, the struggling Mussel Slough settlers won an unintended but significant long-term social and environmental consolation prize in that they did succeed in lastingly imprinting their pattern of small farms on the geography of the Mussel Slough district of the Central Valley. A bastion of giant agribusiness farms worked by year-round employees and itinerant farm workers, the vast southern part of the Central Valley was by the 1940s studded with bleak, dusty towns lacking a wide social base of small farmers possessing their own land.[175] This dreary pattern did not, however, stand up in the case of Hanford, the Mussel Slough metropolis. A community of thirty thousand, Hanford is today one of the loveliest cities of the Central Valley with a spacious, leafy square whose handsome old courthouse has been saved from the wrecker's ball by community-minded local historical preservationists. Outside of Hanford, the Mussel Slough country of our era is, as it was in times of no-duty-to-retreat conflict more than a century ago, an Edenic enclave with ubiquitous mixed-farming plots dotted by stately and graceful orchards and vineyards with small and medium-size farms (such as the original settlers pioneered) watered by flowing irrigation ditches dug originally by the newcomers of the 1870s under the spell of the homestead ethic.[176]

Away from the Mussel Slough country and south of Hanford, toward the Tulare lake bed of today, the Mussel Slough settlers' pattern of small farms was not imprinted on the land, and there the situation is completely different. Instead of a multiplicity of family farms with richly varied crops, there is an austere monoculture featuring vast acreages devoid of human habitation with only, here and there, a shed for storage. Virtually deserted except for a small cadre of corporate employees, this land is owned and operated by some of the greatest agribusiness enterprises of California. The beauty, diversity, and human vitality of the small- and medium-farm Mussel Slough country to the north is entirely absent.[177]

Today one can visit the open, still-fertile field where on May 11, 1880, six men were to suffer death wounds, and one can still see alongside that field the towering, sweeping 160-year-old live oak—the "tragedy oak" as it came to be known—in whose shade the wounded languished on the fatal day.[178] The spirit of no duty to retreat, which energized both sides in the Mussel Slough conflict, pervaded America long after the gunfight of May 11, 1880, was out of mind. That spirit persists in our own time— witness a shooting that took place on a New York City subway train in the 1980s.

4

The Persistence of No Duty to Retreat: Crime, Law, and Society in America from the 1850s to the Present

> "The criminal law, police, courts, and prisons together
> can only restrain common crime if they reinforce
> underlying social forces that are moving in the same
> direction."
> Ted Robert Gurr (1979).*

On December 22, 1984, on a Manhattan subway train, a slight electronics specialist bearing some resemblance to Woody Allen shot four young blacks in what was a no-duty-to-retreat confrontation. The event was front-page news in the next day's Sunday *New York Times* and soon became not just a New York but a national media sensation. The massive show of support for Bernhard H. Goetz, the young white man who fired the shots and whom the media soon labeled the "subway vigilante," was the most significant aspect of the episode, which attracted strong public interest for three months, a relatively long period in a media-sated nation. The case generated heavy newspaper reporting, national newsmagazine cover stories, featured attention by the major television networks, a congressional hearing, and statements by the president, the governor of New York, and the mayor of New York City. More than ten months later, the occasional stories about the aftermath of the Goetz episode were relegated to the inside pages, and the public had largely forgotten the whole thing. Yet the case was one of those news events that had great symbolic significance and the intellectual leverage to focus attention on long-term trends and implications.[1]

The premise of this chapter is that "great social and demographic changes seem to work profound changes on patterns of crime" and that "the criminal law, police, courts, and prisons together can only restrain common crime if they reinforce underlying social forces that are moving in the same direction."[2] Trends in American crime and law, some of them exemplified by the Goetz episode and the spirit of no duty to retreat, will be examined in relation to the long-term evolutions of Industrial Society, Postindustrial Society, and the current Information Society.[3]

The common wisdom used to be that the destabilizing impact of industrialization and urbanization resulted in social chaos and high levels of crime, but careful studies in the last twenty years have shown that just the opposite occurred—that the great forces of industrialization and urbanization were, rather, stabilizing forces that drove down crime. This trend has been charted in England, the protagonist of the Industrial Revolution, and in our own country. Roger Lane's studies of nineteenth-century Boston and Philadelphia reveal a decline of crime in conjunction with the triumph of the Industrial Revolution. As in the case of Boston, Lane found that in Philadelphia the city was " 'working' better as its population grew. The apparent increase of problem behavior of all sorts . . . was not 'real' but 'official,' the product of stricter standards more strictly enforced" by the agents of society.[4] In Boston and other American cities a surge of crime "began in the 1850s and crested in the 1970s."[5] These trends in our social and criminal history were the result "of the discipline demanded by the industrial revolution and taught in the classrooms, on the railroads, and in the factories and offices of nineteenth-century America."[6] Crucial to this process of socialization, which was "broad and continuous" and affected virtually everyone in society—not just those "directly exposed to industrial or bureaucratic discipline"—was "the growing system of public schools" which "inculcated" the "kinds of behavior demanded by the changing economy" of industrialism.[7] Moreover, the downward trend in homicide that began in the 1870s continued (with, perhaps, an upswing from 1900 to about 1930) until the 1950s.[8]

The process of industrialization produced a broad national campaign against the misfits—the "marginal men, those left behind or new to the demands for order and discipline" of the new age.[9] These demands were not restricted to the growing industrial cities of the Northeast but were to be found also on the frontier, where the Western Civil War of Incorporation hinged on such issues. In the West of the middle and late nineteenth century, classic American vigilantism reached a peak as the economic elite and its middle-class compatriots converged in hundreds of local vigilante movements to purge the new country of outlaws so that fields, ranges, and mines could be worked in peace to produce raw materials for the factories of the East and profits for the middle and upper classes of the West.[10] Regular peace officers—exemplified by the Earp brothers of Kansas and Tombstone—joined in this process. Wyatt Earp, leader of the clan, was, as noted in Chapter 2, an ambitious small capitalist and speculator in Tombstone real estate whose strong membership in the Republican party helped make him the chosen instrument of the mining aristocracy of Tombstone against the aggressive outlaw element of surrounding Cochise County. Neovigilante campaigns headed by the coalition of corporate leaders and local members of the middle class continued in the early twentieth-century West as field hands, loggers, sawmill workers, and miners—many of them members of the radical Industrial Workers of the World (IWW)—felt the force of the "conservative mob."[11]

The capitalistic backlash of neovigilantism was also found in the North and East, but in these regions the spearhead of order in behalf of a more stable industrializing, urbanizing society was the growing police establishment. Increasingly stringent and widely approved urban policing was brought heavily to bear upon the drunken and disorderly individuals whose rhythmns were out of tune with Industrial Society, and upon the "the class of transients, drifters, and newcomers to the city" whom Lane found to be the most prone to homicide in Philadelphia.[12] The upward trend of industrialization and the downward trend of crime that characterized America from the 1870s on dissolved in the 1950s and 1960s. The evidence of the crime surge from the 1950s to the 1960s is well summarized by Neal Alan Weiner and Marvin E. Wolfgang and by Ted Robert Gurr.[13] Between the late 1950s and 1973, for example, the urban murder rate increased by 250 percent.[14] As a result of their 1985 reconciliation of the technical indices of crime, Weiner and Wolfgang concluded that the level of violent crime in the United States increased during the 1970s but that, even if it had not, it was "unacceptably high."[15] The figures provided by these two scholars show increases in the years from 1969 to 1982 of 34 percent in criminal homicide, 92 percent in forcible rape, 69 percent in robbery, and 82 percent in aggravated assault.[16]

Lane's statement that since 1952 "the patterns of homicide in the post-industrial city of the 1960s and 1970s [had] reverted in many respects to those of the preindustrial city of the 1840s and 1850s"[17] introduces what some, including myself, see as the most general explanation for the crime surge of the late 1950s to the early 1980s: namely, the destabilizing context of Postindustrial Society. Gurr's comparative cross-national data show that the association of increased crime and Postindustrial Society is a general affliction among the advanced industrial democracies of the world except for Japan. Thus the United States is far from being alone in this pattern, but crime has increased to its highest levels in our own country. Asserting that "the most devastating episodes of public disorder . . . seem to occur" when major "social crises coincide with a change in values," Gurr wrote that the institutions of the criminal justice system and their policies were effective in bygone industrial societies "dominated by a self-confident middle class convinced that prosperity in this life and salvation in the next could be achieved through piety, honesty, and hard work. All authorities spoke with the same voice. The institutions of public order were effective because they reinforced the dominant view. They did not merely punish those who transgressed. They were missionaries to the under class, informing them of the moral order through arrest, trial, and imprisonment."[18] Holding that "it is not entirely convincing to attribute crime increases of 300 or 500 percent [in America] to 50 percent increases in the size of the youthful population," Gurr put his main emphasis on "value change"—on a crucial shift in Postindustrial Society toward an ethic of "aggressive hedonism": that is, "a mutation of Western materialism, stripped of its work ethic and generalized from material satisfactions to social and sexual ones" in coexistence "with a sense of resentment against large, impersonal organizations or indeed any external source of authority that might restrain people from 'doing their own thing.' "[19]

Elliot Currie has reminded us that the Violence Commission's 1969 specter of an American society split between the protected (the "upper-middle and high-income populations" sequestered from street crime by elaborate private security systems) and the unprotected (the remainder of the population moving through high-risk streets and public transportation, or isolated in the terror-ridden urban ghettos) had become the reality of the 1980s.[20] Back in the 1960s the emergent gap between the protected and the unprotected inspired such high-visibility quasi-vigilante movements as the Deacons for Defense and Justice in the South, the Maccabbees of Brooklyn, and the North Ward Citizens' Committee of Newark. These examples of militant urban self-protection were seen in terms of the American vigilante tradition. Yet as neighborhood patrol groups they ordinarily stopped short of taking the law into their own hands.[21] In retrospect they may be seen as the rough nucleus of the by now well-established, well-respected community crime-prevention movement (of which more later).

But the gap between the protected and the unprotected grew during the 1970s and 1980s. It was not merely ghetto blacks (the most victimized of all) but also members of the solid white middle class who were increasingly the prey of murderers, muggers, and rapists on the streets, in their own homes, and on the buses and in the subway and elevated trains of the great cities. A growing but largely silent public resentment seethed below the surface until it broke out in the massive approval for the no-duty-to-retreat shots fired by Bernhard Goetz on December 22, 1984. A nationwide poll taken two months after the event showed that 57 percent (including 39 percent of nonwhites) approved of Goetz's action and that, true to the spirit of no duty to retreat, 78 percent would, following Goetz's presumed example, use deadly force in self-defense.[22]

Inspired by the film *Death Wish* (1974), starring Charles Bronson as the lone avenger of his murdered wife, the *New York Post* led the media in terming Bernhard Goetz the "subway vigilante."[23] In fact, there is no tradition of individual vigilantism in this country, and Goetz was no vigilante. Rightly or wrongly, he acted in what he (and the jury before which he was eventually tried) viewed as self-defense.[24] The historical tradition in which Goetz fitted was not vigilantism but that of no duty to retreat.[25]

While Goetz was no vigilante, the episode in which he was involved was rife with social symbolism for crime and law in America as it moved into the new era of the Information Society. Goetz himself was virtually a personal prototype for the emergent Information Society: a young entrepreneur with a college education in his chosen field of electronics. On the boundary between the protected and the unprotected, Goetz was safe in his comfortable and secure Manhattan apartment, but like so many others he put himself at risk when he took to the city's subways. He was also prototypical as both a victim of crime and active participant in his own neighborhood version of the community crime-prevention movement—that is, he was a leader in FAB 14 (the association "For a Better 14th Street"). Goetz's first moment of victimization came on a day in early 1981 when he was mugged in a Canal Street subway station by three youths who beat him, permanently injured his knee, and robbed him of a thousand dollars' worth of equipment used in his electronics business. Goetz was prototypical, too, in his frustration with the criminal-justice system that alloted only six months of jail time to one of his assailants. Disgusted, Goetz became part of a growing national trend when he obtained a handgun and carried it for the personal protection of which, so he claimed, he availed himself on December 22, 1984.[26] In arming himself, Goetz was imbued with a spirit of aggressive self-defense in the spirit of no duty to retreat. As he made his way about New York City, Goetz stopped wearing gloves in wintertime so that, bare-handed, he could be faster on the draw of his weapon from its concealed, inside-the-belt holster.[27]

On December 22, 1984, Goetz stood his ground against what he (and witnesses on the subway train) saw as the menace of the four young African-Americans who flanked him in the subway car. Goetz could easily have moved to a seat among the other white and black passengers in the car who had given the noisy youths a wide berth or escaped into the next car of the subway train, but he did not retreat. When two of the four young men asked (or ordered) Goetz, in what Goetz saw as a threatening manner, to give them $5, Goetz stood his ground and felled all four—Barry Allen, James Ramseur, Troy Canty, and Darrell Cabey—with shots from his .38 caliber pistol.[28]

The four targets of Bernhard Goetz's bullets may also be seen, like Goetz, as personal prototypes of the current situation of crime, law, and society in America. All four were almost classic examples of the ghetto black underclass of the 1980s: high-school dropouts, products of shattered homes, drug-prone, and crime-prone.[29] One of them, Darrell Cabey, was typical of the black ghetto residents whose lives are permanently ruined by the crime of others: the Cabey family was thriving in a small-business endeavor until the husband and father was killed in a street accident as he defended his truck against theft in Harlem. The bereaved family lost its home and fell into a hapless existence in a dangerous public-housing project in the South Bronx from which the young Darrell lapsed into a pattern of petty theft that brought him, along with the three others, face to face with Bernhard Goetz on the subway train three days before Christmas 1984.[30] These four—Troy Canty, Barry Allen, James Ramseur, and Darrell Cabey—were prime examples of those excluded from today's Information Society: "those left behind" and "more and more out of step" with today's high-technological, computerized life. Even here there is irony and more social symbolism, for Canty, Allen, Ramseur, and Cabey had their own typically underclass relationship with our increasingly pervasive Information Society: their occupation, so to speak, was a criminal one—robbing computerized video machines, an errand on which they were bound when their destinies intersected Goetz's on the subway train.[31]

After a long, hectic show trial of seven weeks, on June 16, 1987, a unanimous lower-middle-class jury composed of nine white, two African-Americans,[32] and one Hispano found Goetz not guilty of the charge of attempted murder. Seven of the jurors had, like Goetz in 1981, been touched by crime: five directly, one through a family member, and another through a friend. In summary, the jury[33] of eight men and four women found Goetz not guilty of ten felony and two lesser charges and found him guilty of only one charge: the minor one of illegal weapons possession in regard to the gun he used in the shootings.[34]

Legal expert George P. Fletcher (who seems not to have agreed with the jury's acquittal of Goetz on the major charges) noted in his study of the Goetz trial that the public reaction in New York City to the outcome of the trial transcended the racial aspect of the shooting on the subway train:

> The fact is that the vast majority of the city's residents supported the [acquittal] verdict. A Gallup poll indicated that the majority was significantly greater for non-Hispanic whites (83 percent) and Hispanics (78 percent) than among blacks (45 percent). But among blacks who supported the verdict, the degree of support was often intense. On the day after the verdict, a black man called into the Sherrye Henry [radio] show with this gripping tale:
>
> > CALLER   I'm a New Yorker, black. Over the past seven years, three members, boys, in my family has been killed, the last one shot,

	with the killer that we see weekly—today— walking around. My wife has been mentally disturbed ever since this happened because no one is serving time for any of this. Members of my family have been robbed, two girls raped, no one is serving time for none of this. The question is: where is the justice? [Governor Mario] Cuomo said that he is against the death penalty. He said that what we should do is put the members away forever if they kill someone. My boys are dead. No one is serving any time. They [the authorities] knew who did it and they say, "not enough evidence" or for one reason or another, this is the case. My wife is crazy because she sees this guy on a daily basis. He spoke to her a few times. And this was the baby son . . . was the last one [son]. And the question is: where is the justice? What do we do? Must we sit there to be robbed? sit there to be raped? sit there to be killed?
SHERRYE HENRY	Let me ask you, sir. I think I know the answer. How do you feel about the Goetz verdict?
CALLER	I think that Goetz did the right thing in defending himself.
SHERRYE HENRY	What a terribly tragic story. We know that the statistics tell us that black crime is usually committed against the black community. Here is a man who is living embodiment of that.
CALLER	You can't do anything until they do something to you. You must sit there and wait for them to attack you.

Serving as a guest interviewer on this radio program, Fletcher himself said to the caller: "Sir, can I ask you this question. I am very moved by your story. Why don't you sympathize with the four victims of Goetz's shooting on the subway? They're black kids who might have been your sons. Why don't you feel with them and their families?" To this, the caller replied:

> Well, as it was brought out in a couple of cases, one [of Goetz's victims] was [out] on parole violation. He should never have been there [on the subway train] to begin with. And the other one should have been in jail. In other words, this is "revolving door justice" and they are right back at our throat again. If the boys were where they were supposed to be, number one: they would never have been shot, and number two: they would never had in mind to do anything. The point is that the justice [system] let them back out again and they were at our throats again. . . . They admit they were going out to steal. . . .[35]

In acquitting Goetz of all charges but the one of illegal weapons possession, the jury in effect accepted his plea of self-defense. The jury seems to have been, like Goetz, animated with the spirit of no duty to retreat. The attitude of the jury in the Goetz trial was in keeping with a hardening, broad national trend in favor of expanded self-defense. Judges and juries, backed by a long-term trend of statutory revision, are widening the the right of self-defense from the justifiable to the excusable. As George P. Fletcher has said of the trend in court decisions favoring violent actions of self-defense, "we can understand and thus, out of compassion, excuse, as against condone" these violent actions of self-defense "as models of behavior." Thus the traditional requirement of a reasonable belief of imminent danger for legal self-defense is being expanded to cover, for example, chronically abused wives and neighbors long afflicted by drug dealers. Accordingly, two men in Detroit who set fire to a drug house were charged with arson but acquitted on the grounds of duress and self-defense.[36]

Yet one must conclude—contrary to the rulings of the jury—that Bernhard Goetz, however threatened he felt himself to be by the noisy, threatening young men, overreacted by shooting them. In referring to the climate of fear in New York City and to Troy Canty's request (on behalf of the four youths) to Goetz for $5 (which Goetz felt, with good reason, was a menacing request), which was the provocation for the shootings, Shirley Cabey (Darrell Cabey's mother) put it best: "There's been so much crime and people have stood for so much, I can understand that they're mad. You work all week for a little bit of money, and they take it away. That's very hurtful. But when somebody comes and asks for five dollars, there's other ways. You can walk to another [subway] car"—that is, retreat—"or you can say no. You don't have to take out a gun and shoot four people."[37]

The Goetz episode—the event itself and the public reaction to it—was a flash of lightning revealing the problems and possibilities of the social scene of our time. It encourages reflection on where we are today and where we are going. To be noted first, however, is another irony: namely, that the massive public outcry in favor of Goetz, widely and correctly interpreted as an index of public frustration over intolerably high levels of crime, occurred at a time when crime in America was going down and leveling off below the peak it reached in 1980–81. Yet public concern over crime in the 1984–85 winter of the Goetz episode was well taken, since the decline in crime from the level of 1980–81 was not steep and was reaching a plateau rather than dropping significantly.[38]

A leading authority has suggested the possibility that "underlying social forces" might move "in the same direction" as current and future efforts of "the criminal law, police, courts, and prisons" to "restrain common crime."[39] Today the underlying social forces at issue are those embodied in our new Information Society. Yet the new age of the Information Society is linked to the still vital attitude of no duty to retreat in that the new public response to crime embodies, very broadly but most significantly, a renewed and redoubled emphasis on the tradition of no duty to retreat.[40] Before returning to the concept of the Information Society it is important to identify elements in the current situation which both exemplified and helped produce decline and leveling off in crime during the 1980s:

○ The 1980s saw a strong trend in favor of a *de facto* nationwide rationalization and regularization of "the laws under which people are sent to prison and in the mechanisms that control how long they stay there," with the result that more hardened, dangerous criminals get to prison and stay there longer. For example, discretionary early-release programs by parole boards are on the wane.[41]

○ Along with this went a sentencing-reform movement aimed at increasing the odds of repeat offenders going to jail and staying there longer. This movement includes the replacement of indeterminate sentencing with the stricter system of determinate sentencing in state after state and, overall, a more rationalized, structured system of sentencing, which, with the exception of the popular panacea of mandatory sentencing, has worked well.[42] One result of this movement was that as early as 1983 the odds of a robbery leading to an arrest and imprisonment had increased to three-to-one from four-to-one in 1978.[43] At the federal level, the sentencing-reform movement was exemplified by a major piece of legislation, the U.S. Sentencing Reform Act of 1984. It was estimated that the result of this law would be harsher sentences, especially for drug offenses, which would increase the federal prison population by 15 percent in the first year of full implementation of the law.[44] Related to the sentencing-reform movement was an effective federal law of 1984 for the pretrial detention of dangerous defendants, major drug offenders, and hardened criminals.[45]

○ Prison space has significantly increased since 1970, and so has the prison population. From 1970 to 1986 the prison population nearly tripled; in line with that increase, the national incarceration rate per 100,000 Americans doubled, rising from 110 in 1970 to 227 in 1986.[46] This increase in overall prison space and population was heightened by a 1979–84 increase of state prison space by 29 percent and of the state inmate population by an even greater 45 percent.[47] These increases, both for the longer term of 1970–86 and the shorter term of 1979–84, were a major reason for the decline of the murder and crime rates in the early 1980s and their leveling off thereafter.

○ Private security expenditures have hugely increased since 1979, and by the early 1980s more money was being spent on private security (over $20 billion) than on public police forces ($15 billion).[48]

○ Community self-help and computerization against crime are very significant. (They are discussed below).

○ With President Ronald Reagan having appointed nearly one-half of its members,[49] a more conservative federal judiciary, in conjunction with a more conservative United States Supreme Court since the 1988 appointment of Anthony M. Kennedy, has been rolling back the 1960s–70s emphasis on due process of law for those accused of crime in favor of the older focus on the repression of crime.[50]

○ Symptomatic are the following movements that cut across the ideological lines of liberal and conservative and have been notable for their vitality and zeal:

    the victim-rights movement[51]

    the drives against child abuse and wife abuse[52]

    movements against rape and incest[53]

    the antipornography movement[54]

    the campaign against drunken driving[55]

    new techniques to detect and forestall serial killers[56]

These developments reflect a trend to tighten the bonds of society that commentator Michael Barone referred to as a new "Age of Restraint."[57] In addition to the waning of sexually permissive behavior (partly in reaction to the threat of the Acquired Immune Deficiency Syndrome and to a resurgence of venereal disease), the use of alcohol and tobacco is off, and among the mainstream population drug use is in significant decline.[58] With the end of the 1980s, a significant hardening of public opinion against crime and in favor of harsh punishment has occurred. Citing 1990 gubernatorial election campaigns in California, Florida, and Texas, a nationally syndicated columnist noted that the 1960s "liberal" approach to crime with its emphasis on the root (social) causes of crime had "been rejected by a preponderance of the American electorate," which strongly prefers a Draconian approach beginning "with a clear, unequivocal denunciation of criminal behavior as beyond the pale." Voters, he declared, are not "simply responding to [politicians'] demagogy. The reason

141

people are afraid of crime"—and, therefore, demanding harsh punishment of offenders—"is rooted in reality; it [crime] has increased geometrically in the last 30 to 40 years. The remorseless savagery of young offenders has shocked even hardened veterans of big-city police forces. And the 1960s-style equation of poverty and discrimination with criminal tendencies is itself stunningly simplistic." Acknowledging that there are, indeed, "deep-rooted reasons for crime," he emphasizes that voters are, however, "saying, 'Enough is enough—there is a right and wrong to crime.' And that sentiment," he concludes, "is as much an expression of common sense as it is of fear."[59]

The new tightening up of society against crime and what Ted Robert Gurr referred to as the ethic of "aggressive hedonism"[60] is, it seems, a part of the increasingly inclusive Information Society whose impact is likely to be, as was that of Industrial Society, "broad and continuous" in terms of "changes in the socialization process" that will affect "virtually every aspect" of our life, and not just the lines of those who are directly engaged in high-technological, computer-oriented occupations.[61] Just as Industrial Society and a decline in crime as well as repression of crime were all linked, it is possible that the Information Society will converge with and reinforce a new decline and a new repression of crime.

Two aspects of the Information Society that are significantly connected to the future of crime in this country are the tandem entities of high technology and computerization and, second, the trend of decentralization in America.

In regard to high technology, science, and computerization, the "war on crime" is increasingly being computerized, and longer and longer strides will be made in that direction. For example, computerized analysis of information now underway holds high hopes for increasing significantly the ability of the criminal-justice system to deal effectively with the elusive serial killers who as recently as 1984 were believed to be responsible for an annual toll of over three thousand unsolved murders.[62] Even more broadly, there is the remarkable expansion in the scope of such criminal-justice data bases as those of the FBI's National Criminal Justice Information Center and the U.S. Treasury Department's Treasury Enforcement Communication System.[63] In thirteen states, highly reliable genetic evidence has been used to convict or exonerate those accused of heinous crimes. California is carrying the new crime-fighting technique of genetic tracking to a higher level by planning a genetic base incorporating such information on those convicted and imprisoned for murder, assault, rape, and other sex crimes. Genetic tracking has high potential for increasing the certainty of the criminal-justice system in dealing with violent crime.[64]

Not all of this is pretty. One of the growth areas of American law enforcement that seems destined to get bigger and bigger is in the realm of undercover work and the high-tech domain of what sociologist Gary T. Marx terms the "new surveillance."[65] The new surveillance is spearheaded by burgeoning, ever-more-sophisticated electronic means that include—among a staggering array of devices—potent lasers, parabolic microphones and other "bugs" with more powerful transmitters, subminiature tape recorders, improved remote camera and videotape systems, advanced ways of seeing in the dark, voice-stress analyzers, and powerful new tracking devices.[66]. In the course of his searching study of the new surveillance, Marx came to be more reconciled to the need for undercover tactics as an aid to law enforcement, but he remained deeply troubled by the frightening potential for the abuse of undercover work in the interest of an oppressive extension of governmental power. Yet in a time when a "choice between anarchy and repression" may too often be forced on society, the new surveillance, concluded Marx, "may be a necessary evil. The challenge," he writes, is to prevent it "from becoming an intolerable one."[67] His forebodings are appropriate, for the trend, noted earlier, away from emphasis on the due process of law toward the bald repression of crime is likely to reinforce the fixation on the new surveillance made possible by the technology of the Information Society.

Much more benign are the Information Society's converging

trends of decentralization and community self-help for neighborhood revitalization and the prevention of crime. Here is an area in which the popular advocate of the Information Society, John Naisbitt, and scholarly criminologists and urbanologists seem to be in agreement. In his prophetic best-selling book, *Megatrends,* Naisbitt presented neighborhood crime prevention as a prime example of decentralization in the Information Society. He wrote that citizens were "responding to the 1980s crime wave with fear, anger and activism. No longer willing to delegate the responsibility for their safety to the government or the police, citizens are taking matters into their own hands. Once an innovation, crime-watch groups and crime-stopper programs are fast becoming commonplace across the country and are compiling an impressive track record."[68] By the same token, a significant recent book, *American Violence and Public Policy* edited by Lynn A. Curtis and emanating from the prestigious Eisenhower Foundation, reveals that community self-help against crime is the avant-garde of scholarly thought on the subject. As contributions by Elliott Currie, James P. Comer, Paul J. Lavrakas, and Curtis himself show, the emphasis in the book is to play down the criminal-justice system (or what might be called "government help") in favor of community self-help. Currie holds "that informal sanctions applied by family, peers, and community have more effect" in deterring crime than " 'tough' criminal justice policies" and advocates "the search for ways of strengthening the infrastructure of local communities and enhancing their capacity to deal with problems of crime and disorder" in preference to the traditional approach of a massive criminal-justice bureaucracy with what he sees as an over-emphasis on incarceration.[69] In this contribution Lavrakas—a leading authority—presents what is virtually a success manual for "citizen self-help and neighborhood crime prevention,"[70] and Curtis in his epilogue for the volume commends model community programs in West Philadelphia and the South Bronx and calls for "neighborhood or community-based crime prevention" as the best hope, one which, he informs us, is being funded and fostered by the Eisenhower Foundation.[71]

The technique of community self-help to prevent crime is being tested as never before in the black ghetto neighborhoods whose residents are both the most crime-prone and the most victimized by crime of all Americans.[72] A triple crisis of epidemic drug use, youthful gang activity, and black-on-black crime in America's inner-city neighborhoods is colliding with the emergent Information Society and its imperatives for a new structure and order in American life. Potent and pervasive youth gangs in the ghettos and barrios of Los Angeles, New York, Miami, Washington, and Chicago have become, in reality, drug-dealing crime confederations specializing in the highly addictive, smokable cocaine known as "crack."[73] The most famous of these gangs are the ubiquitous Crips and Bloods—competing gangs of young African-Americans based in south-central Los Angeles (and environs) and rapidly expanding their operations into Denver, Portland, and other Western cities. Also prominent are similar gangs of young Hispanos, Asians, and Jamaicans. In 1987, 55 percent of the more than eight hundred homicides in Los Angeles were believed to have been drug related, mostly in connection with the gangs. The drive-by shootings of warring gangs have become a dauntingly familiar feature of life in the afflicted urban zones. In some ways resembling the Mafia of the 1920s–40s,[74] these new inner-city gangs are, however, much more violent than their earlier counterparts. The cost, personnel, and time involved in fighting Crips, Bloods, Jamaican "posses," and other gangs is overwhelming the police. As *Newsweek* reported in early 1988, the "war on drugs" is being lost in the inner-city battlegrounds. To many—perhaps the majority of—Americans, the drug danger was the number-one concern in the presidential election year of 1988,[75] and in response to even greater concern in 1989, President George W. Bush III, reacting to a mood of unprecedented national urgency on this issue, presented to the Congress and the nation on September 5, 1989, a $2 billion "National Drug Control Strategy" under the coordinated leadership of William J. Bennett, the federal drug policy director. Although stressing treatment of drug offenders and education of the young against drug use as well as aid to South American nations in their efforts to quell cocaine production, nearly 70 percent of the $2 billion would be spent on increased enforcement of laws against drug sales and use.[76]

In related fashion the carnage inflicted by young black males upon each other is jeopardizing neighborhood after neighborhood of inner-city African-Americans. Statistics show that young black males are by far the most violence-prone and violence-vulnerable of all Americans and have been for some time.[77] At the root of the crime crisis in inner-city African-American life is the shockingly high rate of unemployment among young black males, which has hovered between 40 and 50 percent for a number of years.[78] Elliott Currie has long since made the common-sense point that America will get its problem of crime under control only by a massive publicly funded program of work for African-American youth—and not just low-paid make-work jobs but jobs in which pride may be taken and by which families may be supported above the poverty line.[79]

Aside from the problem, acknowledged by Currie, of gaining political support for such an endeavor, the whole notion of such a massive employment program seems increasingly irrelevant. Once the conventional but arbitrary distinction between legal and illegal employment is put aside, it becomes evident that employment among young black males in inner-city areas is not low but quite heavy in a combination of legal work and drug-dealing illegal gang work. The estimated seventy thousand gang members in Los Angeles are, to greater or lesser degree, employed in illicit but highly remunerative jobs in a drug-dealing hierarchy that brings millions of dollars annually into the city's ghettos and barrios. The illegal employment of drug dealing produces, in effect, wages that are far above the level afforded by the legal private sector or even contemplated in Currie's proposed employment program. Many law-abiding black ghetto residents have, out of economic desperation and without approving illegality, become dependent upon income brought in by those in their families who are affluent drug-dealing gang members.[80]

In his study of crack dealers and addicts in the East Harlem section of New York City, anthropologist Philippe Bourgois found that

> to many, especially the young, the underground economy [of crack dealing] beckons seductively as the ultimate "equal opportunity employer." The rate of unemployment [in comparison to legal employment] for Harlem youth is at least twice the citywide rate of 8.1 percent, and the economic incentive to participate in the burgeoning [criminal] economy is overwhelming.

In regard to their previous roles in the legal economy, recruits to the underground economy

> speak with anger at their former low wages and bad treatment [in legal jobs]. They make fun of friends and acquaintances—many of whom come to buy drugs from them—who are still employed in factories or in service jobs. . . . All of them [the crack dealers] have, at one time or another, held the jobs—delivery boys, supermarket baggers, hospital orderlies—that are objectively recognized as among the least desirable in American society. They see the illegal, underground economy as not only offering superior wages, but also a more dignified workplace.

Bourgois's conclusion was that the crack dealers are not alienated from the values of mainstream society but that

> ambitious, energetic, inner-city youths are attracted to the underground economy precisely because they believe in the rags-to-riches American dream. Like many in the mainstream, they are fanatically trying to get their piece of the pie as fast as possible. In fact, they follow the traditional model for upward mobility: aggressively setting themselves up as private entrepreneurs.[81]

In regard to the inner-city crime crisis, the picture is indeed bleak. There is ample basis for pessimism in regard to a significant decline in the commission of offenses by young black males that is at the center of our late-twentieth century onslaught of crime.[82] Yet neither scholars nor the public should underrate the resiliency of African-Americans in this time of crisis. There is, in

147

fact, a mood among them that the challenge of inner-city crime and disorder must be met and repelled at all costs. In recent years, black leaders and urban residents have come strongly to the view that community self-help more than government aid is the key to the reduction of the size of the underclass of the African-American ghettos.

A precipitating event in the movement stressing African-American community self-help was a 1984 conference in Nashville attended by representatives of one hundred black organizations. Among African-American leaders who have endorsed the self-reliance approach are John E. Jacob, executive director of the National Urban League; William H. Gray III, chairman of the budget committee of the U.S. House of Representatives; Mayor Tom Bradley of Los Angeles; Robert Woodson, chairman of the National Center for Neighborhood Enterprise; Benjamin L. Hooks, executive director of the National Association for the Advancement of Colored People; and two-time presidential candidate Jesse Jackson, leader of People United to Save Humanity. A result was the formation six years later of the National Association of Black Organizations. Convened by the NAACP in a "summit conference of Black Organizations," the NABO is an association of more than a hundred such organizations—all dedicated, said Benjamin L. Hooks, to "taking responsibility for our own destiny."[83]

Typical is the view of the late M. Carl Holman, who in 1985, as president of the National Urban Coalition, reflected upon the future of black children and saw them in trouble, "slipping academically to the point where a shocking percentage of the next generation will be economically expandable—not because of racism but because they will lack the skills to compete in the labor market" of the computer era. "Much of our help," he continued, "has to come from our own community—churches, clubs, fraternities, sororities, fraternal orders, and professional organizations" whose members Holman urged to enlist in an educational crusade for African-American children. "Black people," Holman concluded, "really need to take charge of their own success and not look exclusively to those outside our community."[84] The same theme has been expressed by leading African-American scholars, including psychiatrist James P. Comer, who can recall from his own youth youngsters of "chaotic backgrounds" who became neither criminal nor violent. Comer focuses on child rearing and education within the black community as the realm where progress must be made.[85] Notable too in recent years have been many nationally syndicated newspaper commentaries promoting African-American community self-help, especially in regard to education and the reduction of crime, by columnist William Raspberry, whose home newspaper is the *Washington Post.*[86]

African-American inner-city residents have by the thousands enlisted in the grassroots community self-help movement. One such endeavor is the Fairlawn Coalition, a citizens' quasi-vigilante patrol group which by the summer of 1989 had retaken control of its neighborhood, two miles southeast of the Capitol in the Anacostia section of Washington, D.C. In a city—America's capital—which in 1988 had gained national ignominy for the ravages of crack addiction and its result, the highest murder rate in the United States,[87] the Fairlawn Coalition used a model of community crime-prevention going back a quarter century to 1964,[88] one that stresses radio-equipped patrols of two or three citizens who call in suspicious activity to the quickly responding city police force. After a year of such activity by the two-hundred-odd members of the Fairlawn Coalition in a neighborhood of several thousand residents, one of the earliest members of the Coalition, Alvin Collins (code-named "Elevator Slim" in radio communications), watched with fulfillment and "growing pride" as, in a years's time, the neighborhood drug trade "slowly dried up." Not long before, a typical 1:00 A.M. scene at Seventeenth and R streets would find as many as thirty drug dealers and buyers brazenly making their deals. "Now look," said Collins to a reporter: "nothing."

The Fairlawn Coalition is typical of such undertakings in its nonviolent, quasi-vigilante activity. Along with radio-equipped patrols for calling in illicit activities to police, the Fairlawn Coalition has mobilized neighborhood unity and pride to intimidate the drug suppliers peacefully. The Coalition's relationship with the police has been ideal: "direct confrontation" with the criminal element has been left to the police who have moved in on "the location of a new crack house or some hot street dealing" reported to them by Coalition members. In the opinion of police sergeant J. J. Cummings III, head of a mototcycle unit responsible for Fairlawn, the Coalition is "proof positive" that citizens, with police aid, can reclaim their communities from drug criminals. "The people of Fairlawn," concluded Sergeant Cummings, "have helped themselves, and they've made life a lot easier for me and my officers."[89] In their determination not to surrender their community to the drug dealers who have invaded it, the Fairlawn Coalition exemplifies in broad terms the spirit of no duty to retreat.

In this new mood of anticrime resolve illustrated by the Fairlawn Coalition and many other such grassroots ventures, education is seen as the long-term key to the alleviation of the plight of the demoralized and violence-prone ghetto underclass and, ultimately, to black survival in the era of the Information Society. African-American media magnate John H. Johnson has warned that "we are losing a whole generation" of black youth "in a new high-tech environment in which the disadvantages of one generation multiply in the next" and "create no-win scenarios" that could last until the twenty-first and twenty-second centuries unless the trend is reversed.[90]

With John E. Jacob, president of the National Urban League, also warning that "black survival" is at stake in the present crisis,[91] many are rallying around the revitalization of African-American community educational institutions. A strategy has come to the fore that focuses on creative new model schools. With such great African-American high schools of an earlier generation as Dunbar in Washington, D.C., Frederick Douglass in Baltimore, St. Augustine and Xavier Prep in New Orleans, and Booker T. Washington in Atlanta in decline, there arose a new array of model schools where academic achievement and pride are thriving. Among them are Wheatley Elementary in Dallas, Audubon Junior High and George Washington Preparatory High in Los Angeles, Renaissance High in Detroit, Eastside High in Paterson,[92] Orangeburg-Wilkinson High in South Carolina,[93] Murry Bergstrum High in Manhattan,[94] Kelly Miller Junior High in Washington, D.C.,[95] and Simeon Baldwin and Martin Luther King, Jr., elementary schools in New Haven.[96] In these and other schools, energetic and innovative principals of the 1980s (Joe Clark of Eastside High, George J. McKenna III of George Washington Preparatory High, Gene McCallum of Audubon Junior High, Claude Moten of Kelly Miller Junior High, and Melvin Smoak of Orangeburg-Wilkinson High were only five among many),[97] talented teachers,[98] eager and impressive students,[99] and involved parents led an African-American community educational comeback. In once-chaotic classrooms and crime-ridden hallways discipline was restored, and prideful students responded to the keynote motif that united the ferment and diversity of these vibrant schools: high expectations of student achievement. The black business-magazine publisher Earl Graves of New York City characterized all of this, rightly, as a new battle for education in the postslavery, postsegregation era.[100] There is widespread recognition that African-American students must be trained for "tomorrow's highly technical, super-competitive job market."[101]

Thus local African-American neighborhoods and schools are responding to the crisis of violent, drug-dealing gangs along with the high rate of homicidal deaths among young black males and to the challenge of the Information Society. "Education is the fundamental ingredient in the prescription for saving our children," asserted the Los Angeles African-American principal George J. McKenna III.[102] Blacks will be no less immune than whites and others to the transformation of "the feelings, sensibilities, perceptions, expectations, assumptions, and, above all, the possibilities that define a community" stemming from the creation of the Information Society.[103]

Blacks and all Americans will share, therefore, in the new order and structure to be provided, after decades of Postindustrial chaos, by the Information Society. Japanese scholar and planner Yoneji Masuda has written that the Information Society will "bring about fundamental changes in human values, in trends of thought, and in the political and economic structures" of the times.[104] These changes are well underway in America and are making a revolutionary impact, as Shoshana Shuboff, a thorough and perceptive student of the emerging Information Society, has recently shown. Her case studies of computerized workplaces demonstrate that the alteration in employee attitudes is as significant as that which occurred at the dawn of Industrial Society.[105] Shuboff and other authorities are revealing that the "intellective skills" of the computer-dominated era are producing a new age structured by mental discipline rather than the machine discipline of the earlier Industrial Society.[106]

The radically different ethos of the Information Society (in contrast to that of Industrial Society) is emerging not only in the workplaces but in the minds of the young: by 1985–86 students in 92 percent of the nation's public schools were being exposed to desktop computers.[107] Most adaptable of all to the Information Society are these "microkids"—journalist Fredrick Golden's term for the schoolchildren who, he declares, "will surely confront the world differently from their parents. The precise orderly state of logic required to use and program the machines [i.e., microcomputers] promises to shape—and sharpen—the thought processes of the computer generation."[108] Similarly, Stephen Toulmin, a philosopher of science at the University of Chicago, announces that computers are "re-intellectualizing" the mentally passive members of the TV generation.[109] Mathematician Seymour Papert, developer of LOGO computer language for elementary-school pupils, underscores the potential for educating children according to theorist Jean Piaget's concept of the child as builder of ideas—one who structures reality according to the Piagetian maxim that "to understand is to invent." *"The child programs the computer,"* says Papert, and thus gains a "sense of mastery over a piece of the most modern and powerful technology and establishes an intimate contact with some of the deepest ideas from science, from mathematics, and from the art of intellectual building."[110]

In summary, Americans of the present are determined to have

a more orderly nation and, from a broad but deep belief in no duty to retreat, are prepared to support a harsher policy against crime. The destiny of crime, law, and society in America of the 1990s and into the next century is likely, then, to be governed by a combination of short-term and long-term developments that will affect all Americans:

- An increasing emphasis on education and an increasingly effective educational system (a trend begun in the 1980s)[111] will gradually introduce an important element of structure into society in counteraction to factors that produce crime.

- High technology and computerization will increase the effectiveness of the criminal-justice system and efforts to prevent crime.

- Community self-help will strengthen local neighborhoods and help reduce the inroads of crime.

- An expanded prison population will take out of circulation more and more members of the relatively irreducible hard core of those who commit a highly disproportionate amount of violent crime.[112]

- Leavened by a more conservative federal judiciary, the system of criminal justice will reduce its emphasis on due process of law in favor of repression of crime.

Transcending as well as influencing these short-term developments will be the most important factor of all: a revitalization of education and a freely chosen, self-imposed renewal of social discipline—both resulting from the Information Society[113]—that will shape a new structure and order in American life whose impact will reduce crime in the long run.

With a significant reduction in crime and with other changes in the American and international order of the turn of the century from the twentieth to the twenty-first, will the traditional American attitude of no duty to retreat become obsolete? In the broadest terms of American values and the American character, what has been the significance of no duty to retreat in retrospect, and what are its chances for survival in the nation and the world of the last decade of this century and the early decades of the next?

153

5

Conclusion: No Duty to Retreat in Retrospect and Prospect

"Because I am an American, I will defend. . . . my life, liberty and dignity by whatever legal means I have, including force, if necessary."
Devin S. Standard (1989).*

From the Industrial Society of the nineteenth and the early twentieth century to the Information Society of our own time, the factor of values has been crucial in regard to American violence and crime. Central to understanding the doctrine of no duty to retreat is the realm of values, for the notion of no duty to retreat is an expression of American values as well as American behavior.

In his monumental study of the American dilemma of race relations published in 1944, Gunnar Myrdal found that the then-existing ironclad system of segregation and white supremacy in the South was a standing contradiction to what Myrdal termed the "American Creed" of freedom, equality, and democracy.[1] That is, the notion of white supremacy that many Southerners held as a top value in the 1940s (and long before) contradicted the creed of a majority of Americans. In similar fashion, many have noted the affront of violence to what, along with Myrdal, we might refer to as the American creed.[2] The first significant perception of this inherent contradiction between our values of peace and civility and our all-too-frequent behavior of

155

violence was by Abraham Lincoln, who in 1838 made it the theme of a notable public address. Lincoln was then a youthful lawyer in Illinois, only twenty-eight years old. He was aroused by a surge of violence in the 1830s, that shook the nation—North, South, East, and West—and his conclusion was that the greatest threat to the perpetuation of the political institutions of the American republic would come not from some foreign power but from the internal flaw of violence.[3]

Thus one important issue in regard to violence and American values stems from the Lincolnian proposition that violence is the nemesis of the values Americans cherish. A second issue is, para-doxically, the extent to which violence is not merely opposed to but actually a part of our value system or, put another way, that there are elements (often unacknowledged) in our value system which encourage and sustain violence. Indeed, there is a sort of underground matrix of American values that, although lacking the approval of opinion leaders and citizens in their better moments, has frequently guided Americans in their behavior: a *sub rosa* cluster of values that have provided sanction for actions ordinarily considered shameful and wrong—in short, sanction for violence.

For example, early in the twentieth century (1906, to be exact) a legal scholar mortified by the pervasiveness of extralegal lynch-ings and vigilantism described what he referred to, accurately for the time, as an "unwritten law" of American justice—a "juris-prudence of lawlessness" as it really functioned in America in which, he asserted with good authority, certain maxims guided action more than the moral admonitions of public leaders.[4] This critic, Thomas J. Kernan, enumerated certain late nineteenth-and early twentieth-century practices that were approved by pub-lic opinion and, often, the actions of juries; among them were the following:

○ A rapist may be lynched.

○ An adulterous man may be killed by a wronged husband.

○ A seducer of a virgin may be slain.

- A traducer of a woman may be shot unless he apologizes.
- The survivor of a duel fought fairly may be acquitted by the law.
- The killer in a fair fight may be acquitted by the law.
- An accusation of lying or an opprobious epithet justifies assault.[5]

In late twentieth-century America, this "jurisprudence of lawlessness" is a bit out of date. While there is a vigorous victim-rights movement in our nation[6] and increasingly strong compassion for the victims of rape,[7] the day is long since past when rapists are routinely lynched as in Kernan's time. The killing of the seducer of a virgin is no longer a common occurrence, and unapologetic traducers of women stand in little danger of being shot. Yet even now juries sometimes refuse to convict a husband who does away with his wife's adulterous partner, and an opprobrious epithet is thought by many today to justify assault. Bolstered by the doctrine of no duty to retreat, the killer in what is viewed as a fair fight often wins the approval of a jury in our own time.[†]

Sometimes the official value system sanctioned by the leaders of society and the illicit value system as practiced by the people converge in a way that results in even more widespread approval of violence. In his influential essay of 1893 in which he proclaimed the famous thesis that, more than any other factor, the frontier had determined American history and society, Frederick Jackson Turner concluded that it is "to the frontier [that] the American intellect owes its striking characteristics": a "coarseness and strength combined with acuteness and inquisitiveness"; a "practical, inventive turn of mind"; an overwhelming "grasp of material things"; above all, "that *dominant individualism*,[††] working for good and for evil"—and a "buoyancy and exuberance which comes with freedom." "These are the traits of the frontier," said Turner, "or traits called out elsewhere because of the existence of the frontier."[8]

[†]Such a case is that of Claude Dallas, discussed below in this chapter.
[††]Emphasis added.

Going all the way back to Alexis de Tocqueville's 1840 volume *Democracy in America*,[9] Turner has been only one of many to emphasize American individualism. Two sociologists recently echoed Turner in their stress on the centrality of individualism for "core American values." In their study of "enduring social issues," these scholars found that "all other values are influenced by the emphasis placed upon the individual." Emphasizing the notion of "individual self-determination" as a key to American values, they underscored also the desire of Americans "to master situations" and to have "a manipulative stance toward the world around them."[10]

Such concepts of individualism, individual self-determination, and the desire to dominate situations are, of course, much in phase with the psychology and the norm of standing one's ground without a duty to retreat. Meanwhile, the attitude of individual domination most crucially exemplified by the legal and social doctrine of no duty to retreat has been recently broadened into a far-ranging interpretation of western American history in *The Legacy of Conquest: The Unbroken Past of the American West* by Patricia Nelson Limerick. In this book Limerick stresses the motif of conquest in the pluralistic and multicultural history of the West going back to the sixteenth century. It is a history in which, as she sees it, the principal theme has been conquest— conquest of the land and also conquest of people: the conquest of Indians by other Indians, of Indians by Hispanos, and finally the conquest of all others by Euroamerican pioneers.[11] Limerick does not mention the concept of no duty to retreat, but it is obvious that the legal and individual doctrine of no duty to retreat is highly cognate with the broad social theme of conquest.

A recent widely publicized case unites themes of no duty to retreat and, in individual terms, conquest and mastery. This was the case of the so-called "mountain man," Claude Dallas, who gained his livelihood in the 1970s and 1980s by trapping animals in the wild, isolated country of desert and mountains where the three states of Idaho, Oregon, and Nevada converge. Braced by two state game wardens at his camp on the south fork of the

Owyhee River in Idaho, Dallas was accused by them of poaching. Of the two game wardens, one of them—William Pogue—was the angry protagonist and leader. He was armed, as was Dallas, who ended the heated confrontation by shooting Pogue and his colleague dead.[12] The result was a sensational trial in which Dallas's life hung in the balance. The concept of no duty to retreat was crucial to Dallas's successful plea of self-defense. The legal aim of Dallas and his attorneys, writes Jeff Long, was to counter the prosecution's charge of murder in the first degree by portraying Dallas as "a lone, windswept trapper forced to defend himself against the long arm and heavy hands" of the game-protecting lawmen.[13] In effect, the Western myth of the individualistic mountain man was invoked in Dallas's behalf.[14] All of this was keyed to Idaho law, which in its emphasis on no duty to retreat was "almost tailor-made" to fit Claude Dallas's claim of self-defense.[15]

The official definition of justifiable homicide in Idaho was typically American and included a concise, although legalistic, statement of the doctrine of no duty to retreat:

> Where one, without fault is placed under circumstances sufficient to excite the fears of a reasonable man that another designs to commit a felony, or some great bodily injury upon him, and to afford grounds for reasonable belief that there is imminent danger of the accomplishment of his design, he may, acting under these fears alone, slay his assailant and be justified by the appearances. And as where the attack is sudden and the danger imminent, he may increase his peril *by retreat;* so situated, he may *stand his ground* . . . and *slay his aggressor,* even if it be proved he might more easily have gained by *flight.*[†16]

As Dallas testified before the jury, he—a reasonable man—had had a reasonable fear for his life when confronted by the armed Pogue, had stood his ground, and when Pogue had reached for his holstered revolver had slain Pogue, whom he viewed as his assailant.[17]

Claude Dallas's claim of his right to exercise the legal

---

†Emphasis added

159

privelege of no duty to retreat was no mere opportunistic exploitation of the law hatched up in conference with his attorneys, for Dallas, long before the killings at his riverside camp, strongly identified with the mystique of the gunfight and the walkdown.[†] After the trial, it came out that Dallas had possessed books entitled *No Second Place Winner* and *Kill or Get Killed*— training manuals for the sort of quick-draw gunfight Dallas testified had occurred.[18] In the end, the jury in Dallas's trial was convinced by his plea of self-defense based on no duty to retreat. Thus Dallas escaped conviction for the capital crime of murder, although he was convicted for the lesser offense of manslaughter. After the trial, the foreman explained the jury's thinking in regard to its refusal to find Dallas guilty of murder: "We just figured Pogue drew his gun and Dallas was a better marksman, that he [Dallas] was put in a postion of self-defense. Dallas was a faster draw. He won out."[19] Like Dallas and like President Eisenhower, the jury believed in the concept of the no-duty-to-retreat gunfight of the Wild Bill Hickok type in which, said Eisenhower, if you met your opponent "face to face and took the same risk he did, you could get away with almost anything as long as the bullet was in the front."[††] Yet the judge, not the jury, had the last word in the trial of Claude Dallas when the former pronounced sentence on the latter for the crime of manslaughter. The sentence—a maximum of thirty years in prison—was a very heavy one for manslaughter. Reflecting his own unforgiving attitude, the judge said to Dallas as he imposed the sentence in open court, "I do not believe the issue of self-defense arose. . . . Your actions were motivated by your desire to ensure your own freedom as opposed to an actual threat of life or limb."[20] Thus the judge saw Claude Dallas as an example of the typical American desire to maintain individual self-determination and mastery in all situations—an attitude related to that of no duty to retreat.

[†]See Chapter 2, on the mystique of the gunfight and the walkdown.
[††]On Eisenhower, see Chapter 1, above.

The impact of the change in the common law from the English doctrine of the duty to retreat to the American doctrine of standing one's ground is not confined to the law of homicide, for the broader metaphorical and symbolic significance of the switch to no duty to retreat is evident. Indeed, the concept of no duty to retreat has been strongly imprinted on our foreign affairs and military values as well as the activities of civilian life. Belief in no duty to retreat goes to the core of what it has meant to be an American.

The no-duty-to-retreat attitude is closely related, also, to the trait of courage in everyday affairs. When President Eisenhower invoked the no-duty-to-retreat example of Wild Bill Hickok in his nationally televised speech of November 23, 1953, he did so in the interest of attacking the often anonymous character assassination that had become rampant in the early 1950s, the era of McCarthyism. Eisenhower made an analogy between the Western code of meeting "anyone face to face with whom you disagree . . . as long as the bullet [is] in the front" and the constitutional right of every American "to meet his accuser face to face." The President's 1953 speech was made in response to his receipt of B'nai B'rith's Democratic Legacy Award.[21] Given the climate of opinion in 1953, it was obvious to Eisenhower's nationwide audience that the President saw no-duty-to-retreat courage as the proper antidote to the groundless, destructive charges against individuals so often generated in the hysterical atmosphere precipitated by Senator Joseph R. McCarthy's heedless, irresponsible crusade against Communism.[22]

In one notable American characteristic—competition—the attitude of no duty to retreat is tied to domestic life, for it represents the spirit of competition as well as a perspective on personal combat. Competition is virtually a cult for Americans. Sociologists Jonathan H. Turner and David Musick have found that competitiveness is integrally related to a significant core American value, achievement.[23] So much of the achievement upon which Americans pride themselves—accomplishments in politics, government, science and technology, creative endeavors, the news media, athletics, recreation, education and scholarship, business, the professions, personal careers, and daily activities—is based upon the competitive spirit for which Americans have long since become globally famous.

Examples of the attitude of no duty to retreat also abound in the history of American foreign affairs. Some of these cases quite specifically involve the concept of no duty to retreat; others are more general in their relation to the complementary stand-one's-ground spirit. President James K. Polk's message to Congress on December 2, 1845, in which he laid out the uncompromising policy toward Mexico[24] whose eventual result was the Mexican-American War of 1846–48, expressed an attitude of no duty to retreat at the presidential level. The Polk administration's specific order to General Zachary Taylor to lead his army into disputed territory north of the Rio Grande and to stay there[25]—no matter what armed opposition might be made to him by the Mexicans—was an order to Taylor to stand his ground and not retreat, come what may. Claiming the ground on which Taylor and his men stood, Mexican soldiers attacked a detachment of Taylor's force. This quickly led to an American declaration of war on Mexico.[26] Many Americans then—including the young congressman Abraham Lincoln[27]—and some historians later believed that the Polk policy of insisting on Taylor's standing his ground along the Rio Grande was, given the failure of aggressive but peaceful diplomacy with Mexico, a policy intended to provoke a war with Mexico for the aim of acquiring the Mexican domain of California.[28] Taylor himself had originally recommended that the Polk administration order him to the Rio Grande in order to pressure Mexico into a resolution of the diplomatic conflict that would be favorable to America, while in private correspondence Polk even earlier had expressed his no-duty-to-retreat determination that if diplomacy should not uphold the Texan-American claim to the disputed land above the Rio Grande no Mexican army would be allowed "to occupy a foot of the soil [north] of the Rio Grande."[29]

Whether the Polk-Taylor stand-one's-ground stance on the Rio Grande was, as Lincoln and others believed, an imperialistic plot to draw Mexico into a losing war from the result of which America could exact enormous territorial gains or, rather, a forceful (but not conspiratorial) policy that willingly risked war, this was one of the prime instances of the no-duty-to-retreat spirit in our national history. Its outcome was indeed the acquisition of a huge block of land—California and the remainder of the American southwest. Ironically, Abraham Lincoln—the courageous opponent of James K. Polk's no-duty-to-retreat policy—turned to no duty to retreat himself in the great national crisis of 1860–61. Faced with the dilemma of whether to support or to evacuate the U.S. army force at Fort Sumter or to surrender it to the surrounding Confederate military might in the harbor of Charleston, South Carolina, in the spring of 1861, Lincoln was fearful of being seen as weak in his resolve to preserve the union. To counteract a public perception of weakness on his part, Lincoln chose a no-duty-to-retreat policy of resupplying the beleaguered defenders of Fort Sumter.[30] The Confederacy responded by firing on Fort Sumter. Lincoln's stand-one's-ground action and the Confederate response to it resulted in the Civil War.

In the Cold War era, Harry S Truman's presidential successors, Eisenhower and John F. Kennedy, aggressively sustained the "containment" policy initiated by Truman. Most sweeping and eloquent of all was President Kennedy's 1961 statement of the spirit of standing one's ground worldwide: speaking of America in his inaugural address, the President declared, "Let every nation know, whether it wishes us well or ill, that we shall pay any price, bear any burden, meet any hardship, support any friend, oppose any foe to assure the survival and the success of liberty."[31] Nearly a decade and a half earlier, containment was established in the Truman administration as the basic American approach to the Cold War.[32] The policy designed to contain the power of Soviet Russia within the boundaries it dominated was a diplomatic embodiment of the concept of no duty to retreat. Specifically, there was to be no retreat of American military power from western Europe in which it was lodged at the close of World War II (and still remains). With precedent in some actions of 1946, the cornerstone of the American policy of containment was the no-duty-to-retreat Truman Doctrine of 1947 announced in the president's successful plea to Congress for aid to Greece, Turkey, and all other nations that might be threatened by an internal movement of Soviet-inspired subversion or by the military force of Russia and its allies. The crux of the Truman Doctrine was that "whenever [Soviet] aggression, direct or indirect, threatened the peace, the security of the United States was involved."[33] The Russian blockade of Berlin in the summer of 1948 was met, not by an American and allied retreat from the great metropolis of Germany, but rather by a stand-one's-ground determination to remain in Berlin and to supply it and our forces there through a heroic and successful airlift conducted mainly by the U.S. Air Force.[34]

The policy of containment was not, however, restricted to military action. The Marshall Plan formulated in 1947 by Secretary of State George P. Marshall, who, as General of the Army, had headed all American ground forces in World War II, was a giant American aid program for rebuilding the World War II–devastated economies of the nations of western Europe to forestall social disorder and chaos, which might result in their collapsing into the Russian sphere. Sponsored by President Truman, the Marshall Plan was, of course, strongly approved by Congress.[35]

The containment policy in Europe was capped by the keystone in the arch of the no-duty-to-retreat response to Russian power: the North Atlantic Treaty Organization (NATO) established in 1949, through which, at the behest of the United States, nine western European nations in addition to Iceland and Canada coalesced with America to bind themselves to aid one another against the attack of an aggressor.[36] NATO was a military and diplomatic determination of America and its allies to stand their ground against the perceived Russian threat to western Europe or any part of the North Atlantic region.

Meanwhile, the broad policy of stand-one's-ground anti-Communist containment was extended to the Far East[37] where the powerful new state of Communist China rose alongside the red regime in North Korea and the Russian presence in eastern Siberia. The American attitude of no duty to retreat in the Far East was put to the test in late June 1950, when North Korean Communist troops attacked southward into the territory of the American anti-Communist ally, South Korea. Previously announced United States policy, which seemed to some to exclude South Korea from the American perimeter of defense,[38] was, at any rate, quickly tossed aside by President Truman, who, with South Korea figuratively backed to the wall by the North Korean onslaught, firmly determined that the United States would not retreat from South Korea, where American forces (to be reinforced by token detachments from United Nations members) would stand their ground against the Communist invasion.

Harry Truman's far-reaching presidential policy of no duty to retreat was nowhere better exemplified than in his personal reaction to the compelling crisis of the North Korean invasion of South Korea—an event that put Truman under great national-security deadline pressure. From the very first, Truman's attitude was that of standing one's ground. The president learned of the North Korean attack late in the evening of June 24, 1950. The next day his daughter, Margaret, recorded in her diary her father's mood: "Communist Korea is marching on Southern Korea and we are going to fight."[39] On the same day, June 25, Truman, on his way to an emergency meeting to consider North Korea's thrust, announced to key aides, "By God, I am going to let them have it!"[40] During the meeting itself, General Omar Bradley, chairman of the joint chiefs of staff, opined that somewhere the United States must draw the line against Communist aggression. Truman, in his no-duty-to-retreat mood, emphatically agreed.[41] Truman's leading biographer, Robert J. Donovan, summed up the president's visceral, instinctive response to the emergency: "the shocking way the war began galvanized Truman." The "smashing, unexpected" attack by the North Koreans "was a blow he felt personally." "Characteristically," continued Donovan, "Truman was not a belligerent man, yet *his back went up when he was attacked or put on the defensive.*"†42

American no-duty-to-retreat policy in Korea was lifted to the principle of a regional grand alliance against Communism in east Asia and the western Pacific during the administration of President Eisenhower with the eight-nation South East Asia Treaty Organization (SEATO) modeled on NATO.43

In southeast Asia and in recent American history a most spectacular example of no-duty-to-retreat thinking in foreign and military affairs was President Lyndon B. Johnson's policy of American armed intervention in the Vietnamese civil war. The roots of this intervention went back to the administrations of Johnson's presidential predecessors, Eisenhower and Kennedy, but it was Johnson who escalated their tentative, qualified efforts into one of the greatest wars in American history. A Texan with a family background deeply rooted in the embattled nineteenth-century pioneer era of Texas,44 Johnson thought naturally in terms of concepts strongly held in Texas: no duty to retreat, standing one's ground, and I'll die before I'll run.45 In his presidential autobiography Johnson spoke of his attitude to the conflict going on between our ally, South Vietnam, and its Communist antagonist, North Vietnam, whose military forces had surreptitiously invaded South Vietnam in support of the Vietcong guerrillas in that nation. "I made it clear from the day I took office [in 1963]," wrote Johnson, "that I was not a 'peace at any price man' " and that "we would remain strong, prepared at all times to defend ourselves and our friends."46 The American people who elected him president in his own right in 1964 knew, he said, "that Lyndon Johnson was not going to pull up stakes and run."47 In making the decisive commitment of American ground and air forces to war in Vietnam in the winter and spring of 1965, Lyndon Johnson very much thought in terms of the Texan and American heritage of no duty to retreat. In May 1965, a few months after his decision to embark on the sustained bombing of North Vietnam

†Emphasis added.

166

and in the season that he made the crucial decision fully to Americanize the internal Vietnamese conflict by an all-out commitment of American soldiers to the battlefields of South Vietnam, Johnson took as the model for his belligerent policy the no-duty-to-retreat attitude of a nineteenth-century Texas Ranger of the Lone Star state's frontier era. The ranger, Captain L. H. McNelly, repeatedly exhorted his men with the words, *"courage is a man who keeps coming on."*† With the new American venture in Vietnam clearly in mind, Johnson drew the moral of the example of Captain McNelly: "In the challenging and perilous times of this century, free men everywhere might profitably consider this motto"—courage is a man who keeps coming on.[48]

No duty to retreat as a concept has not been restricted to American soldiers on the land. Famous fighting words of the American navy are imbued with the philosophy of no duty to retreat. In 1779, to a British captain's query, "Have you surrendered?" John Paul Jones made "the immortal reply" from his badly damaged *Bonhomme Richard,* "I have not yet begun to fight."[49] Under similar circumstances in the War of 1812, another American naval hero, the fatally wounded Captain James Lawrence, exhorted his crew of the *Chesapeake:* don't give up the ship![50] During the Civil War, Admiral David G. Farragut refused to retreat in Mobile Bay. Defying a fierce Confederate threat to his fleet, Farragut ordered, "Damn the torpedoes"—full speed ahead![51]

On land, American fighting men have been just as famously loyal to the concept of standing one's ground. In a memorable episode during World War II, General Anthony C. McAuliffe, commanding the beleaguered Hundred-and-First Airborne Division at Bastogne in the great Battle of the Bulge, rejected a German demand for surrender with an intrepid Americanism: "Nuts!"[52] Much earlier, in the Civil War, General Ulysses S. Grant, having absorbed appalling losses at the the hands of the Confederate army of Robert E. Lee, on May 11, 1864, declared

---

†Emphasis added.

his determination not to retreat but "to fight it out on this line if it takes all summer."[53] It was an attitude of no duty to retreat as well as overconfidence that in June 1876 doomed George A. Custer and his men in the face of overwhelming Sioux superiority on the hills above the Little Big Horn River.[54]

In war itself, the theme of no duty to retreat is no monopoly of Americans. For any nation, it goes hand in hand with military doctrine, which condemns surrender or flight from an enemy in battle. Yet American military maxims of nonretreat both reinforced and were reinforced by the prevalence of no duty to retreat in civilian life. Most recently, the presidency of Ronald Reagan revitalized the mood of no duty to retreat for the country at large.[55] In the renaissance of the Central Intelligence Agency under the aggressive, operations-minded William Casey,[56] the overthrow of the radically left-wing government of the island nation of Grenada,[57] the bombing attack on the Libya of Moammar Gadhafi,[58] the 1987–88 deployment of American naval might in the Persian Gulf,[59] and opposition to the Marxist government of Nicaragua,[60] President Reagan's foreign policy was that of vigorously standing one's ground against what he and the nation as a whole perceived as the enemies of the United States. The centerpiece of Reagan's widely popular no-duty-to-retreat national policy was the Strategic Defense Initiative (SDI), a futuristic mix of the highest technology and the most aggressive American self-defense popularly known as "Star Wars" because of its focus on antimissile tactics carried to lofty heights of space.[61] Although Reagan's Star Wars program was the most controversial of his various national-defense efforts, it drew on a linkage in the American mind between the national space program and armed defense against the Russian threat—a linkage most compellingly delineated in Tom Wolfe's study of the 1960s Project Mercury astronauts of the National Aeronautics and Space Administration (NASA). In *The Right Stuff* Wolfe portrayed the deep emotional bond of Americans with the astronauts, whom they saw less as protagonists of a peaceful program for a moon landing than the courageous heroes of what was really seen by the people as an effort crucial for national survival: the attempt to surpass the aggressive space technology of Communist Russia.[62] Thus the astronauts were ultimately seen as America's first line of defense in the Cold War conflict with Soviet Russia. Wolfe characterized the typical American's gratitude to John Glenn, the first astronaut to orbit the globe, in these words: "He is my protector. He risked his life and challenged the Russians in the heavens for me."[63] These words also expressed the national mood of no duty to retreat against the USSR, whether on earth or in space.

Personifying for many Americans the Reagan spirit of no duty to retreat was Lieutenant Colonel Oliver North of the U.S. Marines. Colonel North—whom Ronald Reagan had saluted as a "national hero"[64]—emerged as the star of the Iran-Contra congressional hearings in the summer of 1987.[65] A forthright and charismatic witness before the congressional body, North captured the emotions of the nation with his own personal statement of no duty to retreat by declaring, in regard to a world-famous terrorist, "I'll be glad to meet Abu Nidal on equal terms anywhere in the world."[66] The "Olliemania" which swept America during and after Oliver North's congressional testimony[67] was, in part, a strong national reaction in favor of the concept of no duty to retreat.[68] Although there was a national consensus against direct American military action against the Ortega government in Nicaragua, public opinion strongly approved many actions of the Reagan administration that represented a no-duty-to-retreat spirit. Three of these were episodes in which Oliver North, as a member of the staff of the National Security Council, had a key role: the invasion of Grenada,[69] the capture of four terrorists who murdered an American on the cruise ship *Achille Lauro*,[70] and the bombing of Libya.[71]

In broader terms, Ronald Reagan's personal embodiment of the spirit of no duty to retreat was one of the most admired aspects of the most popular presidency since that of Dwight D. Eisenhower and, earlier, Franklin D. Roosevelt. All in all, the general concepts of no duty to retreat and standing one's ground hit a major twentieth-century peak in the Reagan era of 1981– 89—a time in which such notions were reflected in the popular media where the novels of Tom Clancy glorified American fighting men, their weaponry, and the CIA as the first line of defense against the Russian threat[72] and where Tom Cruise skyrocketed to film superstardom in *Top Gun* (1986) by playing a courageous American naval fighter pilot in training to meet the enemies of America wherever they might be.

The no-duty-to-retreat movie role of Tom Cruise in *Top Gun* was strikingly dramatized as reality for the American people in early January 1989, when two U.S. navy F-14 Tomcat fighter planes, operating from the deck of the aircraft carrier *John F. Kennedy,* shot down a pair of Libyan MiG-23 jet fighters off the Libyan coast. The dialogue between the crews in the cockpits of the two American jets was released. It has much in common with the psychology of the walkdown gunfight in the Old West. The F-14 crewmen call off the miles in this aerial walkdown as they close on their Libyan opponents: "Fourteen miles. . . . Six miles. Six miles. Five miles. Four miles." Of the second F-14, it is reported from the lead F-14, "OK, he's got a missle off" (aimed at the first Libyan MiG), and then the following words are heard on the cockpits' tape:

> Good hit. Good hit on 1.
> Roger that. Good kill. Good kill.

Next, the second Libyan plane is locked into the guidance system of a U.S. Sidewinder missile ("Fox 2") in the second F-14:

> I've got the other one.
> All Right, Fox 2.
> Those. . . .
> Shoot him.
> I don't get a [guidance] tone.
> Lock him up [in the guidance]. Lock him up.
> Shoot him. Fox 2.
> I can't. I don't have a . . . [missle] tone.

Here the pilot of the lead F-14 takes over. He lines up behind the dodging, weaving Libyan jet, hears his missile "growl," and fires it. Abruptly, the words:

> Good kill. Good kill.
> Good kill.[73]

The entire confrontation took six minutes—comparable to the length of time consumed in the process of a Western walkdown from provocation to conclusion.

The Reagan epoch was a time, also, when the space shuttle *Challenger*'s seven astronauts became martyrs to national goals and ideals.[74] In leading the nation's deep mourning for their selfless mortal sacrifice, President Reagan invoked the heroism of the Oregon Trail pioneers of the nineteenth century both to equate the "courage, character, and fortitude" of the *"Challenger* Seven" with theirs and to announce the nation's determination to rebuild the space shuttle program in the same way that the men and women of the Oregon Trail overcame "terrible hardship" to reach their far-Western destination.[75]

Yet in the time since Ronald Reagan left office as an eloquent, widely revered presidential proponent of no-duty-to-retreat values, significant changes in the national situation and mood have occurred. In the last year of his administration, Reagan himself dropped his bellicose characterization of the Soviet Union as the "evil empire" as he, along with Soviet leader Mikhail Gorbachev, made remarkable progress for disarmament and a rapprochement between the long-opposed powers of the United States and the Soviet Union. Since then, President Gorbachev's dramatic alteration of the authoritarian Russian Communist system has rapidly opened up Soviet society in a way long advocated by America and its allies among the Western democracies. By 1989 a newsmagazine cover story appeared whose theme was not merely a renewal of Russian-American *détente* but the utter end of the Cold War,[76] and by the spring of 1990, with the collapse of Communist satellite regimes from East Germany to Romania, the Cold War was, it seemed, over.

171

In the new post–Cold War period, what are the implications for the survival of the American theme of no duty to retreat? The traditional appeal of no duty to retreat may well fade in the aftermath of the Cold War, although it is to be noted that the strong popular approval of President Bush for his successful policy of invading Panama in December 1989 to depose its provocative anti-American dictator, General Manuel Noriega, had strong overtones of no duty to retreat (as did Bush's invasion policy). In the summer of 1990 President Bush responded to Iraq's seizure of the nation of Kuwait by sending a huge American military force into the region and proclaiming a "line drawn in the sand" behind which the American ally against Iraq, Saudi Arabia, was to be protected from invasion. The president's image of a "line drawn in the sand" was clearly a no-duty-to-retreat concept. By fall 1990 it was not clear, however, whether the "line" in the sand would be a stand-one's-ground line to be held until Iraq should peacefully meet American demands or a base point for an American military blow to topple the Iraqi regime of Saddam Hussein and restore the independence of Kuwait. In the middle of November 1990 the extremely high economic cost of this United States military venture—especially if it results in a war not rapidly concluded with victory, the rising public sentiment against the high casualties to be anticipated in anything but a lightning war, and a doubtful national mood in regard to a protracted military presence in the region boded poorly for a long-term no-duty-to-retreat commitment on the large scale of the previous interventions in Korea and Vietnam.

Aside from the demise of the Cold War and difficult choices in international relations and military policy such as those posed by the Iraqi invasion of Kuwait, subtle but significant alterations in an ever-changing America may also challenge the sway of the historic attitude of no duty to retreat. Pulled by a strong revulsion against the death and devastation of the Vietnam War as the epitome of stand-one's-ground thinking and by those who deplore what they see as unduly combative masculine values,[77] a socially strong undertow may be setting in against the long dominant tide of no duty to retreat. Would such a reaction carry into oblivion no duty to retreat? Is America entering a period of post–no duty to retreat in which standing one's ground will have less and less appeal in a nation falling away from no duty to retreat and its web of supporting values? Or are we merely in a lull between eras of enthusiasm for no duty to retreat? In short, is it time to think of writing the epitaph for no duty to retreat? Are we in a stage when the paradigm of American values is shifting? Is a new cluster of values stressing peace (rather than military combat), environmental preservation (instead of environmental exploitation), cooperation (rather than competition), and gentle qualities (rather than the norm of *"macho"* masculinity) slowly but surely eroding the traditional American value of no duty to retreat?

It is much too early to provide completely confident answers to such questions, but speculation is possible. One must be wary of prematurely consigning no duty to retreat to the "dustbin of history," for no duty to retreat is an attribute so deeply embedded in our national character that its end—if it ever comes— seems likely to come only most gradually and in the longest of terms. Indeed, it appears that all Americans of whatever ideological persuasion, race, or sex are united, at least, by a militant temper tightly bound to the spirit of no duty to retreat.[78] Activists for peace, environmental protection, cooperation, community, and feminism demonstrate an ardor of the sort represented by the defiant emotion of no duty to retreat. For example, militant feminist Molly Yard, president of the National Organization for Women, in response to a July 1989 United States Supreme Court decision allowing tighter state restrictions on abortion, announced plans for massive protest against the judicial decision. Yard said, "We're not about to go home and give up. We are going to stay and fight."[79]

If no duty to retreat has indeed been so firmly fixed in the American character, is it not possible, however, that the long-established national character is doomed due to the demographic revolution underway since the 1960s? Enormous immigration from third-world nations[80] has produced a remarkable new America in which the traditional host society of Anglo-Americans (out of which came the idea of no duty to retreat) is threatened with dissolution. Yet dissolution may not occur, for there is much evidence that the multitudes of third-world immigrants are finding no duty to retreat a wholly compatible concept[81] as they adjust to the age-old American character much as did their immigrant predecessors from Europe. Unity in diversity has been one of the grand motifs of American history. Diversity is increasing, but there is, despite the fear of some,[82] no convincing evidence that unity is truly in decline. With domestic crime and international terrorism[83] currently presenting a critical challenge to the United States, unity and the spirit of no duty to retreat may wax rather than wane among all Americans of whatever race or ethnicity.

No more forceful expression of the idea of standing one's ground is to be found than in the recent statement of a young African-American in reaction to the fatal 1989 shooting of an even younger African-American by a band of white New York City teenagers. Noting that his friends, accent, vocabulary, collegiate education, and sweetheart are all white and that his "aspirations of success are the same as those of any American," this twenty-four-year-old black president of his own import-export company in New York City goes on to recount humiliating experiences arising merely from his racial status. "Yet," he says in the aftermath of the wanton shooting of sixteen-year-old Yusuf K. Hawkins,[84] "I cannot walk through the city in which I was born without fearing for my safety—just because I am an African-American. . . . Therefore," he declares in words addressed to the predominantly white readership of the nation's leading newspaper in which his manifesto was published,

> I must state that I will not appease those of you who wish me dead. African-Americans will not be led quietly to their deaths, interned,

or just disappear. Those murderers among you better realize that, *because I am an American, I will defend myself.*

I am not advocating violence. *I will, however, without hesitation, defend my life, liberty and dignity by whatever legal means I have, including force, if necessary.*[85]

For this young black American of the late twentieth century as for so many Americans of the past and present, no duty to retreat is a compelling theme.

Notes

(In the notes to this chapter and others, the form of citation for cases of law follows the standard usage of legal scholarship.)

Chapter 1. No Duty to Retreat in Law and the American Mind

*Quoted in Mark DeWolfe Howe, ed., *Holmes-Laski Letters: The Correspondence of Mr. Justice Holmes and Harold J. Laski, 1916–1935* (2 vols.; Cambridge: Harvard University Press, 1953), I: 335–36.

1. Roy Moreland, *The Law of Homicide* (Indianapolis: Bobbs-Merrill, 1952), 259–61.

2. Joseph H. Beale, "Retreat from a Murderous Assault," *Harvard Law Review* 16 (1902–3):567.

3. Frederic S. Baum and Joan Baum, *Law of Self-Defense* (Dobbs Ferry, N.Y.: Oceana, 1970), 5–9. Blackstone's views on the common law of homicide appeared in his *Commentaries on the Laws of England . . .* (4 vols.; Oxford: Clarendon Press, 1765–69).

4. Baum and Baum, *Law of Self-Defense*, 5–9.

5. *Ibid.*, 6–7.

6. Rollin M. Perkins, "Self-Defense Re-Examined," *UCLA Law Review* 1 (1953–54): 143. The subjects of Foster's critique were William Lambarde (1536–1601), Sir Edward Coke (1552–1634), and Sir Matthew Hale (1609–1676). Foster's essay on the law of homicide appeared in his *A Report of Some Proceedings . . . to Which Are Added Discourses upon a Few Branches of the Crown Law* (Oxford: Clarendon Press, 1762).

7. Beale said Foster distorted the doctrine of duty to retreat, while later Perkins said Foster did indeed clarify it. Beale, "Retreat," 573ff. Perkins, "Self-Defense," 143.

8. Foster, *Crown Law,* quoted in Beale, "Retreat," 573.

9. Edward Hyde East, *A Treatise of the Pleas of the Crown* (2 vols.; London: A. Strahan, 1803), I: 271–72.

10. J. C. Smith and Brian Hogan, *Criminal Law* (London: Butterworths, 1965), 234.

11. Ian McLean and Peter Morrish, *Harris's Criminal Law* (22nd ed.; London: Sweet and Maxwell, 1973), 455.

12. The decision in the *Selfridge* case was to the effect that retreat was not necessary if "an actual danger" threatened at the the time of the encounter and not merely "a bare fear" of one. Francis Wharton, *The Law of Homicide,* 3rd ed. by Frank H. Bowlby (Rochester, N.Y.: Lawyers Cooperative Publishing Co., 1907), 473–74.

13. An example of Francis Wharton's approach to textbook writing is his *A Treatise on the Law of Homicide in the United States* (Philadelphia: Kay and Brother, 1855), the first edition of Wharton's textbook on the law of homicide. On Wharton: "Wharton, Francis," in Allen Johnson *et al.,* eds., *Dictionary of American Biography* (20 vols. and 7 suppl. vols.; New York: Charles Scribner's Sons, 1928–81), XX: 27–28.

14. Joel Prentiss Bishop, *New Commentaries on the Criminal Law upon a New System of Legal Exposition* (8th ed., 2 vols.; Chicago: T. H. Flood, 1892), I: xi. The two-volume first edition of Bishop's book was entitled *Commentaries on the Criminal Law* and published in Boston in 1856–58 by Little, Brown. On Bishop: H. W. Howard Knott, "Bishop, Joel Prentiss," in Johnson *et al.,* eds., *Dictionary of American Biography,* II: 295–96.

15. *Commentaries on the Criminal Law* (3rd ed., 2 vols., Boston: Little, Brown, 1865), II: sections 633–34.

16. Wharton, *Law of Homicide* (3rd ed., 1907, by Bowlby), 473–74.

17. *Erwin v. State,* 29 Ohio St. 186 (1876). *Runyan v. State,* 57 Ind. 80 (1877). Beale, "Retreat," 579–80, states that these two cases were the leading ones on the issue of the duty to retreat. Both of the cases are discussed below.

18. *Erwin v. State* is cited in note 17.

19. *Erwin v. State.* Emphasis added.

20. *Runyan v. State* is cited in note 17.

21. See, for example, Richard Hofstadter and Michael Wallace, eds.,

American Violence: A Documentary History (New York: Alfred A. Knopf, 1970), 82–84, 93–96.

22. Melvyn Hammarberg, *The Indiana Voter: The Historical Dynamics of Party Allegiance during the 1870s* (Chicago: University of Chicago Press, 1977), chap. 7 and *passim*. Charles S. Hyneman, C. Richard Hofstetter, and Patrick F. O'Connor, *Voting in Indiana: A Century of Persistence and Change* (Bloomington: Indiana University Press, c. 1977), 83–96.

23. Keith Ian Polakoff, *The Politics of Inertia: The Election of 1876 and the End of Reconstruction* (Baton Rouge: Louisiana State University Press, 1973), is a general study of the election.

24. John Leggett, *Ross and Tom: Two American Tragedies* (New York: Simon and Schuster, 1974), 82, 95–96. See also De Weese T. Beckner *et al.*, eds., *The Henry County Sesquicentennial Booklet, 1822–1972* (New Castle, Ind.: Community Printing, 1972?), 4, 23; and Herbert L. Heller, *Historic Henry County* (4 vols.; New Castle, Ind.: Courier-Times, 1982), IV: 564–67.

25. Ross Lockridge, Jr., *Raintree County* (Boston: Houghton Mifflin, 1948). Leggett, *Ross and Tom*, 24–25, 79, 95; chaps. 2–8 of this book are a remarkable biographical study of Lockridge's life and tragic early death.

26. On Ross Lockridge, Sr.'s fascination with Indiana local history: Leggett, *Ross and Tom*, 36–37, 158.

27. On Mrs. Lockridge's Henry County heritage: Leggett, *Ross and Tom*, 79, 82, 95–96, 102–3, 132-33.

28. *Ibid.*, 79–82 and *passim*.

29. *An Illustrated Historical Atlas of Henry County, Indiana* (Chicago: Higgins Belden & Co., 1875). This atlas is referred to as the *Illustrated Historical Atlas of Raintree County* in *Raintree County*, 36.

30. The epigraph to *Raintree County* announces that "the clock in the Court House Tower on page five of the *Raintree County Atlas* is always fixed at nine o'clock," as is the clock on the page-five illustration of the Henry County courthouse and its clock tower in the *Illustrated Historical Atlas of Henry County*.

31. *New Castle Mercury*, Nov. 9, 1876, p. 3, col. 3–4.

32. *Ibid.* Cline & McHaffie, *The People's Guide: A . . . Directory of Henry County, Indiana . . .* (Indianapolis: Indianapolis Printing and Publishing House, 1874), 285–86. J. A. Young, comp., *Fall Creek Township, Henry County, Indiana, in the War of the Rebellion . . .* (New Castle, Ind.: Courier Co., 1887), 94–97.

33. *New Castle Mercury*, Nov. 9, 1876, p. 3, col. 3–4

34. *Ibid.*

35. On the strong link between the Republican party and the veterans of the Union army, see, among many works: Wallace E. Davies, *Patriotism on Parade: The Story of Veterans and Hereditary Organizations in America, 1783–1900* (Cambridge: Harvard University Press, 1965), 32–33, 87, 189–211. On the strong activity of Union military veterans in behalf of the Republican party in Indiana in the election of 1876: Emma Lou Thornbrough, *Indiana in the Civil War Era* (Indianapolis: Indiana Historical Bureau and Indiana Historical Society, 1965), 302. On the Republican party's strong majority in Henry County: Hammarberg, *Indiana Voter*, 156, 158, and *passim* (Henry was one of nine Indiana counties studied by Hammarberg). See also *History of Henry County, Indiana . . .* (Chicago: Inter-State, 1884), 315–16. The 1876 presidential vote in Henry County was Hayes (R.)—3,631; Tilden (D.)—1,924; Cooper (Greenback)—123. *Ibid.*

36. Polakoff, *Politics of Inertia*, 155–57.

37. As noted above, the election of 1876 was one of the most controversial in American history. At first Tilden, the Democrat, appeared to be an almost sure winner of the election, since the day after the voting the nationwide count indicated that he had definitely captured 184 electoral votes and needed only one more electoral vote to clinch the victory. It seemed almost certain that he would gain that electoral vote (and more) from among four states (Florida, Louisiana, Oregon, South Carolina) with a total of 20 electorial votes, which each candidate claimed. But Tilden's triumph was not to be, for an Electoral Commission appointed by Congress resolved the dispute in each of the four states in favor of Hayes, who in 1877 was thereby declared the winner by an electoral vote of 185 to 184. Polakoff, *Politics of Inertia*, chaps. 6–7. Indiana was carried by Tilden and was one of only two key Northern states (New York was the other) taken by him. Indiana's 15 electoral votes were thus a key contribution to Tilden's near win over Hayes. On Indiana in the election of 1876: Thornbrough, *Indiana in Civil War*, 295–304.

38. The following account of the events of election day in New Castle and the killing of Charles Pressnall is based on these sources: *New Castle Mercury*, Nov. 9, 1876, p. 2, col. 1–2, and p. 3, col. 3–4. *Runyan v. State*. Appellee's (prosecution's) Brief and Appellant's (Runyan's) Brief in In-

diana State Supreme Court case no. 6168, *John Runyan vs. The State of Indiana* (manuscripts in Archives Division of Indiana Commission of Public Records, Indianapolis).

39. *New Castle Mercury*, Nov. 9, 1876, p. 3, col. 3–4.

40. On Judge Polk: *History of Henry County*, 317–18.

41. *Runyan v. State*.

42. The following sketch of William E. Niblack is based on these sources (listed alphabetically by author or title): *A Biographical History of Eminent and Self-Made Men of the State of Indiana* (Cincinnati: Western Biographical Publishing Co., 1880), 160–61 (where Niblack is admiringly called a "true man"). *Biographical Sketches of Members of the Indiana State Government . . . 1885* (Indianapolis: Indianapolis Sentinel, 1885), 17–20. *History of Pike and Dubois Counties, Indiana* (Chicago: Goodspeed Brothers, 1885), 479, 574–75, 640. Indiana Scrapbook Collection— Cottman (9 bound vols. of machine-copied Indiana biographical sketches, 1880–1935, compiled by George S. Cottman and deposited in the Indiana State Library, Indianapolis), V, containing two clippings on Niblack: (1) a long story written by a veteran reporter with the pseudonym of "Gath" for the Cincinnati *Enquirer* and reprinted in the Indianapolis *Journal*, June 16, 1885; and (2) a story (based on a letter from Niblack) that appeared in the Indianapolis *Journal* on Nov. 7 or 8, 1885. *Indianapolis Sentinel*, May 8, 1893, p. 1, col. 7, p. 2, col. 1–4. Charles Lanman Collection (manuscripts in Indiana Historical Society, Indianapolis) containing two items on Niblack: (1) autobiographical sketch by Niblack, June 1, 1858, and (2) two photographs of Niblack, one *circa* late 1850s and one *circa* late 1860s. Charles W. Moores, comp., *Indiana Society of the Sons of the American Revolution . . .* (Indianapolis: Indiana Society of Sons of the American Revolution, 1908), 39–41, 99. Albert P. Niblack manuscripts (Indiana Historical Society, Indianapolis) containing a folder of William E. Niblack papers (Albert P. Niblack was a son of William E. Niblack and his second wife, Eliza A. Sherman Niblack). John Lewis Niblack, *The Life and Times of a Hoosier Judge* (n.p., n.d.), ix (on William E. Niblack's father, John Hargrave Niblack, Jr.). Joe L. Norris, "Niblack, William Ellis," in Johnson *et al.*, eds., *Dictionary of American Biography*, XIII, 481–82. George Irving Reed, ed., *Encyclopedia of Biography of Indiana* (Chicago: Century Publishing and Engraving Co., 1895), I, 380–83. *The Who-When-What Book . . .* (Chicago: Who-What-When Co., 1900), xviii. George R. Wil-

son, *History and Art Souvenir of Dubois County* (n.p., 1896), 5–7, and *History of Dubois County . . . to 1910* (Jasper, Ind.: G. R. Wilson, 1910), 33, 94, 110, 131.

43. *Runyan v. State.*

44. *Ibid.* Emphasis added. The deceased's name is given as "Pressnal" in *Runyan v. State,* but in all other sources it is "Pressnall," the usage here.

45. *Ibid.*

46. *Ibid.* Emphasis added.

47. *Grainger v. State,* 13 Tenn. (5 Yer.) 459 (1830).

48. *State v. Gardner,* 104 N. W. Rep. (1st Ser.) 971 (1905).

49. *Ibid.* is the source for the following account of the fatal dispute between Garrison and Gardner.

50. *State v. Bartlett,* 71 S. W. Rep. (1st Ser.) 148 (1902).

51 *State v. Meyer,* 164 Pac. 926 (1917).

52. *Miller v. State* and *Bromley v. State,* 119 N. W. 850 (1909). Emphasis added.

53. Joseph H. Beale, Jr., of the Harvard Law School is discussed below.

54. Francis G. Caffey, "George Washington Stone," in William Draper Lewis, ed., *Great American Lawyers . . .* (8 vols.; Philadelphia: John C. Winston, 1907–8), VI: 165–93. Hallie Farmer, "Stone, George Washington," in Johnson *et al.*, eds., *Dictionary of American Biography,* XVIII: 74–75.

55. *Ex parte Nettles,* 58 Ala. 268, 275 (1877). Alice Merchant, "The Historical Background of the Procedural Reform Movement in Alabama," *Alabama Law Review* 9 (1957):284, 286.

56. *Ex parte Nettles,* 274.

57. *Ex parte Wray,* 30 Miss. 673 (1856).

58. *Ibid.*

59. *Ex parte Nettles,* 274.

60. *Judge v. State,* 58 Ala. 406 (1877).

61. The following account of the mortal confrontation between Judge and Wallace is based on *Judge v. State,* 407–8.

62. *Ibid.,* 413–14.

63. *Ibid.*

64. Perkins, "Self-Defense," 145–46, 150. Wayne R. LaFave and Austin W. Scott, Jr., *Handbook on Criminal Law* (St. Paul: West Publishing Co., 1972), 395–96.

65. Arthur E. Sutherland, "Beale, Joseph Henry," in Johnson *et al.*, eds., *Dictionary of American Biography,* suppl. III: 43. The painter Charles

Hopkinson's remarkable portrait of Beale is reproduced in color in Max Hall, "Court Painter of Academia," *Harvard Magazine,* March–April 1990, pp. 74–76; the painting of Beale catches the incisiveness of character that marked his scholarly critique of the doctrine of no duty to retreat (discussed below). Hall, "Court Painter," also, by coincidence, reproduces Hopkinson's portrait of Justice Oliver Wendell Holmes (whose sharp disagreement with Beale on the issue of no duty to retreat is discussed below, this chapter)—a painting that has, however, in contrast to that of Beale, been widely reproduced.

66. Joseph H. Beale, "Homicide in Self-Defense," *Columbia Law Review* 3 (1903):526–45.

67. Beale, "Retreat."

68. Thorington's opinion appears in *Springfield v. State,* 96 Ala. 81 (1891).

69. Beale, "Retreat," 580–81.

70. On the history of Texas violence, see Richard Maxwell Brown, *Strain of Violence: Historical Studies of American Violence and Vigilantism* (New York: Oxford University Press, 1975), chap. 8; W. Eugene Hollon, *Frontier Violence: Another Look* (New York: Oxford Univeristy Press, 1974), 36–55; C. L. Sonnichsen, *I'll Die before I'll Run: The Story of the Great Feuds of Texas* (New York: Devin-Adair, 1962) and *Ten Texas Feuds* (Albuquerque: University of New Mexico Press, 1957); John Bainbridge, *The Super-Americans* (Garden City, N.Y.: Doubleday, 1961), 238–58; and Henry P. Lundsgaarde, *Murder in Space City: A Cultural Analysis of Houston Homicide Patterns* (New York: Oxford University Press, 1977).

71. Lundsgaarde, *Murder in Space City,* 149.

72. *Ibid.,* 162.

73. William M. Ravkind, "Justifiable Homicide in Texas," *Southwestern Law Journal* 13 (1959):508, 515, 518.

74. *Ibid.,* 519–20.

75. *Bell v. State,* 17 Tex. Crim. 538 (1885).

76. *Ibid.,* 550–51. Judge Willson cited article 573 of the Texas penal code.

77. *Bell v. State,* 539–45.

78. *Ibid.,* 553.

79. Lundsgaarde, *Murder in Space City,* 164.

80. George Wilfred Stumberg, "Defense of Person and Property under Texas Criminal Law," *Texas Law Review* 21 (1942–43):17, 32.

81. *Storey v. State,* 17 Ala. 329, 341 (1882).

82. Lundsgaarde, *Murder in Space City,* 145.

83. *Ibid.,* 164. Stumberg, "Defense of Person."

84. *Brown v. United States,* 256 U. S. 335 (1921).

85. *Beard v. United States,* 158 U. S. 550 (1895).

86. On violence in the Indian Territory: Glenn H. Shirley, *Law West of Fort Smith: A History of Frontier Justice in the Indian Territory, 1834–1896* (Lincoln: University of Nebraska Press, 1968).

87. On Parker: Fred Harvey Harrington, *Hanging Judge* (Caldwell, Idaho: Caxton, 1951); Shirley, *Law West of Fort Smith;* and Mary M. Stolberg, "Politician, Populist, Reformer: A Reexamination of 'Hanging Judge' Isaac C. Parker," *Arkansas Historical Quarterly* 47 (1988):3–28.

88. *Beard v. United States.* On Harlan: Louis Filler, "John M. Harlan," in Leon Friedman and Fred L. Israel, eds., *The Justices of the United States Supreme Court, 1789–1969* (4 vols.; New York: Chelsea House and R. R. Bowker, 1969), II: 1281–95.

89. *Beard v. United States.*

90. *Allen v. United States,* 164 U. S. 492 (1896).

91. Beale, "Retreat," 567. Beale probably misconstrued Justice Brown's decision in the *Allen* case as a repudiation of the doctrine of no duty to retreat in the *Beard* case. If so, others probably made the same mistake.

92. *Brown v. United States,* 335–41.

93. *Brown v. United States,* 257 Fed. Rep. 47, 48–49 (1919). This is the case report on Brown's unsuccessful circuit court appeal; it reveals the facts of his conviction in the district court. The common surname of Robert B. Brown and the present author is a coincidence.

94. Paul A. Freund, "Oliver Wendell Holmes," in Friedman and Israel, eds., *Justices of the Supreme Court,* III: 1759. The only truly comprehensive biography of Holmes is Sheldon M. Novick, *Honorable Justice: The Life of Oliver Wendell Holmes* (Boston: Little, Brown, 1989). Briefer but perceptive is Gary J. Aichele, *Oliver Wendell Holmes, Jr.: Soldier, Scholar, Judge* (Boston: Twayne, 1989). Mark DeWolfe Howe's two-volume biography of Holmes's earliest years, 1841–82, is cited in note 95. Brief treatments are Freund, "Oliver Wendell Holmes," 1755–62, and Felix Frankfurter, "Holmes, Oliver Wendell," in Johnson *et al.,* eds., *Dictionary of American Biography,* suppl. I: 417–27. Max Lerner, ed., *The Mind and Faith of Justice Holmes: His Speeches, Essays, Letters, and Judicial Opinions* (Boston: Little, Brown, 1943), is a useful anthology. There are many other editions of Holmes's voluminous writings; see, for example,

Touched with Fire (fully cited in note 97) and *Holmes-Laski Letters* (fully cited in note 101).

95. Mark DeWolfe Howe, *Justice Oliver Wendell Holmes* (2 vols.; Cambridge: Belknap Press of Harvard University Press, 1957–63), I: 75–81. Vol. I of this biography is subtitled *The Shaping Years, 1841–1870* and was published in 1957; vol. II, subtitled *The Proving Years, 1870–1882,* was published in 1963.

96. For example, Freund, "Oliver Wendell Holmes," 1755. Howe, *Justice Holmes,* I: 102, 106, 110, 285, and *passim.* Lerner, ed., *Mind and Faith,* 5.

97. Howe, *Justice Holmes,* I: chaps. 3–4, covers Holmes's Civil War service and is a masterly treatment of it; these two chapters draw heavily, among many sources, on Holmesian writings edited and published earlier in Mark DeWolfe Howe, ed., *Touched with Fire: Civil War Letters and Diary of Oliver Wendell Holmes, Jr.* (Cambridge: Harvard University Press, 1946). See also Novick, *Honorable Justice,* chaps. 5–7.

98. Howe, *Justice Holmes,* I: 87, 109, 115, 133, 165–66; also *passim* in chaps. 3–4.

99. Lerner, ed., *Mind and Faith,* 16.

100. Freund, "Oliver Wendell Holmes," 1760.

101. Mark DeWolfe Howe, ed., *Holmes-Laski Letters: The Correspondence of Mr. Justice Holmes and Harold J. Laski, 1916–1935* (2 vols.; Cambridge: Harvard University Press, 1953), I: 339–40.

102. Howe, *Justice Holmes,* I: 169n.

103. See, for example, Freund, "Oliver Wendell Holmes," 1757–58; Howe, *Justice Holmes,* I: vi; and Morton White, *Social Thought in America: The Revolt against Formalism* (2nd ed., revised; Boston: Beacon, 1957), 15–18, 59–75, 103–6, 172–78, and *passim.* White's influential book is a study of the intellectual impact of five prime contributors to the growth of the American mind: John Dewey, Thorstein Veblen, Charles A. Beard, James Harvey Robinson, and Holmes. A recent treatment is H. L. Pohlman, *Justice Oliver Wendell Holmes: Utilitarian Jurisprudence* (Cambridge: Harvard University Press, 1984). In this chapter I focus on one aspect of the American mind—key attitudes and values (of which of no duty to retreat is one)—and I here (in this sentence of the text) mention another key aspect of the American mind: high thought, of which pragmatism and utilitarianism are examples. Holmes was, of course, a major contributor to the latter aspect of high thought as well as being a key formulator of the dimension of legal thought in the American mind. In regard to the former aspect of key attitudes and values, Holmes had a

dual role: he both shared in the widespread attitude of no duty to retreat and as a Supreme Court justice made a major contribution to its application in law.

104. Oliver Wendell Holmes, *The Common Law* (Boston: Little, Brown, 1881), 1.

105. Howe, ed., *Holmes-Laski Letters,* I: 331–32, 335. Holmes told Laski that he wrote the opinion to relieve Chief Justice Edward D. White of the burden of doing so. White was then in the throes of an illness that would kill him on May 19, 1921. *Ibid.,* 331. *New York Times,* May 19, 1921, p. 1, col. 3. It is evident, however, that dealing with the case was a congenial task for Holmes.

106. Howe, ed., *Holmes-Laski Letters,* I: 331.

107. *Ibid.,* 332.

108. *Brown v. United States,* 342.

109. *Ibid.,* 342–43.

110. The judgment of the lower court against Brown was reversed. Joining Holmes in the seven to two majority in the case were Chief Justice Edward D. White and Associate Justices Joseph McKenna, William R. Day, Willis Van Devanter, James C. McReynolds, and Louis D. Brandeis. Associate Justices Mahlon Pitney and John H. Clarke gave no reasons for their dissents in the case.

111. Holmes, *Common Law,* 1, 36, 247.

112. *Brown v. United States,* 343.

113. *Ibid.,* 336–37. In his opinion (p. 343) Holmes did cite with approval Harlan's decision in *Beard v. United States,* and in a letter to Harold Laski, Holmes spoke well of the negative view of "old Harlan" on the duty to retreat. Howe, ed., *Holmes-Laski Letters,* 335. Harlan had been a very senior colleague of Holmes on the Supreme Court when the latter joined it in 1902.

114. *Brown v. United States,* 343.

115. *Ibid.* Emphasis added.

116. *Ibid.*

117. Howe, ed., *Holmes-Laski Letters,* I: 335–36. Although Holmes did not read his opinion in open court until May 16, he had completed it for circulation to his fellow Supreme Court Justices on May 8. *Ibid.,* 331.

118. Howe, *Justice Holmes,* I: 126 and *passim.* Gerald F. Linderman, *Embattled Courage: The Experience of Combat in the American Civil War* (New York: Free Press, c. 1987), a key study of military valor in the Civil War, prominently mentions Holmes.

119. Howe, *Justice Holmes,* I: 118.
120. *Ibid.,* I: 166.
121. *Brown v. United States,* 344.
122. Howe, *Justice Holmes,* I: 166.
123. Lerner, ed., *Mind and Faith,* 11.
124. *Ibid.*
125. *New York Times,* Nov. 24, 1953, p. 1, col. 2, and p. 20, col. 2–5. Kent L. Steckmesser, *The Western Hero in History and Legend* (Norman: University of Oklahoma Press, 1965), 165, directed my attention to President Eisenhower's 1953 speech. See the next chapter on Wild Bill Hickok as Eisenhower's role model.

Chapter 2. The Gunfighter: The Reality Behind the Myth

*Gunfighter Tom McDonald of Bodie, California, quoted in Roger D. McGrath, *Gunfighters, Highwaymen, and Vigilantes: Violence on the Frontier* (Berkeley: University of California Press, c. 1984), 218.

1. *New York Times,* Nov. 24, 1953, p. 20, col. 2–5. Aside from history and biography, Western novels were Eisenhower's favorite reading; he read for escape and entertainment. At his bedside when he died were six Zane Grey novels. Another preferred author of Westerns was Frederick Faust, who often used the pseudonym of Max Brand. Eisenhower's favorite film was the classic Western *High Noon* (1952) in which Gary Cooper starred as the heroic gunfighter. Merle Miller, *Ike the Soldier: As They Knew Him* (New York: G. P. Putnam's Sons, c. 1987), 72–73. Eisenhower's fascination with Western gunfighting went back to his boyhood game of "Wild West" avidly played with his brother, Edgar, in Abilene. The two boys favored quick-draw gunfighter games in which Dwight and Edgar impersonated Bat Masterson, Billy the Kid, and Jesse James, but their greatest hero was Wild Bill Hickok. Kenneth S. Davis, *Soldier of Democracy: A Biography of Dwight Eisenhower* (Garden City, N.Y.: Doubleday, Doran, 1945), 72. The Eisenhower family moved from Texas to Abilene in 1891 when Dwight was in the first year of his life. Dwight and Edgar played their gunfighting games and hero-worshipped Wild Bill Hickok in the years from 1898 to 1903, a period that came thirty years after Hickok killed Phil Coe in Abilene. Abilene old-timers from the Hickok era, still alive and articulate in the boyhood of Dwight and Edgar Eisenhower, undoubtedly evoked the Hickok mystique for the likes of the future general and president and his brother.

2. Frederick Jackson Turner, *The Frontier in American History* (New York: Henry Holt, 1921), 32–33., keynotes the professional historian's disdain for the historical significance of gunfighters. There are a few worthy general studies of Western gunfighters: Joseph G. Rosa, *The Gunfighter: Man or Myth?* (Norman: University of Oklahoma Press, 1969), and Gary L. Roberts, "The West's Gunmen," *American West* 8 (Jan. 1971):10–15, 64; (March 1971):18–23, 61–62, are perceptive; Nyle H. Miller and Joseph W. Snell, eds., *When the West Was Wild* (Topeka: Kansas State Historical Society, 1963), is an informative documentary collection dealing with Kansas gunfights; Bill O'Neal, *Encyclopedia of Western Gunfighters* (Norman: University of Oklahoma Press, 1969), is a most useful but far from complete collection of biographical sketches.

3. These are my own terms and concepts.

4. On Hickok and Earp, see this chapter, below. On Hardin: John Wesley Hardin, *The Life of John Wesley Hardin, from the Original Manuscript, as Written by Himself* (Sequin, Texas: Smith & Moore, 1896), reprinted in 1961 at Norman by the University of Oklahoma Press; Lewis Nordyke, *John Wesley Hardin: Texas Gunman* (New York: Morrow, 1957); Richard Maxwell Brown, *Strain of Violence: Historical Studies of American Violence and Vigilantism* (New York: Oxford University Press, 1975), 256–58, 261–65, 275–76, 381, and "Hardin, John Wesley," in Howard R. Lamar, ed., *The Reader's Encyclopedia of the American West* (New York: Thomas Y. Crowell, 1977), 483–85. On Billy the Kid: Robert M. Utley, *Billy the Kid: A Short and Violent Life* (Lincoln: University of Nebrasha Press, 1989), is by far the best biography; outstanding in their emphasis on the mythology and popular treatment of the Kid are Stephen Tatum, *Inventing Billy the Kid: Visions of the Outlaw in America, 1881–1981* (Albuquerque: University of New Mexico Press, 1982), and Jon Tuska, *Billy the Kid: A Handbook* (Lincoln: University of Nebraska Press, 1986). On other gunfighters: O'Neal, *Encyclopedia,* and other sources cited in the notes to this chapter.

5. In addition to Tatum, *Inventing Billy the Kid,* and Tuska, *Billy the Kid,* notable studies of the mythology of Western gunfighters include John G. Cawelti, *The Six-Gun Mystique* (Bowling Green, Ohio: Bowling Green University Popular Press, 1975); Kent Ladd Steckmesser, *The Western Hero in History and Legend* (Norman: University of Oklahoma Press, 1965), parts 2–3, and *Western Outlaws: The "Good Badman" in Fact, Film, and Folklore* (Claremont, Calif.: Regina Books, 1983); and William A. Settle, *Jesse James Was His Name, or Fact and Fiction Concerning the*

Careers of the Notorious James Brothers of Missouri (Columbia: University of Missouri Press, 1966). Among thousands of books mythologizing Western gunfighters, two influential works have been Walter Noble Burns, *The Saga of Billy the Kid* (New York: Doubleday, 1926), and Stuart N. Lake, *Wyatt Earp: Frontier Marshal* (Boston: Houghton Mifflin, 1932).

6. On the Code of the West, see the citations to books by Rosenberg and Utley in note 36.

7. Donald Curtis Brown, "The Great Gun-Toting Controversy, 1865–1910: The Old West Gun Culture and Public Shootings (Colorado, Kansas, New Mexico, Oklahoma, Texas)" (Ph.D. dissertation, Tulane University, 1983), treats the gun culture and the unsuccessful movement to curb it.

8. See Chapter 3 at notes 12–20, for some of these conflicts.

9. On the strongly politicized nation, see Chapter 1 at note 36.

10. Hardin and the Civil War: Brown, *Strain of Violence*, 261–62 and *passim*. Earp and the Civil War: see below, this chapter. Wyatt Earp's three older brothers served in the Union army. Dan. L. Thrapp, *Encyclopedia of Frontier Biography* (3 vols.; Glendale, Calif.: Arthur H. Clark, 1988), II: 445–47.

11. William M. Breakenridge, *Helldorado: Bringing Law to the Mesquite* (Boston: Houghton Mifflin, 1928), an autobiography.

12. Leon C. Metz, *Pat Garrett: The Story of a Western Lawman* (Norman: University of Oklahoma Press, 1974). Jack DeMattos, *Garrett and Roosevelt* (College Station, Texas: Creative Publishing Co., 1988). On Hardin: Brown, "Hardin," 484, and *Strain of Violence*, 262, 381n. Although a longtime Democrat himself, Garrett was always close to men of high station whether they were Democrats (like future Vice President John Nance Garner, a Texas friend of Garrett) or Republicans (like President Theodore Roosevelt, who in 1901 appointed Garrett the U.S. collector of customs at El Paso). Garrett was a lifelong, partisan Democrat until the last twelve years of his life when, in order to hold office and please powerful Republicans such as Roosevelt, he became a Republican. Whether a Republican or a Democrat, Garrett, going back to his successful campaign against Billy the Kid, served as a gunfighting sheriff in the interest of the incorporating forces (see this chapter, below) of southern New Mexico. Metz, *Pat Garrett.* DeMattos, *Garrett and Roosevelt.*

13. Quoted in Don Dedera, *A Little War of Our Own: The Pleasant Valley Feud Revisited* (Flagstaff, Ariz.: Northland Press, 1988), 206–7 (I have corrected Graham's spelling and capitalization but have not altered his

wording or grammar). On Graham and the Pleasant Valley feud: Dedera, *A Little War,* and Thrapp, *Encyclopedia,* II: 577. At the center of the Pleasant Valley war was the Graham-Tewksbury family feud, which in turn was focused on factors which made this war in east-central Arizona another episode in a broad regional conflict discussed below: the Western Civil War of Incorporation. The Tewksburys were early settlers in Pleasant Valley who represented the traditional, slow-paced pastoral and farming life Tom Graham aptly (although maliciously) caught in his cutting phrase about "some old cabin with sunflowers growing all round." The Graham newcomers represented a more aggressive ranching and land-enclosing style, and through the social values expressed by Tom Graham they allied themselves with the commercially-oriented, vigilante-minded, large-landholding and ranching elite of interior Arizona. The Tewksbury point men were notable resister gunfighters. One of them, Ed Tewksbury, shot to death Tom Graham in 1892; Graham had earlier killed at least two of the Tewksbury factonists. Tom Graham and his kin and comrades were incorporation gunfighters. The concepts of incorporation and resister gunfighters are presented below.

14. Alan Trachtenberg, *The Incorporation of America: Culture and Society in the Gilded Age* (New York: Hill and Wang, 1982). See also Steven Hahn and Jonathan Prude, eds., *The Countryside in the Age of Capitalist Transformation: Essays in the Social History of Rural America* (Chapel Hill: University of North Carolina Press, 1985), for specialized studies in regard to the process of incorporation. For an influential interpretation of the late nineteenth-century to early twentieth-century period antedating that by Trachtenberg which, although diverging significantly from the incorporation concept on key points, delineates a process resembling incorporation, see Robert H. Wiebe, *The Search for Order, 1877–1920* (New York: Hill and Wang, 1967).

15. David Thelen, *Paths of Resistance: Tradition and Dignity in Industrializing Missouri* (New York: Oxford University Press, 1986), chaps. 4–5.

16. Altina Waller, *Feud: Hatfields, McCoys, and Social Change in Appalachia, 1860–1900* (Chapel Hill: University of North Carolina Press, 1988), dealing with an area where frontier conditions long lingered.

17. On Texas fence cutters: Robert C. McMath, Jr., chap. 7, "Sandy Land and Hogs in the Timber . . . ," in Hahn and Prude, eds., *Countryside.* See also Brown, *Strain of Violence,* 272–79.

18. On New Mexican *gorras blancas* (white caps): Robert W. Larson, *New Mexico Populism: A Study of Radical Protest in a Western Territory* (Boul-

der: Colorado Associated Universities Press, 1974), chap. 4 and *passim,* and Robert S. Rosenbaum, *Mexicano Resistance in the Southwest:* "The Sacred Right of Self-Preservation" (Austin: University of Texas Press, c. 1981), chap. 8. On South Texas *bandidos:* Rosenbaum, *Mexicano Resistance,* chap. 3.

19. Carlos A. Schwantes, "The Concept of the Wageworkers' Frontier: A Framework for Future Research," *Western Historical Quarterly* 28 (January 1987):39–55. For examples of violence on the wageworkers' frontier, see Chapter 3 at notes 12–15. On violence generally in the West: Richard Maxwell Brown, chap. 11, "Historiography of Violence in the American West," in Michael P. Malone, ed., *Historians and the American West* (Lincoln: University of Nebraska Press, 1983). Dealing in general with frequently violent racial, ethnic, and religious conflict in the West is Patricia Nelson Limerick, *The Legacy of Conquest: The Unbroken Past of the American West* (New York: W. W. Norton, 1987), part 2. White-Indian wars were a prime component of the Western Civil War of Incorporation, but they are beyond the scope of this book. On the vast subject of these wars and white-Indian conflict, see, among a huge number of outstanding scholarly works, the chapters by Herbert T. Hoover and Robert C. Carriker in Malone, ed., *Historians;* Roger L. Nichols, ed., *American Frontier and Western Issues: A Historiographical Review* (New York: Greenwood, c. 1986), chap. 10; Francis Paul Prucha, *The Indians in American Society: From the Revolutionary War to the Present* (Berkeley: University of California Press, 1985); Robert M. Utley, *The Indian Frontier of the American West, 1846–1890* (Albuquerque: University of New Mexico Press, 1984); Richard Slotkin, *The Fatal Environment: The Myth of the Frontier in the Age of Industrialization, 1800–1890* (New York: Atheneum, 1985), which focuses mainly on white-Indian conflict; and Richard Drinnon, *Facing West: The Metaphysics of Indian Hating* (Minneapolis: University of Minnesota Press, 1980).

20. On the Johnson County War in Wyoming, see this chapter at notes 28–30. On the Mussel Slough conflict, see Chapter 3. On the Cochise County War, see below, this chapter.

21. On Hickok and Earp, see below, this chapter. On Canton, see at note 29. On Crow, see Chapter 3.

22. E. J. Hobsbawm's concept of the "social bandit" as an outlaw whose actions express general social grievances appears in his *Social Bandits and Primitive Rebels* (Glencoe, Ill.: Free Press, 1959). The social-bandit concept is applied in Richard White, "Outlaw Gangs of the Mid-

dle Border: American Social Bandits," *Western Historical Quarterly* 12 (Oct. 1981):387–408; and Utley, *Billy the Kid*, 270, which notes that the Hispanic plowmen and herdsmen of southern New Mexico viewed Billy the Kid as a social bandit.

23. Utley, *Billy the Kid*.

24. An example of such resistance occurred in Missouri. See Thelen, *Paths of Resistance*, chaps. 4–5. See also Brown, *Strain of Violence*, 104–5ff., for the general phenomenon of resistance.

25. Brown, *Strain of Violence*, chaps. 4–6.

26. Owen Wister, *The Virginian: A Horseman of the Plains* (New York: Macmillan, 1902). For sources on the mythic impact of Wister's *Virginian*, see note 31, below.

27. On Wister's strong conservatism: Darwin Payne, *Owen Wister: Chronicler of the West, Gentleman of the East* (Dallas: Southern Methodist University Press, 1985), 146–47, 204–5, 229, 267–68; on his friendships with Holmes and Roosevelt: *ibid.*, xiii, 64, 70, 94–95, 104, 109, 321, and 327 on Holmes and xiii, 37, 200, 221, 230, 245, 298, 321–23, and *passim* on Roosevelt.

28. Helena Huntington Smith, *The War on Powder River* (New York: McGraw-Hill, 1966). Lewis L. Gould, *Wyoming: A Political History, 1868–1896* (New Haven: Yale University Press, 1968), chap. 6.

29. Payne, *Owen Wister*, 125–27, 140. Smith, *War on Powder River*, 70, 98, 119–20, 145–47, 162–68, 221–25, 260–62, and *passim*. Gould, *Political History of Wyoming*, 140–44 and *passim*.

30. Payne, *Owen Wister*, 205–6; see also 196–97, 203 for the real-life model for the hero in *The Virginian*.

31. Leading authorities who document the significance of *The Virginian* as the model for the formula Western are, among many scholars, James K. Folsom, *The American Western Novel* (New Haven: College and University Press, 1966), 106–7ff.; Richard W. Etulain, *Owen Wister* (Boise: Boise State College, c. 1973); John L. Cobbs, *Owen Wister* (Boston: Twayne, c. 1984), preface and chap. 5; Payne, *Owen Wister*, xi–xii and *passim*. Trachtenberg, *Incorporation of America*, 24–25, contends that the Western myth—generally and as exemplified in *The Virginian*—has a stongly conservative bias. See also Slotkin, *Fatal Environment*, for a similar emphasis, powerfully and lengthily elaborated.

32. Wister, *Virginian*, chap. 35, especially 480–82.

33. Steckmesser, *The Western Hero*, 136–37, in comparing the 1865

post–Civil War walkdown (treated below) to the walkdown in *The Virginian.*

34. Walter Prescott Webb, *The Great Plains* (Boston: Ginn, 1931), 167–79. Samuel Colt's .34-caliber six-chambered revolver was first manufactured in 1838. The initial wide use of it (and subsequent models derived from it) was by the Texas Rangers in the 1840s. Thereafter, the use of the repeating revolver gradually spread northward into the Great Plains country. *Ibid.*

35. On Southern duels: Dickson D. Bruce, Jr., *Violence and Cuture in the Antebellum South* (Austin: University of Texas Press, c. 1979), chap. 1. Bertram Wyatt-Brown, *Southern Honor: Ethics and Behavior in the Old South* (New York: Oxford University Press, 1982), 166–67, 350–61, and *passim.*

36. Bruce A. Rosenberg, *Code of the West* (Bloomington: Indiana University Press, c. 1982), which has a chapter (pp. 159–74) on what Rosenberg terms "that most Western of characters, the gunfighter" (p.1). On the Code of the West and gunfighting, see also Robert M. Utley, *High Noon in Lincoln: Violence on the Western Frontier* (Albuquerque: University of New Mexico Press, 1987), 176–77, and *Billy the Kid,* 4.

37. Steckmesser, *Western Hero,* 137.

38. Joseph G. Rosa, *They Called Him Wild Bill: The Life and Adventures of James Butler Hickok* (2nd ed., revised; Norman: University of Oklahoma Press, 1974), 10–15. Rosa, *They Called Him Wild Bill* and *The West of Wild Bill Hickok* (Norman: University of Oklahoma Press, 1982) are by far the best books devoted entirely to Hickok. Much less detailed but very perceptive is Steckmesser, *Western Hero,* part 3 (on Hickok). A more popular treatment is Richard O'Connor, *Wild Bill Hickok* (Garden City, N.Y.: Doubleday, 1959). Older books on Hickok are Frank J. Wilstach, *Wild Bill Hickok—The Prince of Pistoleers* (Garden City, N.Y.: Doubleday, Page, 1926), and William Elsey Connelley, *Wild Bill and His Era: The Life & Adventures of James Butler Hickok* (New York: Press of the Pioneers, 1933). All in all, the soundest, best balanced, and most judicious studies of Hickok are those by Rosa and Steckmesser.

39. Rosa, *They Called Him Wild Bill,* 14–15, and *West of Wild Bill,* 26.

40. Rosa, *They Called Him Wild Bill,* 14.

41. *Ibid.,* 16. On these early examples of Wild West tales, see Henry Nash Smith, *Virgin Land: The American West as Symbol and Myth* (Cambridge: Harvard University Press, 1950), chap.8.

42. Rosa, *They Called Him Wild Bill,* 16–33.

43. *Ibid.,* chap. 2.

44. *Ibid.,* chap. 3.

45. Charles A. and Mary R. Beard, *The Rise of American Civilization* (2 vols.; New York: Macmillan, 1930), I: chap. 18ff.

46. Rosa, *They Called Him Wild Bill,* 54–55.

47. *Ibid.,* chap. 3.

48. *Ibid.,* 72–73.

49. *Ibid.,* chap. 4. Connelley, *Wild Bill,* 88. Wilstach, *Wild Bill Hickok,* 119.

50. Springfield *Missouri Weekly Patriot,* July 27, 1865, reprinted in Miller and Snell, eds., *Great Gunfighters,* 105. Rosa, *They Called Him Wild Bill,* 54–55. O'Connor, *Wild Bill Hickok,* 87. Connelley, *Wild Bill,* 82–87.

51. Major Albert Barnitz, "Diary" (manuscript in Beinecke Rare Book and Manuscript Library, Yale University), Springfield, Mo., July 21, 1865, copied in Rosa, *West of Wild Bill,* 61. George Ward Nichols, "Wild Bill," *Harper's New Monthly Magazine,* Feb. 1867, p. 277. Rosa, *They Called Him Wild Bill,* 75–76, and *West of Wild Bill,* 47, 61. O'Connor, *Wild Bill Hickok,* 87–88. Steckmesser, *Western Hero,* 109–10.

52. Springfield *Missouri Weekly Patriot,* Aug. 10, 1865, reprinted in Miller and Snell, eds., *Great Gunfighters,* 105–7. The judge's fourth instruction to the jury was specific in regard to Hickok's duty to retreat— that is, his duty to avoid the fight: "4th. To be entitled to acquital [*sic*] on the ground of self-defense, he [Hickok] must have been anxious to avoid a conflict, and must have used all reasonable means to avoid it." *Ibid.* In this case, all reasonable means of avoiding the conflict would have meant flight from the scene, since the town square where the gunfight took place was a very open area. Retreat "to the wall" would not have been necessary for Hickok (or Tutt), because there were many paths of escape from the site of the shooting. As for the judge's instruction to the jury laying down the duty to retreat as the law, not until 1902 did the supreme court of Missouri definitively rule against the duty to retreat in the case of *State v. Bartlett* (see Chapter 1, above and note 50 in Chapter 1). Civil War and ideological animosities may well have also affected the jury's decision, since Connelley (*Wild Bill,* 88) states that some townspeople said Hickok was cleared by the jury because "he was an ex-Federal soldier, and a radical [Republican] in politics" and that Tutt "had been a rebel."

53. George Ward Nichols's long double-columned, vividly illustrated

life profile of Wild Bill, featuring the Hickok-Tutt walkdown, appeared in early 1867 in a widely read national monthly magazine, *Harper's,* and made Hickok an instant American celebrity. Nichols, "Wild Bill." The process of popularizing Wild Bill's career as a gunfighting hero continued with the journalism of Henry M. Stanley in 1867 and after (see note 63, below). By the early 1880s the first of the spurious, low-cost popular biographies of Wild Bill appeared—under the imprint of Beadle & Adams, the publishing house famous for its mass-edition dime novels: Prentiss Ingraham, *Adventures of Wild Bill, the Pistol Prince* (Boy's Library of Sport, Story, and Adventure, No. 3; New York, 1881), and *Wild Bill, the Pistol Dead Shot* (Dime Library, No. 168; New York, 1882). Ingraham was an enormously prolific house author of dime novels at Beadle & Adams. His two books on Hickok were, as Steckmesser says (*Western Hero,* 149), "quasi-biographical dime novels." They were preceded by a highly fictionalized biography of Hickok that was second only to the writings of Nichols and Stanley as a basic source in the creation of the heroic legend of Wild Bill: J[ames] W. Buel, *The Life and Marvellous Adventures of Wild Bill . . .* (Chicago: Belford, Clarke, 1880). On the creation of the legend of Hickok as a mixture of fact and, mostly, fancy: Steckmesser, *Western Hero,* 130–32, 139, 149; Smith, *Virgin Land,* 100, 113, 119–21, 123–24. On Beadle & Adams: Albert Johannsen, *The House of Beadle and Adams* (Norman: University of Oklahoma Press, 1950).

54. Rosa, *They Called Him Wild Bill,* 66–68, 116–17.

55. Settle, *Jesse James,* chap. 3 and *passim.* Settle's book is easily the best and most complete treatment of the Jameses and the Youngers. The gunfights of the Jameses and the Youngers usually broke out during their bank and train robberies. Outstanding studies of the Civil War conflict in Kansas, Missouri, and Arkansas in which Hickok was on the opposite side of that of the Jameses and Youngers are Richard S. Brownlee, *Gray Ghosts of the Confederacy: Guerrilla Warfare in the West, 1861–1865* (Baton Rouge: Louisiana State University Press, 1958); Don R. Bowen, "Guerrilla War in Western Missouri, 1862–65: Historical Explanations of the Relative Deprivation Hypothesis," *Comparative Studies in History and Society* 19 (January 1977):30–51; and Michael Fellman, *Inside War: The Guerrilla Conflict in Missouri during the American Civil War* (New York: Oxford University Press, 1988). On the region's long-lasting post–Civil War aftermath of gunfighting and outlaw activity, see, in addition to the career of Wild Bill Hickok: White, "Outlaw Gangs," and Paul I. Wellman, *A Dynasty of Western Outlaws* (Lincoln: University of Nebraska

Press, 1986). The Confederate maternal grandparents of President Harry S Truman suffered severe property damage from the Red Legs. Truman's maternal grandmother and his mother reared the future president on stories of these depredations. Alfred Steinberg, *The Man from Missouri: The Life and Times of Harry S. Truman* (New York: G. P. Putnam's Sons, c. 1962), 21–22. Truman's lifelong strongly partisan distaste for Republicans was inspired, in part, by family stories about the hated Red Legs who were, of course, Republican and Unionist guerrillas.

56. Settle, *Jesse James*. Thelen, *Paths of Resistance*, 70–77.

57. The popular treatment of Hickok by Nichols appeared in the monthly *Harper's*, which, although a national magazine, had a predominantly Northern, pro-Unionist readership. In Nichols's profile of Hickok the climactic event was the Hickok-Tutt gunfight, but Nichols also gave heavy emphasis to Wild Bill's Civil War role as a Union military operative, and he presented Hickok's first famous victim, David McCanles, incorrectly as a Confederate conspirator. Nichols, "Wild Bill." Steckmesser, *Western Hero*, 122.

58. Rosa, *They Called Him Wild Bill*, chap. 5.

59. *Ibid.*, 90–91. Although best known as a Union war hero second only to Ulysses S. Grant, Sherman was, like his guide, Hickok, a strong Republican, and Sherman's brother Senator John Sherman (to whom General Sherman was close) was one of the leading Republican statesmen of the 1860s–1890s period. Lloyd Lewis, *Sherman: Fighting Prophet* (New York: Harcourt, Brace, 1958), on the general; on the senator: Jeannette P. Nichols, "Sherman, John" in Allen Johnson *et al.*, eds., *Dictionary of American Biography* (20 vols. and 7 suppl. vols; New York: Charles Scribner's Sons, 1928–81), IX: 84–88.

60. Rosa, *They Called Him Wild Bill*, chap. 6.

61. *Ibid.*, 116–17.

62. Stephen Z. Starr, *Jennison's Jayhawkers: A Civil War Cavalry Regiment and Its Commander* (Baton Rouge: Louisiana State University Press, 1974).

63. Contributing to the national media coverage of Hickok was journalist Henry M. Stanley, later famous for his successful search in Africa for the missing explorer, Dr. David Livingstone. Stanley wrote on Wild Bill in the St. Louis *Weekly Missouri Democrat* and the New York *Tribune*. Steckmesser, *Western Hero*, 110–11, 124; see also Rosa, *They Called Him Wild Bill*, 109–10. Stanley's pieces in the *Weekly Missouri Democrat* were reprinted in other newspapers, while the New York *Tribune* was widely

read in the North and West. While Stanley's reporting on Hickok (who deeply impressed Stanley in the latter's interviewing of the gunfighter) was a mixture of fact and fiction, it strongly emphasized Wild Bill's heroic stature. Stanley later reprinted some of his writing on Hickok in *My Early Travels and Adventures in America and Asia* (2 vols.; New York: Charles Scribner's Sons, 1895).

64. *Galaxy Magazine,* reprinted in Custer, *My Life on the Plains* (New York: Sheldon, 1874), 33–34, and quoted in Rosa, *They Called Him Wild Bill,* 111.

65. In Hickok's time the present Hays, Kansas, was known as Hays City. On Hickok in Hays: Rosa, *They Called Him Wild Bill,* chap. 8, and *West of Wild Bill,* 102–3, 115–17; Steckmesser, *Western Hero,* 113; Miller and Snell, eds., *Great Gunfighters,* 119–27. On the killing of Tom Smith: Rosa, *They Called Him Wild Bill,* 178–80.

66. Joseph G. McCoy, *Historic Sketches of the Cattle Trade of the West and Southwest* (Kansas City, Mo.: Ramsey, Millett & Hudson, 1874). Edward Everett Dale, *The Range Cattle Industry: Ranching on the Great Plains from 1865 to 1925* (Norman: University of Oklahoma Press, 1960). Robert R. Dykstra, *The Cattle Towns* (New York: Alfred A. Knopf, 1968). Don Worcester, *The Chisholm Trail: High Road of the Cattle Kingdom* (Lincoln: University of Nebraska Press, 1980).

67. Rosa, *They Called Him Wild Bill,* 174–75. McCoy, *Historic Sketches,* chap. 8. A highly realistic fictional account of Texas cowboys on the long cattle drive north (punctuated by bouts of wild pleasure in Great Plains cattle towns) is Andy Adams's classic novel, *The Log of a Cowboy: A Narrative of the Old Trail Days* (Boston: Houghton Mifflin, 1903). On prostitution in Kansas cowtowns: Carol Leonard and Isidor Wallimann, "Prostitution and Changing Morality in the Frontier Cattle Towns of Kansas," *Kansas History* 2 (Spring 1979):34–53.

68. Dykstra, *Cattle Towns,* chap. 3. C. Robert Haywood, *Cowtown Lawyers: Dodge City and Its Attorneys, 1876–1886* (Norman: University of Oklahoma Press, 1988), chap. 1 and pp. 106–7, 123–26, 240.

69. Rosa *They Called Him Wild Bill,* 181–82, 190, 196. Dykstra, *Cattle Towns,* 116 and *passim.* McCoy, *Historic Sketches,* 131–42, 145.

70. Dykstra, *Cattle Towns,* 116, 132. McCoy, *Historic Sketches,* 137. Steckmesser, *Western Hero,* 105 and *passim.* Rosa, *They Called Him Wild Bill,* 175–81. See also Adams, *Log of a Cowboy,* 191–92.

71. Topeka *Chronicle,* Nov. 30, 1871, quoted in Rosa, *They Called Him Wild Bill,* 201–2. Steckmesser, *Western Hero,* 114–15.

72. Rosa *They Called Him Wild Bill,* 186, 194, and *passim.*

73. On Thompson: Floyd B. Streeter, *Ben Thompson: Man with a Gun* (New York: Frederick Fell, 1957); Lauran Paine, *Texas Ben Thompson* (Los Angeles: Westernlore Press, 1966); O'Neal, *Encyclopedia,* 69–70. On Coe: O'Neal, *Encyclopedia,* 69–70.

74. Rosa, *They Called Him Wild Bill,* 180–81.

75. Hardin, *Life,* 42.

76. Rosa, *They Called Him Wild Bill,* 194.

77. *Ibid.,* 188–89. Hardin, *Life,* 42–45. In an 1888 letter, Hardin wrote that "no braver man [than Hickok] ever drew breath." Rosa, *West of Wild Bill,* 136.

78. Steckmesser, *Western Hero,* 117.

79. Rosa, *They Called Him Wild Bill,* 194. In early July, Thompson left Abilene on a personal errand, met with an accident, and was unable to return to Abilene that year. Meanwhile, Coe remained in the cattle town as house gambler at the Bull's Head after selling its license to another on August 2. O'Neal, *Encyclopedia,* 316. Rosa, *They Called Him Wild Bill,* 189–90.

80. Abilene *Chronicle,* Oct. 12, 1871, reprinted in Miller and Snell, eds., *Great Gunfighters,* 131–32.

81. *Ibid.* See also Rosa, *They Called Him Wild Bill,* 196–201. These sources reveal that in the bad light and a scene confused by a pressing crowd of Coe partisans, Hickok, as he fired at Coe, also shot and killed a peacekeeping colleague and friend, Mike Williams, special policeman in the employ of the Novelty Theater of Abilene. Williams, rushing to Wild Bill's assistance, suddenly came around a corner and took two of Hickok's shots that were meant for Coe. The elation of Hickok's triumph over Coe was quickly dampened by his immediate grief and anger over the unintended fatal shooting of Williams. Hickok vented his outrage over the death of Williams (for which he blamed Coe and the troublemaking Texans much more than himself) by rampaging, that night, through the streets of Abilene: "Like a man possessed he swept into the saloons and gambling houses and in no uncertain manner kicked everybody out. Those who resisted he knocked aside. Others took one look at the death in his eyes and fled." Rosa, *They Called Him Wild Bill,* 197.

82. *Ibid.,* 142.

83. *Ibid.,* 251–61.

84. *Ibid.,* 234–40. Rosa, *West of Wild Bill,* 172–73, 180–82. Wild Bill's

wife was known professionally as Agnes Lake. There is no truth to the oft-told tale that Wild Bill and "Calamity Jane" (Martha Jane Cannary) were intimate. *Ibid.*, 184–86.

85. Rosa, *They Called Him Wild Bill*, 288–89, 295–96.

86. *Ibid.*, 272–77.

87. *Ibid.*, 267–71.

88. *Ibid.*, 270. Rosa, *West of Wild Bill*, 179.

89. Rosa, *They Called Him Wild Bill*, 281, 288–90. For overall historical context of Wild Bill's final phase in the Black Hills of present South Dakota: Howard Roberts Lamar, *Dakota Territory, 1861–1889: A Study of Frontier Politics* (New Haven: Yale University Press, 1956), and Watson Parker, *Deadwood: The Golden Years* (Lincoln: University of Nebraska Press, c. 1981).

90. Rosa, *They Called Him Wild Bill*, 288.

91. *Ibid.*, 290, 295.

92. *Ibid.*, 297–98. McCall was tried and convicted in federal court and on March 1, 1877, was hanged at Yankton (in present South Dakota) for the murder of Hickok. *Ibid.*, 335–36. McCall's motive in shooting Hickok has never been definitely settled. Rosa, *West of Wild Bill*, 201, sums up the scholarly opinion: Many authorities "believe he [McCall] was the tool of others [i.e., enemies of Hickok]; some think he attempted, in a druken stupor, what many others had tried and failed to do: kill Hickok. But rather than confront such a man face to face, McCall shot hom from behind."

93. Rosa, *They Called Him Wild Bill*, 298. Afficionadoes of Western lore who watched the classic John Ford film, *Stagecoach* (1939), would have noted that, as he played cards, the villain (acted by John Carradine) held aces and eights—the dead man's hand—and thus would have correctly anticipated the outcome of the movie's climactic gunfight, in which the hero (John Wayne in his first starring role) killed the villain.

94. Utley, *Billy the Kid*.

95. Settle, *Jesse James*, chap. 11 and *passim*.

96. Brown, "Hardin."

97. O'Neal, *Encyclopedia*, 3–16 and *passim*.

98. This was Walter J. Crow of California, who is treated in the next chapter.

99. It would be possible to attempt a tabulation of these deaths in order to reach a proximately accurate figure, but it would require, at

the least, page-by-page research in all the extant newspapers, *ca.* 1860–1900, from the Great Plains to the Pacific Coast. Even so, the exact total yielded by such research would be an undercount (although far less an undercount than currently available figures), because not all gunfights were reported in newspapers and many newspapers which reported gunfights have not survived. Still, a count of this sort would afford a minimal approximation of the number of Westerners who were gunfighters, the total number of and data on their gunfights, and the total casualties. Such a tabulation would require enormously time-consuming and expensive team research of a sort unlikely ever to be subsidized and undertaken.

100. McCoy, *Historic Sketches,* 145–46.

101. Epigraph to C[harles] L. Sonnichsen, *I'll Die before I'll Run: The Story of the Great Feuds of Texas* (2nd ed., revised: New York: Devin-Adair, 1962), a remarkable treatment of its subject and one with many episodes of no-duty-to-retreat violence. The complete words of the verse of the ballad used as the epigraph: "Wake up, wake up, darlin' Corie! / And go get me my gun. / I ain't no hand for trouble, / But I'll die before I'll run."

102. Galveston *News,* Oct. 11, 1867, reprinted in C[harles] L. Sonnichsen, *Ten Texas Feuds* (Albuquerque: University of New Mexico Press, 1971), 210–11. Punctuation and capitalization, but not grammar and dialect, have been slightly altered in the quotation.

103. This and previous paragraphs on Bodie and the following treatment of it are based on Roger D. McGrath, *Gunfighters, Highwaymen, and Vigilantes: Violence on the Frontier* (Berkeley: University of California Press, c. 1984), especially chap. 11. See also an earlier version of McGrath's study: "Frontier Violence in the Trans-Sierra West" (Ph.D. dissertation, University of California, Los Angeles, 1978). On Hammond in Bodie: John Hays Hammond, *The Autobiography of John Hays Hammond* (2 vols.; New York: Farrar & Rinehart, c. 1935), I: 86–87.

104. McGrath, *Gunfighters,* 199 and *passim.*

105. *Ibid.,* 221.

106. *Ibid.*

107. Emphasis added. See Chapter 1, above, on Harvard Law Professor Joseph H. Beale, Jr.'s notion of "hip-pocket ethics" as the social basis of the legal doctrine of no duty to retreat.

108. *Ibid.,* 199. Hammond, *Autobiography,* I: 86–87, also emphasized that Bodie gunfighters mostly left "unoffending" citizens alone as they shot and killed each other.

109. McGrath, *Gunfighters*, 199. Utley, *High Noon*, 176, also stresses the consumption of alcohol as a major contributor to violence in the West generally.

110. McGrath, *Gunfighters*, 199—emphasis added.

111. Similar to McGrath's concept of the role of "reckless bravado" is Robert M. Utley's emphasis on the Code of the West as a key inspiration for Western violence. Utley, *High Noon*, 176–77.

112. McGrath, *Gunfighters*, 203, 217–18.

113. *Ibid.*, 213.

114. *Ibid.*, 218–19.

115. The following overview (whose sources are in notes 116–205) of Wyatt Earp, Tombstone, Cochise County, and the gunfight near the O.K. Corral is an expansion of my interpretation as published in my editor's introduction to William M. Breakenridge, *Helldorado: Bringing Law to the Mesquite*, ed. Richard Maxwell Brown (Lakeside Classics; Chicago: R. R. Donnelley & Sons, 1982), xxvi–xxxvii (Breakenridge's *Helldorado* was originally published in 1928—see note 11).

116. On Wyatt Earp: John D. Gilchriese, "The Odyssey of Virgil Earp," *Tombstone Epitaph*, National Edition, Fall 1968, has material on Wyatt. The most strongly anti-Earp books are Ed Bartholomew, *Wyatt Earp, 1848 to 1880: The Untold Story* (1963) and *Wyatt Earp, 1879 to 1882: The Man and the Myth* (1964), both published in Toyahvale, Texas, by Frontier Book Company; and Frank Waters, *The Earp Brothers of Tombstone* (New York: Clarkson N. Potter, 1960). Despite his choleric anti–Wyatt Earp bias, Bartholomew's two books are valuable for his prodigious research in primary sources. Noteworthy for its balance and perceptiveness is the book by Paula Mitchell Marks cited in note 125 below. Significant contributions are made in the publications of Glenn G. Boyer and Alford E. Turner—works cited in the notes below. Most valuable also are the contributions, cited below, of Gary L. Roberts, Dan L. Thrapp, John Myers Myers, and Odie B. Faulk. On Wyatt Earp's parentage and northern Illinois background: Glenn G. Boyer, ed., *Wyatt Earp by Wyatt S. Earp* (Sierra Vista, Ariz.: Loma V. Bissette, 1981), 20. William Urban, "Wyatt Earp's Father," *True West*, May 1989, pp. 30–32, 37–39.

117. Gary L. Roberts, "Earp Brothers," in Lamar, ed., *Reader's Encyclopedia*, 327.

118. Roberts, "Earp Brothers," 327. Gilchriese, "Odyssey."

119. Roberts, "Earp Brothers," 327.

120. O'Neal, *Encyclopedia*, 100. Thrapp, *Encyclopedia*, I: 448.

121. Roberts, "Earp Brothers," 327. Thrapp, *Encyclopedia*, I: 448.

122. Roberts, "Earp Brothers," 328.

123. On turbulent Wichita, see H. Craig Miner, *Wichita: The Early Years: 1865–80* (Lincoln: University of Nebraska Press, c. 1982), especially chap. 6.

124. Roberts, "Earp Brothers," 328.

125. *Ibid.* Thrapp, *Encyclopedia*, I: 448. It is possible but not proven that "Sallie Earp" and "Bessie Earp" were consorts of, respectively, Wyatt and James Earp, who were then in Wichita. Paula Mitchell Marks, *And Die in the West: The Story of the O.K. Corral Gunfight* (New York: William Morrow, 1989), 34.

126. Roberts, "Earp Brothers," 328.

127. *Ibid.* In Dodge City, Wyatt took a wife, Mattie, whom he deserted in his Tombstone period for Josephine Sarah Marcus (see below), who eventually became his last wife (see note 180).

128. *Ibid.*, 327.

129. *Ibid.*, 328.

130. O'Neal, *Encyclopedia*, 101.

131. Roberts, "Earp Brothers," 328.

132. O'Neal, *Encyclopedia*, 100.

133. Marks, *And Die,* 30. For Arizona history generally in the era of the Tombstone boom: Howard Roberts Lamar, *The Far Southwest, 1846–1912: A Territorial History* (New Haven: Yale University Press, 1966), part 4.

134. Boyer, "Postscripts to Historical Fiction about Wyatt Earp in Tombstone," *Arizona and the West* 18 (Autumn 1976):223. Glenn G. Boyer, ed., *I Married Wyatt Earp: The Recollections of Josephine Sarah Marcus Earp* (Tucson: University of Arizona Press, c. 1976), 46. Marks, *And Die,* 31, 43, 82–83, 115, 149, 151.

135. Odie B. Faulk, *Tombstone: Myth and Reality* (New York: Oxford University Press, 1972), 141. Tucson *Arizona Daily Star,* March 26, 1882, p. 1, col. 3–5.

136. Tucson *Arizona Daily Star,* March 26, 1882, p. 1, col. 3–5.

137. Roberts, "Earp Brothers," 328.

138. John P. Clum mss. (University of Arizona Library, Tucson).

139. Frank D. Ashburn, *Peabody of Groton: A Portrait* (New York: Coward McCann, 1944).

140. Henry Pickering Walker, "Preacher in Helldorado," *Journal of Arizona History* 15 (Autumn 1974):223–48.

141. *Ibid.*, 235–39.

142. *Ibid.*, 239.

143. George W. Parsons, *The Private Journal of George W. Parsons: Adventure in the American West—Tombstone in Its Troubled Days* (Tombstone: Tombstone Epitaph, 1972), covering the period from January 1880 to June 1882.

144. On Gage: John Myers Myers, *The Last Chance: Tombstone's Early Years* (New York: E. P. Dutton, 1950), 232; and William Hattich, *Tombstone in History, Romance, and Wealth* (Norman: University of Oklahoma Press, c. 1981), 18–19. On Hammond: Hammond, *Autobiography*, I: 79, 82.

145. Gary L. Roberts, "The Wells Spicer Decision: 1881," *Montana, the Magazine of Western History* 20 (January 1970):64–65.

146. *Ibid.*, 65. Thrapp, *Encyclopedia*, I: 449.

147. The Spicer decision is discussed above and below.

148. Boyer, "Postscripts," 225.

149. Boyer, ed., *I Married Wyatt Earp*, chap. 4.

150. Boyer, "Postscripts," 224.

151. Myers, *Last Chance*, 142–44. Marks, *And Die*, 107–9.

152. Breakenridge, *Helldorado*, 105. Marks, *And Die*, 26, 95, 127.

153. All authorities stress the enmity of the Earps (and Holliday) versus the Clantons and McLaurys. In the sources of the time "McLaury" was often given as "McLowry."

154. Roberts, "Earp Brothers," 328–29.

155. Boyer, ed., *Wyatt Earp*, 226–27.

156. *Ibid.*

157. Alford E. Turner, *The O.K. Corral Inquest* (College Station, Texas: Creative Publishing Co., 1981), 29; see also Turner, ed., *The Earps Talk* (College Station, Texas: Creative Publishing Co., 1982).

158. Turner, *O.K. Corral*, 100.

159. *Ibid.*

160. Boyer, ed., *I Married Wyatt Earp*, 88–93. In public, Wyatt Earp always denied that his side fired first, but his third wife disclosed in her memoirs (*ibid.*) that Doc Holliday and Morgan Earp had fired first. Spicer in his decision absolving the Earps and Holliday of murder said that even if the Earp side had fired first it was entitled to do so in the interest of "self-preservation." Roberts, "Wells Spicer Decision," 70.

161. Turner, *O.K. Corral*, 240.

162. *Ibid.*, 101.

163. *Ibid.*, 80. Holding that Wyatt Earp fired first, Gary L. Roberts, "The Fremont Street Fiasco . . . ," *True West*, July 1988, pp. 14–20, is a careful study of the gunfight.

164. Boyer, ed., *Wyatt Earp*, 226–27, 239. John P. Clum, "It All Happened in Tombstone," *Arizona Historical Quarterly* 2 (October 1929):46, 55–56. Parsons, *Private Journal*, 189.

165. The Republicans lost the municipal election of January 3, 1882. Parsons, *Private Journal*, 204. See, also Faulk, *Tombstone*, 153–54.

166. Faulk, *Tombstone*, 171–72.

167. On the post-boom history of Tombstone, see Faulk, *Tombstone*, chaps. 7–8. In recent decades tourism focused on the lure of Tombstone's Wyatt-Earp era has made it a lively "ghost town" with a population of about sixteen hundred. In recent years new technology resulted in a modest revival of mining.

168. Dave Brown, "Were the McLaurys Peaceful Ranchers or Gunslingers?," *Des Moines Sunday Register,* Nov. 1. 1981, pp. 1A, 10A. C. L. Sonnichsen gave me a copy of this article.

169. On Will McLaury organizing the legal and illegal campaign: Marks, *And Die*, 265–69, 318, 340–41, and *passim*.

170. Roberts, "Earp Brothers," 329.

171. Douglas D. Martin, *Tombstone's Epitaph* (Albuquerque: University of New Mexico Press, 1951), 207–8, 211–12. Myers, *Last Chance*, 199.

172. Larry D. Ball, *The United States Marshals of New Mexico and Arizona Territories, 1846–1912* (Albuquerque: University of New Mexico Press, c. 1978), 123–27, 132. Myers, *Last Chance*, 188–90.

173. Myers, *Last Chance*, 192, 193–95, 198–99. Faulk, *Tombstone*, 155.

174. Myers, *Last Chance*, 201–2.

175. *Ibid.*, 204, 206–7. Recent authorities who accept Wyatt Earp's claim to killing Curly Bill are Gilchriese, "Odyssey," and Roberts, "Earp Brothers," 329.

176. Myers, *Last Chance*, 207.

177. Faulk, *Tombstone*, 155.

178. Myers, *Last Chance*, 216.

179. Roberts, "Earp Brothers," 329.

180. On Josephine Sarah Marcus Earp, see Boyer, ed., *I Married Wyatt Earp*.

181. Boyer, ed., *I Married Wyatt Earp*, 137n.

182. *Ibid.*, chaps. 7–18.

183. *Ibid.*, 113, 126n., 141–46, 147n., 149n., 194–205, 211–216.

184. *Ibid.*, chap. 7 and pp. 119–20n. On Tabor and Baby Doe: Duane A. Smith, *Horace Tabor: His Life and the Legend* (Boulder: Pruett, 1973).

185. *Ibid.*, 142–45, 148n. On Baldwin: C. B. Glasscock, *Lucky Baldwin* (Indianapolis: Bobbs-Merrill, 1933).

186. Boyer, ed., *I Married Wyatt Earp*, chap. 13 and p. 180n.

187. *Ibid.*, chap. 16 and pp. 215–16n. On Tasker L. Oddie: Loren B. Chan, *Sagebrush Statesman: Tasker L. Oddie of Nevada* (Reno: University of Nevada Press, 1973).

188. Boyer, ed., *I Married Wyatt Earp*, 147n.

189. *Ibid.*, 205n. Earp made $85,000 on this 1901 sale, but press reports inflated his profit to as high as $300,000. The $85,000 of 1901 would amount to many times more in present-day dollars.

190. *Ibid.*, 206–7. Boyer concludes (215n.) that by the 1920s the Earps were supported not only by their Alaska nest egg but by Sadie's family inheritance from the Marcus business in the San Francisco Bay area and her income from oil royalties as well as Wyatt's small-mining and gambling activity, which he carried on up to about 1928.

191. Boyer, ed., *I Married Wyatt Earp*, 201.

192. *Ibid.*, chap. 11 and 155–57n. Jack DeMattos, *The Earp Decision* (College Station, Texas: Creative Publishing Co., 1989). This famous prizefight was decided by referee Wyatt Earp's controversial decision awarding the victory to Sharkey as a result of a foul by Fitzsimmons. This episode brought another major burst of fame for Earp after the renown of his Tombstone days. As late as 1911, Earp may have regressed at least once to a low rounderism; in that year he was charged with operating a $25,000 bunco game in Los Angeles. It does not appear, however, that he was convicted of the charge. Marks, *And Die*, 419.

193. Boyer, ed., *I Married Wyatt Earp*, chaps 12–13 and 172n. On Rex Beach see Stanley J. Kunitz and Howard Haycraft, eds., *Twentieth Century Authors* (New York: H. W. Wilson, 1942), 91.

194. Boyer, ed., *I Married Wyatt Earp*, chaps. 12, 16 and 172n.

195. *Ibid.*, chap. 14 and p. 189n. and *passim*. On Wilson Mizner: Addison Mizner, *The Many Mizners* (New York: Vere, 1932).

196. Charles Samuels, *The Magnificant Rube: The Life amd Times of Tex Rickard* (New York: McGraw-Hill, 1957).

197. Boyer, ed., *I Married Wyatt Earp*, 238–39. In this last meeting between them, Earp and Mizner discussed the recent death of their old

friend, Tex Rickard. *Ibid.* About this time, John P. Clum also made his last visit to Earp. *Ibid.,* 240.

198. Samuels, *Magnificent Rube.*

199. Boyer, ed., *I Married Wyatt Earp,* chap. 18 and pp. 236–37n.

200. *Ibid.,* chaps. 18–19 and pp. 236n., 239.

201. *Ibid.,* 230–31, 236–37n.

202. *Ibid.,* 242.

203. Thrapp, *Encyclopedia,* 449. The minister of the Wilshire Congregational Church preached the sermon at Earp's funeral. *Ibid.*

204. Boyer, ed., *I Married Wyatt Earp,* 242.

205. *Ibid.*

206. O'Neal, *Encyclopedia,* 249–50.

207. See Chapter 3, below.

Chapter 3. California Conflict and the American Dream

VWD = Visalia Weekly Delta, a newspaper published in Visalia, California, the county seat of Tulare County, in which the Mussel Slough district was located. Also used in research for this chapter were the few surviving issues of two weeklies published in Hanford, California—*The Public Good,* 1878, and the *Mussel Slough Delta,* 1881–82.

*Quoted in James L. Brown, *The Mussel Slough Tragedy* (n.p., 1958), 140–47.

1. The settlers' version of the American dream is elaborated below.

2. On the ideology of individual enterprise in a market economy: Irvin G. Wyllie, *The Self-Made Man* (New Brunswick, N.J.: Rutgers University Press, 1954), chaps. 2–3. John G. Cawelti, *Apostles of the Self-Made Man* (Chicago: University of Chicago Press, c. 1965), 43–46. Moses Rischin, ed., *The American Gospel of Success: Individualism and Beyond* (Chicago: Quadrangle Books, 1965), 4–5, 91ff. As men who rose from poor or modest circumstances to great wealth, the railroad owners and leaders—Leland Stanford, Collis P. Huntington, Mark Hopkins, and Charles Crocker—personified Henry Clay's concept of the self-made man, which he expressed in an 1832 speech in which he praised "enterprising and self-made men, who have acquired whatever wealth they possess by patient and diligent means." Cawelti, ed., *Apostles,* 43–46. In an 1884 letter, Collis P. Huntington credited his great success in life to "a determination to be self-sustaining by [my] own industry" and noted

that he had "been continuously at work, almost without a holiday for thirty years" and advised his correspondent, "I cannot too strongly impress upon you the importance of actual work." Huntington to Howard Morton, New York City, June 3, 1884, in Huntington Family Papers (mss. in Huntington Library, San Marino, Calif.). See also the biography of Huntington by David Lavender, *The Great Persuader* (Garden City, N.Y.: Doubleday, 1970), 268–69. For Leland Stanford's similar version of the doctrine of individual enterprise in a market economy: Hubert Howe Bancroft, *History and Life of Leland Stanford: A Character Study* (Oakland, Calif.: Biobooks, 1952), 58 and *passim;* and Norman E. Tutorow, *Leland Stanford: Man of Many Careers* (Menlo Park, Calif.: Pacific Coast Publishers, 1971), 131, 135.

3. The corporate history of the Southern Pacific is a complex, technical, and tangled one. Chartered in 1866, the Southern Pacific received a land grant along its prescribed coastal route from San Francisco to Los Angeles, but because old Mexican land grants tied up so much land along the coast, the railroad in 1867 changed its route (and its entitlement to the land grant) to a route through the Central Valley of California, an action confirmed by Congress and the California legislature in 1870. Not until 1871 did the "Big Four" of Stanford, Huntington, Hopkins, and Crocker take over the Southern Pacific, which thereafter was operated in close conjunction with the Central Pacific. Lavender, *Great Persuader,* 265, 283, 289.

4. Typical of an often-repeated viewpoint of the railroad leaders was Collis P. Huntington's 1883 declaration to the New York *Journal* "that California and the entire West and the Southwest owe what they are to the energy and enterprise" of the railroad builders (i.e., himself, Stanford, *et al.*) "who have risked their money to build them up." Lavender, *Great Persuader,* 422. See also *ibid.*, 268; Collis P. Huntington to F. H. Gassaway, New York City, Oct. 22, 1894, in Huntington Family Papers; and Bancroft, *Leland Stanford,* 53–54, 61.

5. On the Big Four/Big Three and the Southern Pacific Railroad: Oscar Lewis, *The Big Four: The Story of Huntington, Stanford, Hopkins, and Crocker and of the Building of the Central Pacific* (New York: Alfred A. Knopf, 1938). On individuals: Lavender, *Great Persuader,* and Cerinda W. Evans, *Collis Potter Huntington* (2 vols.; Newport News, Va.: Mariner's Museum, 1954), on Huntington. Tutorow, *Leland Stanford;* Bancroft, *Leland Stanford;* and George T. Clark, *Leland Stanford: War Governor of California, Railroad Builder, and Founder of Stanford University* (Stanford: Stan-

ford University Press, 1931). John H. Frederick, "Crocker, Charles," in Allen Johnson *et al.*, eds., *Dictionary of American Biography* (20 vols. and 7 suppl. vols.; New York: Charles Scribner's Sons, 1928–81), IV: 552. "Hopkins, Mark," *The National Cyclopaedia of American Biography*, XX (New York: James T. White, 1929), 49–50. There is no adequate general work on the Southern Pacific before 1901, but a specialized study is Stuart Daggett, *Chapters on the History of the Southern Pacific* (New York: Ronald Press, 1922).

6. Richard Maxwell Brown, "Back Country Rebellions and the Homestead Ethic in America, 1740–1799," in Richard Maxwell Brown and Don E. Fehrenbacher, eds., *Tradition, Conflict, and Modernization: Perspectives on the American Revolution* (New York: Academic Press, 1977), 73–98.

7. Henry George, *Social Problems* (1883), in Henry George, *Complete Works* (10 vols.; New York: Doubleday, Page, 1871–1904), II: 232. On Henry George: Charles A. Barker, *Henry George* (New York: Oxford University Press, 1955); and John L. Thomas, *Alternative America: Henry George, Edward Bellamy, Henry Demarest Lloyd, and the Adversary Tradition* (Cambridge: Harvard University Press, c. 1983).

8. Henry George, *The Land Question* (1881), in George, *Complete Works*, III: 75.

9. Henry George, *Our Land and Land Policy* (1871), in George, *Complete Works*, VIII: 5, 7, 20, 33–34, 36, 36–38, 71–72, 94.

10. Henry George, *The American Republic: Its Dangers and Possibilities* (1877), in George, *Complete Works*, VIII: 171.

11. George, *Our Land*, 95.

12. On the Coeur d'Alene region in the 1890s: Vernon H. Jensen, *Heritage of Conflict* . . . (Ithaca: Cornell University Press, 1950), chaps. 4, 7; Robert W. Smith, *The Coeur d'Alene Mining War of 1892* . . . (Corvallis: Oregon State University Press, 1961); Stanley S. Phipps, *From Bull Pen to Bargaining Table: The Tumultuous Struggle of the Coeur d'Alene Miners for the Right to Organize, 1887–1942* (New York: Garland, 1988).

13. On Cripple Creek 1904: Jensen, *Heritage of Conflict*, chap. 10. Stewart H. Holbrook, *The Rocky Mountain Revolution* (New York: Henry Holt, 1956). George C. Suggs, Jr., *Colorado's War on Militant Unionism* . . . (Detroit: Wayne State University Press, 1972). On Ludlow 1914: George S. McGovern and Leonard F. Guttridge, *The Great Coalfield War* (Boston: Houghton Mifflin, 1972); Zeese Papanikolas, *Buried Unsung: Louis Tikas and the Ludlow Massacre* (Salt Lake City: University of Utah Press, 1982).

14. On Wheatland 1913: Cletus E. Daniel, "In Defense of the

Wheatland Wobblies: A Critical Analysis of the IWW in California,"
Labor History 19 (Fall 1978):485–509.

15. On Everett 1916: Norman H. Clark, *Mill Town* . . . (Seattle: University of Washington Press, 1970). On Centralia 1919: John McClelland, Jr., *Wobbly War: The Centralia Story* (Tacoma: Washington State Historical Society, 1987).

16. On Los Angeles, 1910: Graham Adams, Jr., *Age of Industrial Violence, 1910–15* . . . (New York: Columbia University Press, 1966), chap. 1. Robert Gottlieb and Irene Wolt, *Thinking Big: The Story of the Los Angeles Times* . . . (New York: Putnam, c. 1977), chap. 5. On San Francisco 1916: Richard H. Frost, *The Mooney Case* (Stanford: Stanford University Press, 1968).

17. Richard Maxwell Brown, *Strain of Violence: Historical Patterns of American Violence and Vigilantism* (New York: Oxford University Press, 1975), 270–72. Also in Nebraska was a similar conflict in the Sandhills; it is vividly re-created in Mari Sandoz, *Old Jules* (Lincoln: University of Nebraska Press, 1962).

18. Helena Huntington Smith, *The War on Powder River* (New York: McGraw-Hill, 1966). The Johnson County War was the real-life inspiration for the social conflict depicted in Owen Wister's novel, *The Virginian*. See Chapter 2, above, in which it is emphasized that Wister, as a friend of key members of the faction of large cattlemen that precipitated the war, ardently opposed the resistant opponents of the large cattlemen in life and in his fiction.

19. Brown *Strain of Violence,* 279. Robert C. McMath, Jr., "Sandy Land and Hogs in the Timber . . . ," in Steven Hahn and Jonathan Prude, eds., *The Countryside in the Age of Capitalist Transformation* . . . (Chapel Hill: University of North Carolina Press, c. 1985), 217–18.

20. Robert W. Larson, *New Mexico Populism: A Study of Radical Protest in a Western Territory* (Boulder: Colorado Associated Universities Press, 1974), chap. 4 and *passim.* Robert S. Rosenbaum, *Mexicano Resistance in the Southwest: "The Sacred Right of Self-Preservation"* (Austin: University of Texas, c. 1981), chap. 8.

21. George, *Land Question,* 74.

22. *Alta California* (San Francisco), May 15, 1880, p. 1, col. 4. William L. Preston, *Vanishing Landscapes: Land and Life in the Tulare Lake Basin* (Berkeley: University of California Press, c. 1981), occasionally treats the Mussel Slough area in the context of an excellent environmental history of the Tulare Lake region.

23. *Business Directory and Historical and Descriptive Handbook of Tulare County, California* (Tulare City, Calif.: Pillsbury and Ellsworth, 1888), 16–17, 129–30. See also the nine-part series of articles on irrigation in the Mussel Slough area in *VWD*, Aug. 22–Oct. 31, 1879.

24. *Alta California*, Dec. 8, 1880.

25. *San Francisco Examiner*, Dec. 16, 1880, p. 2, col. 3.

26. Eugene L. Menefee and Frederick A. Dodge, *History of Tulare and Kings Counties, California* (Los Angeles: Historical Record Co., 1913), 209.

27. Drawing their water from the Kings River were five main canals or ditches: People's Ditch, Mussel Slough Canal, Last Chance Ditch, Lower Kings River Canal, and Rhoads Ditch. These five irrigation canals totaled 110 miles in length. Two lesser canals drew their water from Cross Creek (a branch of the Kaweah River that, like Kings River, drained into Tulare Lake): Settlers' Ditch and Lakeside Ditch. *Business Directory*, 129–30. See also *History of Tulare County, California, with Illustrations . . .* (San Francisco: Wallace W. Elliot, 1883), 108–9. For a general history of irrigation in California see Donald J. Pisani, *From the Family Farm to Agribusiness: The Irrigation Crusade in California and the West, 1850–1931* (Berkeley: University of California Press, c. 1984).

28. *VWD* 1879: March 7, p. 2, col. 3; Sept. 12, p. 2, col. 3. James L. Brown, *The Mussel Slough Tragedy* (n.p., 1958), 143. The current author is not related to the late James L. Brown.

29. John J. Doyle, *Memorial of the Settlers on Lands Claimed by the Southern Pacific Railroad; and Argument for the Settlers* (n.p., n.d. [1876?]), 4–16. In the Mussel Slough area, says this pamphlet, there are 512,000 acres claimed by the railroad; on this land are about five hundred settlers claiming 80,000 acres at 160 acres each. *Ibid.*, 9. According to William Clyde McKinney, "The Mussel Slough Episode: A Chapter in the Settlement of the San Joaquin Valley, 1865–1880" (M.A. thesis, University of California, Berkeley, 1948), 81, California was the nation's leading wheat producer in 1874.

30. *History of Tulare County*, 168–69.

31. *Ibid. VWD*, July 18, 1879, p. 3, col. 4. Interview with Frank Latta, Santa Cruz, Calif., Aug. 11, 1978.

32. *History of Tulare County*, 168–69.

33. Brown, *Mussel Slough*, 140–47.

34. Brown, *Strain of Violence*, 306–7. Wallace Smith, *Garden of the Sun* (Los Angeles: Lymanhouse, 1939), 267.

35. John A. Larimore, "Legal Questions Arising from the Mussel Slough Land Dispute," *Southern California Quarterly* 58 (1976):75–94.

36. Various contemporary sources (see, for example, note 29) estimated the size of the Mussel Slough area as being from 100,000 to 512,000 acres with from 25,000 to 80,000 acres in dispute between the railroad and the settlers. The Southern Pacific land grant stretched for ten miles on each side of its line from Goshen to Hanford to Huron.

37. Settlers' Committee, *The Struggle of the Mussel Slough Settlers for Their Homes!* . . . (Visalia, Calif.: Delta Printing, 1880), 4–11. The settlers contended that the railroad had twice violated the terms of its land grant with each violation being sufficient, according to the settlers' interpretation of the law, to void the grant: (1) in 1867 by changing its route from the coast to the Central Valley and (2) by failing to complete the Tres Pinos–Huron section of its altered route. Of course, the railroad denied that any of its actions had invalidated its land grant, a view eventually upheld in court (see below).

38. Settlers' Committee, "An Appeal to the People: A History of the Land Troubles in Tulare and Fresno [Counties]," in *VWD,* May 7, 1880. See also Brown, *Mussel Slough,* 33–35; and McKinney, "Mussel Slough," 85. Yet in Jerome Madden, *The Lands of the Southern Pacific Railroad Company of California* (San Francisco: Southern Pacific Railroad Co., 1876), Madden, the land director for the entire Southern Pacific Railroad, issued a *caveat* cautioning that the assurances about land prices and improvements were not promises equivalent to a "contract." On page 9, the pamphlet declared that "true market value" would be the pricing criterion for Southern Pacific lands, a statement that in effect nullified the assurance about not charging settlers for the improvements they had made.

39. *VWD* 1878: April 12, p. 3, col. 1; April 19, p. 2, col. 2; May 17, p. 2, col. 4.

40. That is, 25,000 acres × $20.00 per acre = $500,000.00 For the 25,000 acres, see note 36.

41. Richard J. Orsi, "*The Octopus* Reconsidered: The Southern Pacific and Agricultural Modernization in California," *California Historical Quarterly* 54 (Fall 1975):197–220. In an effective justification of the railroad's Mussel Slough land policy, the Southern Pacific land director, Jerome Madden, denied that the railroad's prices were excessive but were, rather, cognate with prices being charged in the open market for land in the nonrailroad even-numbered sections, a policy Madden claimed had

been announced in all of its promotional pamphlets. Moreover, Madden charged that John J. Doyle had engineered the entire Mussel Slough protest movement of many years' duration for his own private gain—private gain to be made either by the railroad buying him off or from money contributed to the antirailroad movement by credulous settlers. In making this charge, Madden did not mention the name of Doyle, but readers with a solid knowledge of the Mussel Slough controversy would have easily known that he was referring to Doyle. Madden's long, detailed statement first appeared in the *Pacific Rural Press,* April 12, 1879, and was reprinted in *VWD,* April 18, 1879, p. 2, col. 3–4. Although he strongly sympathized with the settlers against the railroad, Ambrose Bierce shared Madden's view that John J. Doyle was motivated by selfishness. Brown, *Mussel Slough,* 101. Agreeing with the Madden-Bierce view of John J. Doyle and holding that the Southern Pacific and its Big Three leaders were more sinned against (by Doyle and the settlers) than sinning in the Mussel Slough conflict is Richard J. Orsi, "The Confrontation at Mussel Slough," in Richard B. Rice, William A. Bullough, and Richard J. Orsi, *The Elusive Eden: A New History of California* (New York: Alfred A. Knopf, c. 1988), 217–36.

42. Brown, "Back Country Rebellions," 78.

43. The entire petition to President Hayes is reproduced in Brown, *Mussel Slough,* 140–47. The particular lure and mystique of California are strikingly treated in Kevin Starr, *Americans and the California Dream, 1850–1915* (New York: Oxford University Press, 1973).

44. Irrigating 15,000 acres, 15,000 acres, and 25,000 acres, respectively, were the Lower Kings River Ditch (completed 1870–71), the People's Ditch (1870–71), and the Last Chance Ditch (1873–74). Robert R. Brown and J. E. Richmond, *History of Kings County* (Hanford, Calif.: A. H. Caviston, 1940), 49.

45. *VWD,* June 4, 1880, p. 2, col. 3–4. See also Mrs. Chambers's additional statement in *ibid.,* May 6, 1881, p. 2, col. 3–4. Mrs. Chambers's brother, Archibald McGregor, was one of the five settlers fatally shot in the gunfight of May 11, 1880.

46. The figure of 128 acres derived from the case files of 136 Mussel Slough settlers (all of whom lost their cases to the railroad) in Old [Federal] Circuit Court (1865–1911) case files (manuscripts in Federal Archives and Records Center, San Bruno, Calif.). The numbers of the Mussel Slough case files are 2034–38, 2160–65, 2282, 2317, 2320–22,

2358, 2361–2479. About 16,000 acres were in dispute in these particular cases.

47. Judgment Roll and Loose Papers of Case No. 2037, *Southern Pacific Railroad vs. Robert B. Huey* in Old (Federal) Circuit Court (1865–1911) case files.

48. *Ibid.* Other settlers were also the targets of ejectment suits by the railroad in 1878. *Ibid. History of Tulare County*, 195–97.

49. Ezra S. Carr, *The Patrons of Husbandry of the Pacific Coast* (San Francisco: A. L. Bancroft, 1875), 131–33, 135, 137–42, 179–80, 183–93, 212, 226. Many of those in the Mussel Slough settlers' movement were Grange members, and the village significantly named "Grangeville" was a stronghold of the settlers' movement. *Ibid.*, 252, 254, 278–79.

50. *History of Tulare County*, 189–90.

51. So said Thomas Jefferson McQuiddy. *History of Tulare County*, 187–88.

52. *S. F. Examiner*, Dec. 17, 1880.

53. *Ibid.*, Dec. 16, 1880 p. 2, col. 3. *VWD* 1880: Apr. 19, p. 2, col. 2; May 7, p. 2, col. 2–7. The Settlers' League was also called the "Settlers' Grand League" and the "Settlers' Land League." In these pages it will ordinarily be referred to as the Settlers' League. Three years earlier—in 1875—a settlers' meeting, keynoted by John J. Doyle, resulted in a petition to Congress by 500 signers. Brown, *Mussel Slough*, 41.

54. *S. F. Examiner*, Dec. 16, 1880, p. 2, col. 3. Brown, *Mussel Slough*, 40–41, 43.

55. *History of Tulare County*, 197. Brown, *Mussel Slough*, 45–46. *Alta California*, Dec. 3, 1880; Dec. 7, 1880. *VWD*, Nov. 29, 1878, p. 2., col. 3; March 7, 1879, p. 3, col. 1; July 25, 1879, p. 3, col. 6. See also *VWD*, Dec 20, 1878, p. 3 col. 1–2; Jan. 3, 1879, p. 3, col. 7, for extralegal daytime activity, which was less frequent than nighttime extralegal activity.

56. *VWD*, Dec. 6, 1878, p. 2, col. 2. *History of Tulare County*, 195. Brown, *Mussel Slough*, 54. It is ironic that the Southern Pacific was, in effect, the subject of vigilante violence, since Leland Stanford had himself been a rank-and-file member of the great San Francisco vigilance committee of 1856 and at the same time Collis P. Huntington was a leader of an affiliated vigilance committee in Sacramento. Brown, *Strain of Violence*, 163–64, on Stanford. Lavender, *Great Persuader*, 65–66, on Huntington.

57. *VWD*, Nov. 19, 1878, p. 2, col. 3.

58. For example, *VWD*, March 7, 1879, p. 3, col. 1. Smith, *Garden of Sun*, 267. Brown, *Mussel Slough*, 45–46. McQuiddy, the former Confederate major, headed the military arm of the settlers movement. *Ibid.*

59. *History of Tulare County*, 197.

60. Smith, *Garden of Sun*, 265.

61. *S. F. Examiner*, Dec. 16, 18, 1880. Hartt had been the Southern Pacific station agent at Goshen, 15 miles east of Hanford.

62. *Ibid.*, Dec. 16, 1880, p. 2, col. 3. Other leading members of the prorailroad faction included or came to include Welcome Fowler, E. Giddings, Theodore Marsh, W. L. Morton, Perry C. Phillips, C. Railsback, and Daniel Spangler. Brown, *Mussel Slough*, 127.

63. Menefee and Dodge, *Tulare and Kings*, 801–2.

64. *History of Tulare County*, 20, 187–88. See also *Sacramento Daily Record-Union*, Oct, 23, 1882, p. 3, col. 6–7, and *Hanford Morning Journal*, Feb. 21, 1915, p. 1, col. 2–3, and p. 8, col. 1–2.

65. *Alta California*, Dec. 3, 1880. Hawley was a staunch and quite radical member of the Settlers' League until he defected from the cause after the violence of May 11, 1880. *Ibid.* Biographical details on Hawley are in Menefee and Dodge, *Tulare and Kings*, 395–96.

66. *History of Tulare County*, 189–90.

67. For example, Patterson was in command of the detachment of settlers in the shootout of May 11, 1880. *VWD*, May 21, 1880, p. 3, col. 1–3.

68. Their portraits: McQuiddy—*History of Tulare County*, 23; Doyle and Patterson—Brown, *Mussel Slough*, 44; Hawley—Menefee and Dodge, *Tulare and Kings*, 395–96.

69. Marshal A. W. Poole to Attorney General Wayne MacVeagh, San Francisco, April 5, 1881, in National Archives and Records Service, Record Group 60, Records of the Department of Justice: Records Relating to the Mussel Slough Affair, 1880–81 (microfilm in Bancroft Library, University of California, Berkeley). *History of Tulare County*, 188. The case against McQuiddy was finally dismissed in 1886. Brown, *Mussel Slough*, 112.

70. *History of Tulare County*, 187–88.

71. On Hawley in the Civil War: Menefee and Dodge, *Tulare and Kings*, 395–96. On McQuiddy in the Civil War: *History of Tulare County*, 187–88.

72. For a rejoinder to the prorailroad charge that the Mussel Slough

dissidents were predominantly rebellious Southerners, see Settlers' Committee, *Struggle*, 30–31. Southerners were, it was admitted, a significant presence among the settlers but with Confederate "treachery and duplicity" being no part of "their natures." *Ibid.*

73. Menefee and Dodge, *Tulare and Kings*, 395–96.

74. McQuiddy and Wright were majors. *History of Tulare County*, 187, 189.

75. The Union army captain was Hawley. Menefee and Dodge, *Tulare and Kings*, 396.

76. Smith, *Garden of Sun*, 265. Collis P. Huntington was, indeed a major patron of African-American employment and education in the South and was thus from the viewpoint of dominant white Southerners indirectly a carpetbagger. Lavender, *Great Persuader*, 350–51. See also Richard J. Orsi, "The Big Four: Villains or Heroes?," in Rice, Bullough, and Orsi, *Elusive Eden*, 248, for Huntington as "a lifelong opponent of racial prejudice" who condemned white oppression of Chinese, American Indians, Filipinos, and Japanese as well as supporting black education and employment in the South.

77. Brown, *Mussel Slough*, 84–85.

78. *S. F. Examiner*, Dec, 16, 1880.

79. *History of Tulare County*, 197.

80. For example, *VWD*, April 8, 1881, p. 3, col. 5.

81. *VWD* 1879: May 23, p. 2, col. 6; June 6, p. 2, col. 1, 6.

82. *S. F. Examiner*, Dec. 19, 1880.

83. Brown, *Mussel Slough*, 45. Stopping legal processes was a principal feature of violent rural protest action going all the way back to the eighteenth century. Brown, "Back Country Rebellions," 92.

84. *VWD*, Dec. 19, 1879, p. 2, col. 1, announcing Sawyer's prototypical decision against the settlers in the case of *Southern Pacific Railroad Company vs. Pierpont Orton. Southern Pac. R. Co. v. Orton*, 32 F. 457 (C.C.D. Cal. 1879), for the case. Also *The Southern Pacific Railroad Company vs. Pierpont Orton: Opinion of Hon. Lorenzo Sawyer, Circuit Judge, District of California* (San Francisco: n.p., 1879). In most of the other cases (see the numbers of the case files in note 46, above) Sawyer simply repeated his decision and reasoning from the Orton case (case-file number 2035).

85. Linda C. A. Przybyszewski, "Judge Lorenzo Sawyer and the Chinese: Civil Rights Decisions in the Ninth Circuit," *Western Legal History* 1 (Winter/Spring 1988):27.

86. Sawyer's close relationship with the Stanford family postdated the death of Leland Stanford, whose expected place as the first president of Stanford University's board of trustees Sawyer was given, Stanford having died in 1893 before the board members were appointed. P. O. Ray, "Sawyer, Lorenzo," *Dictionary of American Biography,* XVI: 395–96. Przybyszewski, "Judge Lorenzo Sawyer," 53n.

87. In his will Sawyer named Charles Crocker as his executor, but the railroad magnate never served in that capacity since he predeceased Sawyer.

88. Przybyszewski, "Judge Lorenzo Sawyer," 53.

89. The chief architect of this procorporation jurisprudence was another Californian of the Gold Rush days, Associate Justice Stephen J. Field of the U.S. Supreme Court. As was required at the time, Justice Field also served as a member of the federal circuit court of which Sawyer was the judge. Field headed an economically conservative Pacific Coast federal judicial clique that included, in addition to Sawyer, Judges Matthew P. Deady of Oregon, Ogden Hoffman of northern California, and George M. Sabin of Nevada. Sawyer and Field were personally as well as judicially close. On Field, see footnote, p. 107. On the Sawyer-Field relationship, see Carl Brent Swisher, *Stephen J. Field: Craftsman of the Law* (Washington, D.C.: Brookings Institution, 1930), 326–27, 331–37, 342, 352–59, and *passim;* and Malcolm Clark, Jr., ed., "My Dear Judge . . . ," *Western Legal History* 1 (Winter/Spring 1988), 97 and *passim.*

90. *VWD,* Jan. 23, 1880, p. 3, col. 3.

91. *History of Tulare,* 197.

92. Brown, *Mussel Slough,* 80, 84–85.

93. *Congressional Record,* 46th Congress, House of Representatives, 2941–42 (May 1, 1880).

94. Senators Newton Booth and James T. Farley and Representative Campbell P. Berry later expressed this sympathy. *VWD,* March 4, 1881, p. 4, col. 4.

95. *VWD,* May 7, 1880, p. 2, col. 2–7. Menefee and Dodge, *Tulare and Kings,* 111.

96. *VWD* 1880: March 19, p. 3, col. 2; May 7, p. 2, col. 2–7. Settlers' Committee, *Struggle,* 24ff.

97. Menefee and Dodge, *Tulare and Kings,* 111.

98. Smith, *Garden of Sun,* 283. Irving McKee, "Notable Memorials to Mussel Slough," *Pacific Historical Review* 17 (Feb. 1948):2.

99. Smith, *Garden of Sun*, 273.

100. A. Russell Buchanan, *David S. Terry of California: Dueling Judge* (San Marino, Calif.: Huntington Library, 1959). David S. Terry was known as Judge Terry because he had served on the California state supreme court in the late 1850s.

101. On the significance of Stephen J. Field in American constitutional history, see, among many authorities, Robert G. McCloskey, *American Conservatism in the Age of Enterprise: A Study of William Graham Sumner, Stephen J. Field, and Andrew Carnegie* (Cambridge, Mass: Harvard University Press, 1951); and Charles W. McCurdy, "Stephen J. Field and the American Judicial Tradition," in Philip J. Bergan *et al., The Fields and the Law* (San Francisco: U.S. District Court for the Northern District of California Historical Society and New York: Federal Bar Council, 1986), 5–19.

102. On the Terry-Neagle-Field episode and its complicated background in the Sharon divorce case: Buchanan, *David S. Terry,* chaps. 12–13 and *passim;* Robert M. Kroninger, *Sarah and the Senator* (Berkeley: Howell-North, 1964); Gary L. Roberts, "In Pursuit of Duty," *American West,* Sept. 1970, pp. 26–33, 62–63; Swisher, *Stephen J. Field,* chaps. 11–13 and *passim;* R. Hal Williams, *The Democratic Party and California Politics, 1880–1896* (Stanford: Stanford University Press, 1973), 47–50, 54, and *passim.* On Neagle's service as a "fearless [law] officer and a good one" in Tombstone: William M. Breakenridge, *Helldorado: Bringing Law to the Mesquite* (Boston: Houghton Mifflin, 1928), *passim.* On Field's armed no-duty-to-retreat phase in California, 1850–51: Swisher, *Stephen J. Field,* 37–51. During the late 1850s Terry and Field had served together on the supreme court of California and were on good terms, sharing the no-duty-to-retreat attitude. It was not until the 1880s that bitter political differences and personal hatred divided these two hot-tempered and extremely proud men.

103. *VWD,* May 21, 1880, p. 3, col. 1–3, and *passim.* Brown, *Mussel Slough,* 64–65.

104. *VWD,* May 21, 1880, p. 3, col. 1–3, and *passim.* The confrontation between the Patterson-led settlers and the foursome of Hartt, Crow, Clark, and Poole actually came on a tract held solely by Brewer—land which adjoined the half-section claimed jointly by Brewer and Storer. Brewer's singly held plot, where the confrontation and gunfight took place, was the west half of the southwest quarter of Section 4, Township 18 South, Range 21 East. Brown, *Mussel Slough,* 64–65.

105. *VWD,* May 21, 1880, p. 3, col. 1–3, and *passim.*
106. *Ibid.*
107. *Ibid. S. F. Examiner,* Dec. 16, 1880.
108. *VWD.* May 21, 1880, p. 3, col. 1–3, and *passim.* Of the four other settlers who died as a result of the shootout, Iver Knutson was killed on the spot while John E. Henderson, Daniel Kelly, and Archibald Mc-Gregor were mortally wounded.
109. *VWD,* May 14, 1880, p. 3, col. 3.
110. In November 1880 a California state supreme court decision ruled on the duty to retreat, but the opinion was not clear, and the duty to retreat remained in doubt legally until the state supreme court decision in the case of *People v. Lewis,* 117 Cal. 186 (1897), held that in defending oneself there was no duty to retreat.
111. Brown, *Mussel Slough,* 74. Wallace Smith, *Prodigal Sons: The Adventures of Christopher Evans and John Sontag* (Boston: Christopher, 1951), 58–60, 417n, which, however, mistakenly identifies the killer of Crow as James Flewelling.
112. McKee, "Notable Memorials," 21. Latta, interview.
113. On Commodore Perry Owens, see Chapter 2, above. Twenty years earlier, on Oct. 16, 1867, a grassroots gunfighter, Mart Frost, by accounting for three lives in a shootout at Little Lake, Mendocino County, California, had equaled what would become Commodore Perry Owens's fatal toll. Frost's three kills were part of an election-day fray in which three members of the partisan Democratic, pro-Confederate Frost family battled it out with three members of the Republican, Unionist Coates family. Altogether, six lives were lost (one less than in Mussel Slough for the entire day of May 11, 1880) in the Little Lake shootout, of which five were Coateses and one was a Frost. With two members of the Coates family also wounded, the Coateses were badly defeated on October 16 by their Frost rivals. Yet these deaths were only the sanguinary high point in the complicated, more than two decades long Coates-Frost feud, which resulted in fourteen fatalities. John Boessenecker, *Badge and Buckshot: Lawlessness in Old California* (Norman: University of Oklahoma Press, c. 1988), chap. 11. Like the Karnes County, Texas, gunfight of the same year, 1867 (see Chapter 2, above), the Little Lake shootout far exceeded the number of deaths in the 1881 Tombstone gunfight near the O.K. Corral. As a grassroots gunfight the Little Lake shootout attracted little attention aside from stories in San Francisco's *Call,* Oct, 22, 1867, and *Bulletin,* Oct, 25, 1867 (both disclosed in

Boessenecker, *Badge and Buckshot,* chap. 11), and was not known to authorities on Western gunfighting until the recent publication of Boessenecker's book. Five of the six Little Lake gunfighters of Oct. 16, 1867, used repeating hand-guns, while the sixth used a shotgun. Located about 120 miles north of San Francisco as the crow flies, the village of Little Lake was, along with its twin, Willitsville, eventually merged into the present town of Willits.

114. *The Wasp* (San Francisco), 1881, p. 293.

115. Henry Nash Smith, *Virgin Land: The American West as Symbol and Myth* (Cambridge, Mass.: Harvard University Press, 1950). Kent Ladd Steckmesser, *The Western Hero in History and Legend* (Norman: University of Oklahoma Press, 1965). John G. Cawelti, *The Six-Gun Mystique* (Bowling Green, Ohio: Bowling Green University Popular Press, 1975).

116. For example, Bill O'Neal's *Encyclopedia of Western Gunfighters* (Norman: University of Oklahoma Press, 1979), an authoritative reference work, takes no notice of the Mussel Slough shootout and while listing 255 gunfighters omits Crow. Not generally known is that what seems to have been the bloodiest of all gunfights between American civilians took place not in the West but in Matewan, West Virginia, on May 19, 1920, when a labor dispute resulted in ten deaths with seven of those fatalities owing to the gunfire of Sid Hatfield, the local police chief, who was pro-union. Hatfield's toll of seven lives exceeded Walter J. Crow's five and is apparently the record for one American gunfighter on a single occasion. The "Matewan Massacre" of 1920 was an outgrowth of southern Appalachia'a violent tradition, which resembled that of the incorporating West. John Alexander Williams, *West Virginia: A Bicentennial History* (New York: W. W. Norton, c. 1976). Altina L. Waller, *Feud: Hatfields, McCoys, and Social Change in Appalachia, 1860–1900* (Chapel Hill: University of North Carolina Press, c. 1988). David Alan Corbin, *Life, Work, and Rebellion in the Coal Fields: The Southern West Virginia Miners, 1880–1922* (Urbana: University of Illinois Press, c. 1981), 195–224.

117. Frank Norris, *The Octopus: A Story of California* (New York: Doubleday, Page, 1901). Although the political cartoons of G. Frederick Keller (see below) were apparently responsible for popularizing (and perhaps originating) the Southern Pacific's image as an octopus, a book predating Frank Norris's *Octopus* was John R. Robinson, *The Octopus: A History of the Construction, Conspiracies, Extortions, Robberies, and Villainous Acts of the Central Pacific, Southern Pacific of Kentucky, Union Pacific, and*

Other Subsidized Railroads (San Francisco: n.p., 1894), a nonfiction exposé by an aggrieved Southern Pacific stockholder. Glen A. Love and David A. Carpenter, "The Other *Octopus*" (unpublished paper), notes similarities between Robinson's book and Norris's novel and argues that the former was an important source for the latter.

118. *VWD* 1880: May 21, p. 2, col. 2; May 28, p. 2, col. 5. *Harper's New Monthly Magazine*, Nov. 1882, pp. 874–75. McKee, "Notable Memorials," 19.

119. Other antirailroad color cartoons by Keller appeared in the *Wasp* on March 12, July 8, and Nov. 11, 1881; the *Wasp* was the first American publication to publish color cartoons on a sustained basis. Kenneth M. Johnson, *The Sting of the Wasp* (San Francisco: Book Club of California, 1967).

120. *Wasp*, Dec. 2, 1881, p. 358. Bierce's view that the railroad was legally right but morally wrong in its conflict with the settlers was shared by philosopher and novelist Josiah Royce (see note 124, below). Bierce's antirailroad writings, often keyed to the Mussell Slough conflict, appear in the *Wasp*, 1880–82. See also Johnson, *Sting of the Wasp*. In the *Wasp* of April 2, 1881, Bierce paid this anti-Stanford tribute (entitled "After Mussel Slough") to the five Mussel Slough settler martyrs of May 11, 1880:

"These mounds are green where lie the brave
  Who fought and fell at Hanford [*sic*];
O, point me out, I pray, the grave
  Of Leland Stanford.

"Twas here he fell"—the Granger thus
  Replied, with tears in torrents—
"Twas here he fell afoul of us
  With writs and warrants.

"Our fallen brave sleep well; each keeps
  This ground, where none besets him.
And well the fallen Stanford sleeps—
  When conscience lets him."

Quoted in Ernest Jerome Hopkins ed., *The Ambrose Bierce Satanic Reader* ... (Garden City, N.Y.: Doubleday, 1968), 195. On Bierce's antirailroad, anti–Big Three vendetta: Hopkins, ed., *Ambrose Bierce*, chaps. 12–13. Richard Saunders, *Ambrose Bierce* ... (San Francisco:

Chronicle Books, c. 1983), 33, 36–39, 70–74. See also Carey Mc-Williams, *Ambrose Bierce: A Biography* (New York: A. C. Boni, 1929), which perceptively treats Bierce's antirailroad idealism of the 1880s.

121. Przybyszewski, "Judge Lorenzo Sawyer," 48–49. On the "Sand-lotters" (who were allies of the Mussel Slough settlers), see below at note 133.

122. *VWD*, Dec. 3, 10, 17, 20, 24, 1880, on the trial. On sentencing, the jail term, and the mass movement for pardon of the prisoners: *ibid.*, Jan. 28, Feb. 4, 18, 25, March 4, 1881. On the triumphant return to Hanford: *ibid.*, Oct. 7, 1881, and *History of Tulare County*, 195–97. On the entire episode, see also Brown, *Mussel Slough*, 89–94ff., and Lavender, *Great Persuader*, 332.

123. Brown, *Mussel Slough*, 120.

124. Josiah Royce, *The Feud of Oakfield Creek* (Boston: Houghton Mifflin, 1887). The parallels between the fictional Oakfield Creek feud and the real Mussel Slough feud are obvious and have long been acknowledged by specialists—for example, James D. Hart, *A Companion to California* (New York: Oxford University Press, 1978), 360. John Clendenning, *The Life and Thought of Josiah Royce* (Madison: University of Wisconsin Press, 1985), 159, shows a parallel also to a land feud in Contra Costa County in the San Francisco Bay region, 1878–82. In Royce's novel a leading character, Tom Eldon, said of the Oakfield Creek land claimants what appears to have been Royce's view of the Mussel Slough settlers—an opinion Ambrose Bierce and many other Californians shared: "The plain facts are that the settlers have no legal rights whatever, and that they have all the moral rights you please." Royce, *Feud of Oakfield Creek*, 184.

125. Norris, *Octopus*. In addition to that of Josiah Royce, the three other novels based on the Mussel Slough conflict are William C. Morrow, *Blood-Money* (San Francisco: F. J. Walker, 1882); Charles C. Post, *Driven from Sea to Sea; or Just a Campin'* (Philadelphia: Elliott & Beezley, c. 1884); and May Merrill Miller, *First the Blade* (New York: Alfred A. Knopf, 1938). Although not distinguished literature, Miller's is by far the best of these three novels. Morrow, a onetime editor of the outstanding *Visalia Weekly Delta*, is best at describing the Mussel Slough country, especially its barren, sandy state before the irrigation efforts of the settlers. Charles C. Post was a radical newspaper editor in Chicago and later a Populist leader in Georgia. Post's Mussel Slough novel is poorly written and propagandistic but significant for its prosettler, quasi-

socialistic ideology. On Post: C. Vann Woodard, *Tom Watson: Agrarian Rebel* (New York: Oxford University Press, 1963), 182–83 and *passim*.

126. Karl Marx to Friedrich A. Sorge, London, Nov. 5, 1880, in Karl Marx and Frederick Engels, *Letters to Americans: 1848–1895: A Selection*, ed. Alexander Trachtenberg (New York: International Publishers, 1953), 126. Williams, *Democratic Party and California Politics*, chap. 1, attracted my attention to this passage by Marx.

127. See notes 85–89, above.

128. Larimore, "Legal Questions," 75–94. David J. Bederman, "The Imagery of Injustice at Mussel Slough: Railroad Land Grants, Corporation Law, and the 'Great Conglomerate West,' " *Western Legal History* 1 (Summer/Fall 1988):237–69.

129. The legal sequence of the dispossession of many individual farmers may be followed in the case files listed in note 46. The township maps of tract-by-tract land occupancy in Thomas H. Thompson, *Official Historical Atlas-Map of Tulare County* (Tulare, Calif.: Thomas H. Thompson, 1892), show the replacement of the original setttlers by new occupants. See also Brown, *Mussel Slough,* 108. For the original settlers who came to terms with the railroad and retained their land, Brown and Richmond, *History of Kings County,* 63, assert that "it is a fact that most lands on which the corporation had demanded $24 to $30 per acre were actually sold to the 'squatters' for less than one-half of those prices." Turbulence continued in the Mussel Slough country during the early 1880s. The murder of Edwin McAuliffe of San Francisco, who (along with two others) had purchased railroad land occupied (and claimed) since 1875 by John W. Cockrell, a settler near Hanford, almost touched off a second Mussel Slough gun battle. John J. Doyle and Thomas J. McQuiddy led the local antirailroad opposition to McAuliffe. The murder of McAuliffe was never solved, but it is likely that he was murdered by Settlers' League vigilantes. Brown, *Mussel Slough,* 112–14.

130. *History of Tulare County,* 187–88. Brown, *Mussel Slough,* 110–11.

131. Neil L. Shumsky, "San Francisco's Workmen Respond to the Modern City," *California Historical Quarterly* 55 (Spring 1976):46–57.

132. Kenneth M. Johnson, "Progress and Poverty—a Paradox," *California Historical Society Quarterly* 42 (March 1963):27–32.

133. P. O. Ray, "Kearney, Denis," *Dictionary of American Biography*, X: 268–69. The WPC grew rapidly on the strength of the mass audiences aroused by Kearney's impassioned speeches in the vacant sandlots of

San Francisco in the summer and fall of 1877. As a result, San Francisco members of the WPC were referred to as "sandlotters."

134. M. M. Marberry, *The Golden Voice: A Biography of Isaac Kalloch* (New York: Farrar, Straus, 1947), 227–31.

135. Marberry, *Golden Voice*, 244–76, 297–309, 337–41. Irving Mc-Kee, "The Shooting of Charles de Young," *Pacific Historical Review* 16 (August, 1947):271–84.

136. Hart, *Companion to California*, 113.

137. William Issel and Robert W. Cherny, *San Francisco, 1865–1932: Politics, Power, and Urban Development* (Berkeley: University of California Press, c. 1986), 127–28. The WPC and Kearney were famous for being anti-Chinese, for, aside from the the general racial prejudice of the time, there was strong fear that Chinese workingmen were taking or would take jobs away from whites and/or would depress the wages and working conditions of the whites, with whom they sometimes competed for employment. Alexander Saxton and all authorities have rightly emphasized the anti-Chinese thrust of the WPC. Without at all playing down the anti-Chinese aspect, the broad radical reform tenor of the WPC must also be stressed, for in California and the West in the late nineteenth century, radical labor sentiments and anti-Chinese passions often went hand in hand. Indeed, the rank and file and leadership of all political parties in California was decidedly anti-Chinese. Anti-Chinese feeling was strong in the Mussel Slough district, as it was throughout California. Alexander Saxton, *The Indispensable Enemy: Labor and the Anti-Chinese Movement in California* (Berkeley: University of California Press, 1971), is the best study of the issue. Significantly, the Big Three (especially Huntington) and their judicial allies, Field and Sawyer, defended the Chinese against assault and loss of civil liberties. On Field: Swisher, *Stephen J. Field*, chap. 8; and McCurdy, "Stephen J. Field," 12–17. On Sawyer: Przybyszewski, "Judge Lorenzo Sawyer."

138. Walton Bean and James J. Rawls, *California: An Interpretive History* (4th ed.; New York: McGraw-Hill, c. 1983), 194–96. Williams, *Democratic Party*, 16–17. Carl B. Swisher, *Motivation and Political Technique in the California Constitutional Convention, 1878–79* (Claremont: Pomona College, 1930).

139. On the Nob Hill mansions: Issel and Cherny, *San Francisco*, 69. On white worker resentment of the Nob Hill mansions of the Southern Pacific owners: *ibid.*, 127.

140. *VWD* 1879: March 28; April 6, p. 2, col. 1, 6.

141. Bean and Rawls, *California*, 196–97. Unlike others, Henry George was quick to perceive (in 1880) that the impact of the 1879 constitution would ultimately disappoint reformers and radicals. Issel and Cherny, *San Francisco*, 129.

142. Bean and Rawls, *California*, 196–97.

143. Robert A. Burchell, "Opportunity on the Frontier: Wealth-Holding in Twenty-six Northern California Counties, 1848–1880," *Western Historical Quarterly* 18 (April 1987):195, who thus cites the Western habit of "transience." Wallace Stegner, *The American West as Living Space* (Ann Arbor: University of Michigan Press, c. 1987), 21–22, notes the "footloose" trait of Westerners and of Americans for whom "the road has always led west." Departure to new places, says Stegner, has always been "associated in our minds with escape from history and oppression" and "with absolute freedom."

144. This trend of research was inspired by Stephan Thernstrom, *Poverty and Progress: Social Mobility in a Nineteenth Century City* (Cambridge: Harvard University Press, 1964), whose scholarly title significantly reverses Henry George's famous title, *Progress and Poverty*.

145. Don Harrison Doyle, "Social Theory and New Communities in Nineteenth-Century America," *Western Historical Quarterly* 8 (April 1977):155.

146. *Ibid.* Doyle cites eleven communities, including five on the West Coast: Seattle, Washington; Roseburg, Oregon; and San Francisco, Nevada City, and Grass Valley, California.

147. *Ibid.*

148. Burchell, "Opportunity and the Frontier," 195–96. Stegner, *American West as Living Space*, 22, holds of Americans that "our migratoriness has hindered us from becoming a people of communities, especially in the West."

149. Ira B. Cross, *A History of the Labor Movement in California* (Berkeley: University of California Press, 1935), 128. Roger W. Hite, "The Public Speaking of Denis Kearney, Labor Agitator" (M.A. thesis, University of Oregon, 1967), 27–28.

150. Marberry, *Golden Voice*, 349–50.

151. David A. Johnson, *Charters for the Far West: State-Building in California, Oregon, and Nevada, 1840–1890* (University of California Press, forthcoming), perceptively treats the embrace of the "individualist ethos."

152. Hahn and Prude, eds., *Countryside.*

153. Menefee and Dodge, *Tulare and Kings,* 801–2. On December 30, 1883, the United States Supreme Court upheld the railroad by confirming the findings of the Circuit Court in *John T. Phillips vs. Southern Pacific Railroad* and *James H. Cox vs. Southern Pacific Railroad.* Manuscript Volume of the Minutes of the Supreme Court of the United States, Vol. 45, April 23, 1883, to January 8, 1884, cited in Brown, *Mussel Slough,* 61.

154. Floyd L. Otter, *The Men of Mammoth Forest: A Hundred-Year History of a Sequoia Forest and Its People in Tulare County, California* (Ann Arbor: Edwards Brothers, 1963), 51, 101–2, plate 4, and *passim.* See note 157 below on the Hollow Log.

155. On the success ideology and the American dream: Cawelti, *Apostles of Self-Made Man;* Richard M. Huber, *The American Idea of Success* (New York: McGraw-Hill, 1971); Kenneth S. Lynn, *The Dream of Success: A Study of the Modern American Imagination* (Boston: Little, Brown, 1955); Donald Meyer, *The Positive Thinkers* (Garden City, N.Y.: Doubleday, 1965); Rischin, ed., *American Gospel of Success;* and Richard Weiss, *The American Myth of Success: From Horatio Alger to Norman Vincent Peale* (New York: Basic Books, 1969).

156. By coincidence, both Doyle and Thomas Jefferson McQuiddy died in 1915. On McQuiddy: *Hanford Morning Journal* 1915: Feb. 21, p. 1, col. 2–3, and p. 8, col. 1–2; Feb. 24, p. 8, col. 3. On Doyle: *Visalia Morning Delta,* Dec. 16, 1915, p. 1, col. 2.

157. Otter, *Men of Mammoth,* 35, 51, 91–92, 101–2, 104. Thompson, *Atlas-Map,* 70, 104. *The Way It Was: The Colorful History of Tulare County* (Fresno: Valley Publications, 1976), 103, says that in 1885 John J. Doyle filed on Talbott Meadows, which he developed into "Summer Home Resort." Doyle sold out in 1905 or 1906 to an electric utility company. His "Summer Home" development in the Hollow Log area is now the center of Tulare County's Balch County Park, high in the mountains northeast of Porterville. The Hollow Log campground at 6,400 feet elevation is one of the most beautiful spots in the giant sequoia redwood country of the Sierra Nevada, stretching south from Kings Canyon and Sequoia National Parks. It is reached by a steep, narrow, winding mountain highway across which black bears and their cubs freely wander and whose route goes back to a road built by John J. Doyle in the 1880s. The Hollow Log area is a favorite of today's nature lovers. Standing next to the Hollow Log is a lofty, gracefully symmetrical redwood *(Sequoiaden-*

dron giganteum), "Lady Alice," which Doyle named after his wife, born Lillie Alice Holser. The Hollow Log in its lovely mountain location is still, as it was in the time of the Doyles, one of the leading landmarks of Tulare County. Before the Doyles lived in the Hollow Log, it had sheltered Indians, fur trappers, prospectors, and an 1870 pioneer, Clinton T. Brown. Otter, *Men of Mammoth,* 101–2. *Guide to the Forestry Information Trail* (pamphlet; Visalia, Calif.: Tulare County Parks Division of Building Services and Parks Department, n.d.). Personal visit to Balch County Park and the Hollow Log.

158. Menefee and Dodge, *Tulare and Kings,* 801–2. Otter, *Men of Mammoth,* 101–2. *Visalia Morning Delta,* Dec. 16, 1915, p. 1, col. 2. The "Doyle Colony" located on the edge of Porterville and mentioned in Hunter S. Thompson's *Hell's Angels* was originally a real estate development of John J. Doyle. The Doyle Colony was one focus of outlaw motorcycle-gang activity in the Porterville area on Labor Day 1963. Hunter S. Thompson, *Hell's Angels* (New York: Ballantine Books, 1967), quoting the *Porterville Farm Tribune,* Sept. 5, 1963.

159. Lavender, *Great Persuader,* 376.

160. Bean and Rawls, *California,* 267–68. A sensitive study of long-term opposition to the Southern Pacific Railroad culminating in Hiram Johnson's victorious crusade is William F. Deverell, "Building an Octopus: Railroads and Society in the Late Nineteenth-Century Far West" (Ph.D dissertation, Princeton University, 1989). Broad studies of Hiram Johnson and progressive reform in California are George Mowry, *The California Progressives* (Berkeley: University of California Press, 1951); and Spencer C. Olin, Jr., *California's Prodigal Sons: Hiram Johnson and the Progressives* (Berkeley: University of California Press, 1968).

161. Tutorow, *Leland Stanford,* chap. 11.

162. Lavender, *Great Persuader,* 376. Although Henry E. Huntington eventually created his own traction and real-estate empire in the Los Angeles area, the nucleus of his great wealth was his one-third share of Collis P. Huntington's estate inherited upon the latter's death, to which was joined in 1913 a second one-third share. The union of the two one-third shares of Collis P. Huntington's estate came about when Henry E. Huntington, following a divorce from his first wife, married Collis P. Huntington's widow, Arabella, who had inherited one-third of Collis P. Huntington's estate. *Ibid.*

163. Issel and Cherny, *San Francisco,* 37–38.

164. On lingering voter resentment over the Mussel Slough episode

as a factor leading to Hiram Johnson's election victory on an antirailroad platform in 1910, see Smith, *Garden of Sun,* 260, 288.

165. Brown, *Mussel Slough,* 14.

166. McKinney, "Mussel Slough Episode," 120.

167. E. J. Hobsbawm, *Social Bandits and Primitive Rebels* (Glencoe, Ill.: Free Press, 1959).

168. Richard White, "Outlaw Gangs of the Middle Border: American Social Bandits," *Western Historical Quarterly* 12 (October 1981): 387–408, holds that Jesse James, his gang, and later outlaws who "metaphorically rode out of Missouri and Oklahoma into America at large quickly transcended the specific economic and political conditions of the areas that produced them and became national cultural symbols."

169. Smith, *Prodigal Sons.* Evans and Sontag conform very well to the model of the American social bandit in White, "Outlaw Gangs."

170. Smith, *Prodigal Sons,* 31.

171. Eva Evans (Mrs. Perry McCullough), "An Outlaw and His family" (1934; manuscript in Huntington Library, San Marino, Calif.), 43–44. Smith, *Prodigal Sons,* 50. Also contributing to Evans's animus against the Southern Pacific was his friendship with farmer Bart Patterson, the son of James N. Patterson, a key leader of the antirailroad Mussel Slough settlers' movement. *Ibid.,* 32.

172. In *The Octopus* Frank Norris based Dyke, and embittered railroader turned train robber, on the outlaw career of Sontag.

173. On the last two shootouts of Evans and Sontag: Smith, *Prodigal Sons.* According to Eva Evans, Ambrose Bierce wrote sympathetically of Evans and Sontag in his *San Francisco Examiner* columns, including the one of July 9, 1893, in which he saluted the fallen John Sontag as a man of courage. Evans, "An Outlaw," 146–47.

174. *Ibid.,* 122–28. Smith, *Prodigal Sons,* chap. 14.

175. Such a town was Arvin in Kern County—the object of a classic 1940s study by anthropologist Walter Goldschmidt. Walter Goldschmidt, *As You Sow: Three Studies in the Social Consequences of Agribusiness* (1947; reprinted Montclair, N.J.: Allanheld, Osmun & Co., 1978), part II. See also Donald Worster, *Rivers of Empire: Water, Aridity, and the Growth of the American West* (New York: Pantheon, c. 1985), 248–49.

176. This sketch of Hanford and the Mussel Slough country of our time is based on recent visits to those localities. See also Preston, *Vanishing Landscapes,* 231 (fig. 60) and 242 (figs. F–G), on the survival of small- and medium-size agricultural plots in the Mussel Slough area. Marinus

Bakker, who farmed for forty years in the Mussel Slough country (and who in 1950–54 worked under lease the gunfight field), told me that Mussel Slough farms of 40 to 160 to 260 acres are common nowadays.

177. This sketch of the agribusiness mode north of Tulare Lake (often dry since 1898) is based on recent visits to the locality and on interviews with H. E. (Hal) Weisman, Eddie Warmerdam, and Marinus Bakker—all of Hanford. See also Preston, *Vanishing Landscapes*, 231 (fig. 60) and 242 (figs. F–G).

178. This field (Brewer's plot) of the gunfight of May 11, 1880, is, in terms of the Kings County street grid of 1990, bounded on the west by Fourteenth Avenue and on the south by Elder Avenue—a vicinity northwest of Hanford. It is part of a 120-acre farm that in recent decades has been owned and operated by Mr. Eddie Warmerdam of a long-established Central Valley family whose most famous member, a first cousin of Eddie Warmerdam, was Cornelius Warmerdam—the world-record-setting pole vaulter of the 1940s. The Warmerdams came to the Central Valley after the conflict with the railroad ended and were not involved in that episode. At times the gunfight field has been planted in milo, winter wheat, cotton, and alfalfa. Interviews with Eddie Warmerdam and with Marinus Bakker; the latter farmed the property under lease from Mr. Warmerdam in 1950–54. Adjacent to the field on the east side of Fourteenth Avenue is an impressive monument to the "Mussel Slough Tragedy" erected in 1950 by the California Centennial Commission as State Registered Landmark No. 245.

Chapter 4. The Persistence of No Duty to Retreat: Crime, Law, and Society in America from the 1850s to the Present

In the notes to this chapter both the regular (New York City) edition of *The New York Times* and the national edition of *The New York Times* are cited. Unless otherwise indicated, the citation is to the regular edition.

*Ted Robert Gurr, "On the History of Violent Crime in Europe and America," in Hugh Davis Graham and Ted Robert Gurr, eds., *Violence in America: Historical and Comparative Perspectives* (Beverly Hills: Sage Publications, 1979), p. 370.

1. Additional discussion of the Goetz episode is below. All four of Goetz's targets were hospitalized with gunshot wounds. Barry Allen, James Ramseur, and Troy Canty recovered, but Darrell Cabey was per-

manently paralyzed from the waist down as the result of a severed spinal cord.

2. Ted Robert Gurr, "On the History of Violent Crime in Europe and America," in Hugh Davis Graham and Ted Robert Gurr, eds., *Violence in America: Historical and Comparative Perspectives* (Beverly Hills: Sage Publications, 1979), 353, 370.

3. The Information Society is discussed below.

4. Roger Lane, *Violent Death in the City: Suicide, Accident, and Murder in Nineteenth-Century Philadelphia* (Cambridge: Harvard University Press, 1979), 119. See also Lane, *Policing the City: Boston, 1822–1885* (Cambridge: Harvard University Press, 1967).

5. Gurr, "History of Violent Crime," 359.

6. Lane, *Violent Death*, 124.

7. *Ibid.*, 359–61.

8. Ted Robert Gurr, "Historical Trends in Violent Crime: England, Western Europe, and the United States, chap. 1, in Gurr, ed., *Violence in America* (2 vols.; Newbury Park, Calif.: Sage Publications, 1989); the full titles of the two volumes of this work are *Violence in America: Volume 1— The History of Crime* and *Violence in America: Volume 2—Protest, Rebellion, Reform;* citations in the following notes will not be by main title and volume number but will be by editor and the subtitle of each volume, thus: Gurr, ed., *History of Crime* and Gurr, ed., *Protest, Rebellion, and Reform.* Two contributors to Gurr, ed., *History of Crime,* are in disagreement over whether homicide increased significantly in the period from 1900 to about 1930: Margaret A. Zahn, chap. 10, "Homicide in the Twentieth Century: Trends, Types, and Causes," finds a significant increase; Roger Lane, chap. 2, "On Social Meaning of Homicide Trends in America," disagrees. Accepted by all is Zahn's finding that the American homicide rate was at its lowest in the late 1950s.

9. Lane, *Violent Death*, 131.

10. Richard Maxwell Brown, *Strain of Violence: Historical Studies of American Violence and Vigilantism* (New York: Oxford University Press, 1975), chaps. 4–6, and Chaps. 2–3, above, on the Western Civil War of Incorporation.

11. Brown, *Strain of Violence*, 127–28, 134. Two recent studies of the widespread phenomenon of neovigilantism (classic frontier/Western vigilantism updated for a twentieth-century age of urbanization and industrializaton) against industrial laborers and IWW members are James W. Byrkit, *Forging the Copper Collar: Arizona's Labor-Management*

War of 1901–1921 (Tucson: University of Arizona Press, c. 1982); and John McClelland, Jr., *Wobbly War: The Centralia Story* (Tacoma: Washington State Historical Society, 1987).

12. Lane, *Violent Death*, 131.

13. Neil Alan Weiner and Marvin E. Wolfgang, "The Extent and Character of Violent Crime in America, 1969 to 1982," in Lynn A. Curtis, ed., *American Violence and Public Policy: An Update of the National Commission on the Causes and Prevention of Violence* (New Haven: Yale University Press, 1985). Gurr. "History of Violent Crime" and "Historical Trends in Violent Crime."

14. Gurr, "History of Violent Crime."

15. Weiner and Wolfgang, "Extent and Character," 34.

16. *Ibid.*, 25.

17. Lane, *Violent Death*, 137.

18. Gurr, "History of Violent Crime," 370.

19. *Ibid.*, 369–70.

20. National Commission on the Causes and Prevention of Violence, *To Establish Justice, To Insure Domestic Tranquility: Final Report of the National Commission on the Causes and Prevention of Violence* (Washington, D.C.: U.S. Government Printing Office, 1969), 44–45 (the commission was chaired by Milton S. Eisenhower). Elliott Currie, "Crimes of Violence and Public Policy: Changing Directions," in Curtis, ed., *American Violence*, 41–42. See also Currie, *Confronting Crime: An American Challenge* (New York: Pantheon, 1985), 7–9; this elegant piece of scholarship has devastating critiques of the wrong-headed ways in which both the "conservative" and the "liberal" schools of criminology have reacted to 1960s–1980s crime. Currie's own views, which transcend the conservative and liberal schools, are compellingly presented throughout his book.

21. Brown, *Strain of Violence*, 129–30.

22. *Newsweek*, March 11, 1985, pp. 50–53.

23. George P. Fletcher, *A Crime of Self-Defense: Bernhard Goetz and the Law on Trial* (New York: Free Press, 1988), 2.

24. Fletcher states that "self-defense was always the central issue in the Goetz case." *Ibid.*, 18.

25. Widespread fears that the example of Goetz would result in a wave of vigilantism (group or individual) in New York City and elsewhere were not realized. Not being a vigilante, Goetz inspired no vigilante emulators. Fletcher, *Crime of Self-Defense*, 201–2. On the American

vigilante tradition—a tradition of group, not individual, activity—see Brown, *Strain of Violence*, chaps. 4–6.

26. Robert D. McFadden, "Bernhard Goetz: A Private Man in a Public Debate," *New York Times*, Jan. 6, 1985, sec. 1, pp. 1, 22. See also the psychological study of Goetz by Lillian B. Rubin, *Quiet Rage: Bernie Goetz in a Time of Madness* (New York: Farrar, Straus & Giroux, 1986). A critique of Rubin's book is George P. Fletcher, "Goetz on Trial," in *New York Review of Books*, April 23, 1987.

27. Fletcher, *Crime of Self-Defense*, 103.

28. The law of New York state is divided on the duty to retreat: (1) a self-defender has a duty to retreat (if the retreat can be made with safety to oneself and others) against an impending attack of deadly physical force; (2) a self-defender has no duty to retreat in the face of an impending robbery. Fletcher, *Crime of Self-Defense* (p. 26), citing the relevant statute as codified in *New York Penal Law*, sec. 35, #15. Fletcher comments: "The best explanation for this apparent contradiction (duty to retreat from the more, not the less serious attack) is that the statute combines two distinct traditions in the theory of using deadly force. One theory, generating a duty to retreat, is based on personal defense. The other, not requiring retreat, is based on the authority of every citizen to prevent the occurrence of a serious felony." Fletcher, *Crime of Self-Defense*, 222, n12. Because the issue in the Goetz case was whether or not Canty *et al.* were attempting to rob Goetz, the duty to retreat was not a factor in the trial of Goetz. With attempted robbery as the issue (as all agreed it was), Goetz had no duty to retreat. Whether or not Goetz understood that he had no legal duty to retreat, the evidence is abundant that, as he was confronted by the four youths, his attitude was very much one of no duty to retreat.

29. Before they encountered Goetz on December 22, 1984, both Canty and Ramseur had served short sentences for petty theft, and Allen had twice pleaded guilty to disorderly conduct. Between December 22, 1984, and the beginning of Goetz's trial on April 27, 1987, Ramseur had been convicted of and was serving time in prison for rape and sodomy; Allen had been arrested for snatching a chain; and Cabey had allegedly used a shotgun to rob three men. Fletcher, *Crime of Self-Defense*, 3, 107–8.

30. Derrick Jackson and Marily Milloy of *Newsday*, "A Victim of a Vigilante," Eugene (Ore.) *Register-Guard*, March 24, 1985, pp. 1E–2E.

31. *Ibid.*, 2E.

32. In jury deliberations one of the African-Americans was a strong advocate of Goetz's acquittal. Fletcher, *Crime of Self-Defense*, 205.

33. Fletcher, *ibid.*, 180–81, commended the jury for being unusually conscientious.

34. *New York Times*, national edition, June 17, 1987, A15. Eugene *Register-Guard*, June 17, 1987, pp. 1A, 4A. Portland *Oregonian*, June 17, 1987, pp. 1, 3. A splendid legal study of the trial is Fletcher, *Crime of Self-Defense*. On the composition of the jury: *Register-Guard*, June 17, 1987, p. 5A, and *USA Today*, June 17, 1987, p. 3A. Goetz unsuccessfully appealed his conviction for the minor weapons offense for which he was sentenced to six months (which he served in full) in prison, a fine of $5,075, and four and a half years of probation (including 280 hours of community service). Fletcher, *Crime of Self-Defense*, 216–17. Delayed by the appeals process, Goetz's prison term was completed in September 1989. He still faced, however, a $50,000,000 lawsuit by his paralyzed victim, Darrell Cabey. *New York Times*, national edition, Dec. 2, 1989, p. 16, col. 1. Cabey's lawsuit went to trial in 1990.

35. Fletcher, *Crime of Self-Defense*, 199–200. Legal scholar Nadine Klansky cited another New York City subway self-defense case in which the racial roles of the Goetz case were reversed, noting that "on April 13, 1980, Austin Weekes, a 23-year-old black man riding on a southbound F train in Brooklyn, shot two white teenagers when they confronted him and said, 'What are you looking at?' In that case, one of the teens was shot dead. Weekes later confessed and stated before a grand jury that he began carrying a gun because he had before been the victim of a mugging. The jury refused to indict him and all charges were dropped." Nadine Klansky, "Bernard [*sic*] Goetz, A 'Reasonable Man': A Look at New York's Justification Defense," *Brooklyn Law Review* 53 (Winter 1988):1150.

36. *New York Times*, national edition, Nov. 11, 1988, A23, col. 3–6. The recent judicial trend in favor of expanded self-defense apparently reflects, in part, the increasing use and effectiveness of armed self-defense—see *Newsweek*, Sept. 24, 1990, pp. 81–83.

37. Rubin, *Quiet Rage*, 7, 151. Exploring the racial aspects of the Goetz case, Fletcher, *Crime of Self-Defense*, 201–2, 205, found that, contrary to fears, the not-guilty verdicts in the trial of Goetz did not inspire open-season attacks on African-Americans in New York City. Yet since the white Goetz's shooting of the four young blacks in 1984, the city has been shaken by three racially polarizing events of violence, in none of

which self-defense or no duty to retreat was an issue: (1) The 1986 death of an African-American who was the victim of murderous behavior by young whites in the Howard Beach section of Queens. *Newsweek*, Jan. 12, 1987, p. 25, and Feb. 23, 1987, p. 29 (reporting on the trial of the killers). (2) The brutal multiple rape of a young white female in Central Park, Manhattan, on April 19, 1989, by a band of black and Hispanic teenagers who described their action as "wilding"—violently running wild in a youthful rampage. *New York Times*, April 29, 1989, p. 30, col. 1–6. *Newsweek*, May 8, 1989, p. 65. (3) The shocking fatal shooting of Yusuf K. Hawkins, an inoffensive sixteen-year-old African-American, by racially antagonistic white teenagers on August 23, 1989, in the Bensonhurst section of Brooklyn. *New York Times*, national edition, Aug. 25, 1989, p. A16, col. 1–5. Richard Cohen, "The Ugly Truth about Bensonhurst, U.S.A.," *Washington Post National Weekly Edition*, Sept. 11, 1989, p. 29. In the long term, the racially divisive effect of these three crimes may have been offset in fall 1989 by black candidate David Dinkin's election to the office of mayor of New York City. Dinkins has been applying his healing approach to race relations to the spring 1990 black-white racially polarizing outcome of the trials of those accused of murdering Yusuf Hawkins and also to an embittering dispute between African-Americans and Korean-Americans in the Flatbush neighborhood of Brooklyn. On Dinkins and the Hawkins-murder trials: Sam Roberts, "People Apart: Can Politics Get to the Roots of Racial Strife?," *New York Times*, national edition, May 20, 1990, sec. 4, p. 1, col. 1–4, and p. 4, col. 1–4. On the Flatbush dispute: Laurie Goodstein, "New York's Racial Tinderbox," *Washington Post National Weekly Edition*, May 21, 1990, p. 9.

38. The "murder rate" (i.e., the number of murders and non-negligent manslaughters per 100,000 Americans) peaked at 10.2 and 9.8 in 1980 and 1981, respectively and fell to 9.1 in 1982. From 1983 through 1987 it has held steadily at a lower but still high level in the range of 7.9 (1984, 1985) to 8.6 (1986). The figure for both 1983 and 1987 was 8.3; for 1988 it was 8.4, while it rose to 8.7 for 1989. U.S. Department of Justice, Federal Bureau of Investigation, *Uniform Crime Reports for the United States: Crime in the United States*—annual reports for 1980–89. The "crime rate" (i.e., the percentage of American households affected by the crimes of rape, robbery, assault, personal theft, and theft or burglary in the residence) was 24.4 percent in 1987 and has been holding steady at about 25 percent since 1985, as such way down

from the 1985 figure of 32 percent. *National Journal,* June 11, 1988, p. 1576, reporting figures from the U.S. Department of Justice's Bureau of Justice report on the crime rate for 1987.

39. The words quoted are from Gurr, "History of Violent Crime," 370.

40. In recent years, for example women have increasingly identified with the violent tradition of self-defense by more and more arming themselves with guns. Paxton Quigley, *Armed and Female* (New York: Dutton, 1989). Quigley is a strong advocate of female use of guns for self-defense.

41. *Society,* July/Aug. 1984, p. 3. On the waning of discretionary early-release programs: Robert J. Sampson, "Crime in Cities: The Effects of Formal and Informal Social Control," in *Crime and Justice: An Annual Review off Research 8, Communities and Crime,* ed. Albert J. Reiss, Jr., and Michael Tonry (Chicago: University of Chicago Press, 1986), 271–311. Sampson (271) found that the the "high risk of jail incarceration" had a significant deterrent effect on robbery.

42. Michael Tonry, "Structuring Sentencing," in *Crime and Justice* 10, ed. Michael Tonry and Norval Morris (1986): 267–337. Tonry found that mandatory sentencing was largely a failure, because attorneys and judges frequently managed to evade it and because it often produced injustice in individual cases.

43. *National Journal,* March 30, 1985, p. 215.

44. *New York Times,* national edition, Aug. 25, 1988, A8. Recently in Oregon, for example, prosecutors have shifted drug cases from an overburdened state judicial and penal system to the federal system with its greater availability of prison space and more effective sentencing.

45. U.S. Department of Justice, Bureau of Justice Statistics, *Special Report: Pretrial Release and Detention: The Bail Reform Act of 1984* (Feb. 1988), 2, 5.

46. Alfred Blumenstein, "Prison Populations: A System Out of Control?," in *Crime and Justice* 10, ed. Tonry and Morris (1986), 232. Despite the very high rate of incarceration in 1986 which found one of every 300 Americans in jail, Blumenstein found, also, that, contrary to the "conventional wisdom" of scholars, the United States is not one of the most punitive nations in the world. *Ibid.,* 236.

47. U.S. Department of Justice, Bureau of Justice Statistics, *Special Report: Population Density in State Prisons* (Dec. 1986), 1.

48. Joseph Kraft, "Law Is in Disorder in America Today," Eugene

Register-Guard, Jan. 10, 1985, p. 11A. See also Currie, "Crimes of Violence," 42–43.

49. *New York Times,* national edition, Aug. 9, 1988, A1, A8.

50. For the distinction between an emphasis on due process of law versus an emphasis on the repression of crime in regard to the criminal-justice system, see Herbert L. Packer, *The Limits of Criminal Sanction* (Stanford: Stanford University Press, 1968), 149–73.

51. Robert Reiff, *The Invisible Victim: The Criminal Justice System's Forgotten Responsibility* (New York: Basic Books, 1979), an advocacy book. The National Organization for Victim Assistance is a strong advocacy organization that has effectively joined in the movement resulting in "a rising tide of victim-assistance legislation in . . . both state and federal codes" since 1980—a trend spearheaded by the federal Victim and Witness Assistance Act of 1982. *Washington Post National Weekly Edition,* May 15, 1989, pp. 11–12. Public outrage activated by sympathy for the victim of a heinous hammer-and-knife attack on one Pamela Small in 1973 by John Mack resulted in the latter's resignation in 1989 from his powerful position as executive director of the Democratic party's Steering and Policy Committee in the U.S. House of Representatives. After serving only 27 months in jail for his crime, Mack became a staff employee in the House of Representatives and worked his way up to the high post from which he resigned when his crime of 1973 became generally known as a result of a *Washington Post* exposé. *Ibid.*

52. Terry Davidson, *Conjugal Crime: Understanding and Changing the Wifebeating Pattern* (New York: Hawthorn, 1978), is an advocacy book, while Jean Giles-Sims, *Wife Battering: A Systems Theory Approach* (New York: Guilford, 1983), is a scholarly study.

53. On rape: Susan Brownmiller, *Against Our Will: Men, Women, and Rape* (New York: Simon and Schuster, 1975), which significantly raised the consciousness of people on the subject; and Susan Estrich, *Real Rape* (Cambridge: Harvard University Press, 1987), a legal study. On incest: W. Arens, *The Original Sin: Incest and Its Meaning* (New York: Oxford University Press, 1986), a cultural study.

54. *Newsweek,* March 18, 1985, pp. 58–66. Andrea Dworkin, *Pornography: Men Possessing Women* (New York: Perigee Books, 1981). A quite new initiative has been the movement against child pornography resulting in, among various actions, an increase in federal child-pornography prosecutions from 3 to 249 annually in the last five years. *New York Times,* July 8, 1988, p. A27.

55. James B. Jacobs, "The Law and Criminology of Drunk Driving," in *Crime and Justice* 10, ed. Tonry and Morris (1988), 171–229. A profile of Candy Lightner, founder of Mothers Against Drunk Driving (MADD), appears in Bill Berkowitz, *Local Heroes* (Lexington, Mass.: Lexington Books, 1987).

56. Elliott Leyton, *Compulsive Killers: The Story of Modern Multiple Murder* (New York: Washington Mews Books, 1986). Ronald M. Holmes and James DeBurger, *Serial Murder* (Beverly Hills: Sage Publications, 1987). *Newsweek,* Nov. 26, 1984, pp. 100, 104–5, discusses the creation of the National Center for the Analysis of Violent Crime (Quantico, Va.) with its focus on serial killers.

57. Michael Barone, "An Age of Restraint," *Washington Post National Weekly Edition,* Sept. 30, 1985, p. 27.

58. *National Journal,* Oct. 17, 1987, p. 2628. *New York Times,* national edition, July 10, 1988, sec. 4, p. 5, on the decline in alcohol use. On the decline of drug use: *New York Times,* national edition, July 10, 1988, sec. 4, p. 5, citing two recent research studies and the opinion of David F. Musto, a historian of drug-abuse trends. The mainstream decline in drug use is countered by a powerful surge of inner-city drug activity (discussed below).

59. Jeff Greenfield, "Enough's Enough!: Americans Reject Liberal Approach toward Crime and Punishment," Portland *Oregonian,* March 23, 1990, p. D7, col. 1–3. See also a recent *New York Times*/CBS News poll showing that 72 percent of Americans support the death penalty (much more to avenge crime than to deter it). Public support for the death penalty has moved steadily upward since the 1960s in phase with the rise of the murder rate since then. E. J. Dionne, "The Death Penalty: Getting Mad and Getting Even," *Washington Post National Weekly Edition,* May 21, 1990, p. 37. Symptomatic of the changing attitude to crime and punishment is the moderately liberal *New York Times,* which in response to New York City's climbing murder rate of 1989–90 called for a $500 million program of 5,000 more police officers, 6,000 more jail cells, 90 more judges to bring down the annual criminal-case load, and a strengthened probation system. *New York Times,* national edition, Sept. 6, 1990, A22, col. 1–2. In its tough editorial the *Times* said nothing about the root causes of crime.

60. Gurr, "History of Violent Crime," 369–70.

61. The quotations are from Lane, *Violent Death,* 120–21.

62. *Newsweek,* Nov. 26, 1984, pp. 100, 104–5.

63. Gary T. Marx, *Undercover: Police Surveillance in America* (Berkeley: University of California Press, 1988), 208–9.

64. *New York Times,* national edition, April 8, 1989, p. 1, col. 1–2 and p. 8, col. 5–6.

65. Marx, *Undercover,* 3.

66. *Ibid.,* 54–59, 208–16.

67. *Ibid.,* 206, 233.

68. John Naisbitt, *Megatrends: Ten New Directions Transforming Our Lives* (New York: Warner Books, 1982), 114; see also pp. 154–55. A more recent popular prophet of the Information Society, Alvin Toffler, *Powershift: Knowledge, Wealth, and Violence at the Edge of the 21st Century* (New York: Bantam, 1990), also emphasizes the trend of decentralization.

69. Currie, "Crimes of Violence," 44–45, 48, 57.

70. Paul J. Lavrakas, "Citizen Self-Help and Neighborhood Crime Prevention Policy," in Curtis, ed., *American Violence,* 87–115.

71. Lynn A. Curtis, "Neighborhood, Family, and Employment: Toward a New Public Policy against Violence," in Curtis, ed., *American Violence,* 206–9, 213, 217–18. A balanced, perceptive study of the movement as a whole is Wesley G. Skogan, "Community Organizations and Crime," in *Crime and Justice* 10, ed. Tonry and Morris, 39–78. For recent highly successful examples of neighborhood movements against crime, see below at notes 87–89.

72. Weiner and Wolfgang, "Extent and Character," 27, 29, 32, 34.

73. In a powerful editorial succinctly tracing the disastrous impact of crack, the *New York Times* in the spring of 1989 called for "a national mobilization as if for war headed, by a President . . . who is willing to . . . fight for victory" against the threat to national security from "the crack invasion." *New York Times,* national edition, May 28, 1989, sec. 4, p. 14, col. 1–2. See also *ibid.,* Aug. 20, 1989, sec. 1, p. 1., col. 1–2, and p. 17, col. 1–4, for a resurgence of syphilis and the rapid spread of Acquired Immune Deficiency Syndrome among the poor as a result of crack use.

74. Humbert S. Nelli, *The Business of Crime: Italians and Syndicate Crime in the United States* (New York: Oxford University Press, 1976). Joseph L. Albini, *The American Mafia: Genesis of a Legend* (New York: Appleton-Century-Crofts, 1971). Francis A. J. Ianni, *A Family Business: Kinship and Social Control in Organized Crime* (New York: Russell Sage Foundation, 1972).

75. *Newsweek,* March 14, 1988, pp. 16–18, and March 28, 1988, pp. 20–27.

76. *New York Times,* national edition, Sept. 6, 1989, p. A1, col. 4–6, p. A2, col. 1–5 and p. A11, col. 1–6.

77. Weiner and Wolfgang, "Extent and Character," 34. Gurr, chap. 1, Zahn, chap. 10, and Wesley G. Skogan, chap. 11, "Social Change and the Future of Violent Crime," in Gurr, ed., *History of Crime.*

78. Currie, "Crimes of Violence," 58–59. Colin Loftin, David McDowall, and James Boudouris, chap. 7, "Economic Change and Homicide in Detroit, 1926–1979," in Gurr, ed., *History of Crime,* found that homicide was not significantly related to the unemployment rate per se, but they did find a significant connection with the level of poverty—the basic issue addressed by Currie (see below) and other advocates of a crime-alleviating full-employment policy for black youth.

79. Currie, *Confronting Crime,* chap. 7.

80. *New York Times,* national edition, April 2, 1989, sec. 1, p. 12, col. 5; Richard E. Rubenstein, chap. 11, "Rebellion in America: The Fire Next Time," in Gurr, ed., *Protest, Rebellion, and Reform,* 321. See also Skogan, chap. 11, in Gurr, ed., *History of Crime,* on "rational choice theory" applied to the propensity of young black males to join high-profit drug-dealing gangs.

81. Philippe Bourgois, "Just Another Night on Crack Street," *New York Times Magazine,* Nov. 12, 1989, pp. 53, 60–65, 94. Although focusing on a gang Hispanic (that is, Dominican) in character, another study also stresses the entrepreneurial character of youthful drug dealers: Terry Williams, *The Cocaine Kids: The Inside Story of a Teenage Drug Ring* (Reading, Mass.: Addison-Wesley, 1989).

82. Gurr, chap. 1; Lane, chap. 2; and Skogan, chap. 11, in Gurr, ed., *History of Crime.* Countervailing trends in 1990 were a national decline in cocaine use and a surge in big-city homicide. *New York Times,* national edition, July 1, 1990, sec. 1, p. 11, col. 1–4, and July 18, 1990, A1, col. 1–2, A10, col. 1–6.

83. *Ibid.,* June 15, 1986, sec. 1, pp. 1, 18; and Aug. 20, 1990, A10, col. 1–2.

84. Quoted by William Raspberry in Portland *Oregonian,* Oct. 29, 1985, B7.

85. Comer, "Black Violence and Public Policy," in Curtis, ed., *American Violence,* 63, 80, 84–85, and below for Comer's own effort to revitalize education in the African-American ghetto of New Haven.

86. See, for example, Raspberry, "Blacks' Ability Must Rest in Attitude," Portland *Oregonian,* Sept. 27, 1985, D7; "Blacks Need to Seize

Own Educational Reins," *ibid.*, Oct. 29, 1985, B7; and many subsequent columns. An African-American intellectual who, although not always in agreement with Raspberry, also advocated black community self-help for education and against crime is Stanley Crouch—see his *Notes of a Hanging Judge: Essays and Reviews, 1979–1989* (New York: Oxford University Press, 1990), including chap. 19, a 1985 essay on the broader implications for self-help in "the Negro-American community" of the violent, criminal, and racial aspects of the Bernhard Goetz episode.

87. Washington, D.C., led the nation in 1988 with its rate of 59.5 murders and non-negligent homicides per 100,000 residents. Federal Bureau of Investigation, *Uniform Crime Reports*—annual report for 1988.

88. The first such group was the Maccabees movement in the Crown Heights section of Brooklyn, N.Y. Brown, *Strain of Violence*, 129.

89. *New York Times*, national edition, Aug. 20, 1989, sec. 1, p. 14, col. 1–4. Another successful example of the African-American community self-help movement is in the vast section of south-central Los Angeles, with a population of 550,000, where a combination of black self-help organizations (including Community Youth Gang Services, Brotherhood Crusade, Nation of Islam, and Southern Christian Leadership Conference) used a campaign (focusing, but not exclusively, on civilian street patrols) against youth-gang activity in early 1990 to bring down the crime rate of such youths by "a stunning 36 percent" with murders involving gang members dropping 45 percent. The early stages of this community effort "coincided with a series of massive police round-ups on gang-ridden streets, dubbed Operation Hammer. . . . But the dramatic reduction in crime was not seen until the police crackdowns were supplemented with community group efforts." *Los Angeles Times* report in *Denver Post*, May 6, 1990, 2A, col. 3–6. Later in 1990 Mayor David Dinkins of New York City called for a great increase in the city's more than 400 citizen patrol organizations to help "take back our streets" from the violence that "threatens to tear our city apart." *New York Times*, national edition, Sept. 10, 1990, A15, col. 5–6.

90. *Ebony*, Aug. 1988, p. 31. The quotations are from Johnson's keynote editorial for this special issue of *Ebony* devoted entirely to the problem of revitalizing education in the inner-city black areas. Aside from its informative content, this special issue is significant because *Ebony* is a high-circulation "slick" magazine catering to the affluent

African-American middle class that has often been accused of indifference to the plight of crime-plagued ghetto blacks.

91. *Ebony*, Aug. 1988, p. 164.

92. *Ibid.*, 52–63.

93. *Newsweek*, May 2, 1988, pp. 56–65.

94. Allyson Reid-Dove, "Of Minds and Money," *Black Enterprise*, Sept. 1988, pp. 67–70.

95. William Raspberry, "Black Children Succeed at Strong D.C. School," Portland *Oregonian*, Sept. 24, 1985, B11.

96. James P. Comer, "The Social Factor," *New York Times*, Aug. 7, 1988, sec. 4A, pp. 27–31, in which Comer recounts the success of a "social-skills" approach in the two schools in the course of a five-year project directed by him.

97. On McCallum and McKenna: *Ebony*, Aug. 1988, pp. 58, 124–26, respectively. On Clark: *ibid.*, 120, 122, and *Newsweek*, Jan. 18, 1988, pp. 80–81. On Moten: Raspberry, "Black Children Succeed." On Smoak: *Newsweek*, May 2, 1988, pp. 56–65.

98. Profiles of ten such teachers appear in *Ebony*, Aug. 1988, pp. 78–87.

99. For example, the ten "top achievers" presented in *ibid.*, 40–50.

100. *Black Enterprise*, Sept. 1988, Graves edits and publishes this magazine.

101. Reid-Dove, "Of Minds and Money," 67.

102. *Ebony*, Aug. 1988, p. 124.

103. The quotation is from Shoshana Shuboff, *In the Age of the Smart Machine: The Future of Work and Power* (New York: Basic Books, 1988), 388.

104. Yoneji Masuda, *The Information Society as Post-Industrial Society*, trans. Bernard Halliwell (Bethesda: World Future Society, 1981), viii. Masuda was the formulator of a nationwide cooperative public/private plan for an "Information Society" in Japan which, with 2000 as its target year for completion, is being impressively realized.

105. Shuboff, *Age of Smart Machine*, xiii and *passim*.

106. *Ibid.*, 70–76 and *passim*. See also J. David Bolter, *Turing's Man: Western Culture in the Computer Age* (Chapel Hill: University of North Carolina Press, 1984), 232–33, 236–37; Eugene F. Provenzo, *Beyond the Gutenberg Galaxy: Microcomputers and the Emergence of Post-Typographic Culture* (New York: Teachers College, Columbia University, 1986), 16–17, 73, 75; Tom Forester, ed., *High-Tech Society: The Story of the Informa-*

tion Technology Revolution (Cambridge: MIT Press, 1987), 167; Tom Forester, ed., *The Information Technology Revolution* (Cambridge: MIT Press, 1985), 227–28; Masuda, *Information Society*, 30–31. "Intellective skills" is Shuboff's appropriate term for a concept that all these authorities, in their own terminology, emphasize. A significant statement is by Daniel Bell, "The Social Framework of the Information Society" (1979), reprinted in Tom Forester, ed., *The Microelectronics Revolution* (Cambridge: MIT Press, 1981), 500–549.

107. *National Journal,* May 7, 1988, p. 1220.

108. Frederick Golden, "Here Come the Microkids," in Forester, ed., *Information Technology Revolution,* 227.

109. Quoted in *ibid.,* 228.

110. The emphasis in the quotation is by Papert, who is cited and quoted in Provenzo, *Beyond the Gutenberg Galaxy,* 15, 76.

111. For example, *Newsweek,* May 2, 1988, pp. 54–55, which mentions among other things the widely noted improvement in Scholastic Aptitude Test (SAT) scores, and *USA Today,* Sept. 12, 1989, p. 5D, which reports that since 1979 a closing of the gap between the higher average SAT score for the white majority and the lower average SAT scored for the racial minorities has occurred.

112. On this disproportionately violent element, see Weiner and Wolfgang, "Extent and Character," 32. On May 15, 1989, President George W. Bush announced an ambitious new $1.8 billion anticrime program stressing 24,000 new prison cells as well as more federal agents and prosecutors and expansion of the scope of the death penalty. *New York Times,* national edition, May 16, 1989, A1, col. 1, and A12, col. 4–6. *USA Today,* May 16, 1989, p. 1A, col. 6 and p. 5A, col. 1–5. There was a notable 115 percent increase in the federal and state prison population from 1980 to 1989 culminating in a record 274 sentenced prisoners per 100,000 Americans in 1989, *National Journal,* Oct. 6, 1990, p. 2428.

113. Shuboff in *Age of the Smart Machine* is far from being a Pollyanna, but she has high hopes for humanity in the Information Society in which, on the basis of trends discoverd in her field research, she envisions a "socially integrated high technology workplace" in which the "hierarchical or other status-based distinctions" of Industrial Society will dissolve or at least "hold less power." Shuboff, *Age of Smart Machine,* 206, 404, and *passim.* Her view is typical of many authorities on the Information Society.

Chapter 5. Conclusion:
No Duty to Retreat in Retrospect and Prospect.

In the notes to this chapter, both the regular (New York City) edition of the *New York Times* and the national edition of the *New York Times* are cited. Unless otherwise indicated, the citation is to the regular edition.

*New York Times, national edition, Sept. 2, 1989, p. 13, col. 2–6. See the conclusion of this chapter for the background of Devin S. Standard's statement.

1. Gunnar Myrdal, *An American Dilemma* (New York: Harper, 1944), 4, 23–25, and *passim.*

2. For example, National Commission on the Causes and Prevention of Violence, *To Establish Justice, To Insure Domestic Tranquility: Final Report of the National Commission on the Causes and Prevention of Violence* (Washington, D.C.: U.S. Government Printing Office, 1969), xiii–xxxii.

3. Roy P. Basler *et al.,* eds., *The Collected Works of Abraham Lincoln* (9 vols.; New Brunswick: Rutgers University Press, c. 1953–55), I: 108–15.

4. Thomas J. Kernan, "The Jurisprudence of Lawlessness," *Reports of American Bar Association,* XXIX (1906): 450–67.

5. *Ibid.*

6. See Chapter 4, above, on the victim-rights movement.

7. For example, the public outrage over the brutal group rape and beating of a 28-year-old New Yorker in Central Park on April 19, 1989. Eight juveniles were arrested and became the subjects of legal proceedings. The shocking episode attracted heavy media attention nationwide as well as in New York City. *New York Times,* April 28, 1989, B2, col. 1–2, and April 29, 1989, p. 30, col. 1–5, for examples of the voluminous press coverage of the event and its aftermath in law and public opinion. See also Chapter 4, above, in note 53 and note 37. Emphasizing that rape is a hate crime against women is Ann Pellegrini, "Rape Is a Bias Crime," *New York Times,* national edition, May 27, 1990, sec. 4, p. 13, col. 3–6.

8. Frederick Jackson Turner, *The Frontier in American History* (New York: Henry Holt, 1921), 37.

9. Tocqueville coined the word "individualism" and presented the modern concept of the individual in *Democracy in America: Part the Second, The Social Influence of Democracy,* trans. Henry Reeve (New York: J. and H. G. Langley, 1840), Book 2, chap. 2. Although Tocqueville's book

focused on America, he did not restrict his notion of individualism to our country.

10. Johnathan H. Turner and David Musick, *American Dilemmas: A Sociological Interpretation of Enduring Social Issues* (New York: Columbia University Press, 1985), 14–18.

11. Patricia Nelson Limerick, *The Legacy of Conquest: The Unbroken Past of the American West* (New York: W. W. Norton, 1987).

12. Two excellent studies of Claude Dallas and his killing of the two game wardens are Jeff Long, *Outlaw: The True Story of Claude Dallas* (New York: William Morrow, c. 1985); and Jack Olsen, *Give a Boy a Gun: A True Story of Law and Disorder in the American West* (New York: Delacorte, 1985). Dallas's second victim was Conley Elms.

13. Long, *Outlaw*, 218.

14. On the myth and the reality of the beaver-trapping "mountain men" of the 1820s–1830s upon which Claude Dallas based his self-image (one widely accepted by his many admirers in the Idaho-Oregon-Nevada region), there is a vast scholarly literature including the following salient treatments: Bernard De Voto, *Across the Wide Missouri* (Boston: Houghton Mifflin, 1947). William H. Goetzmann, "The Mountain Man as Jacksonian Man," *American Quarterly* 15 (Fall 1963):402–15. Kent Ladd Steckmesser, *The Western Hero in History and Legend* (Norman: University of Oklahoma Press, 1965), chaps. 2–5. David J. Wishart, *The Fur Trade of the American West, 1807–1840: A Geographical Synthesis* (Lincoln: University of Nebraska Press, 1979). Many other worthy studies are cited by Gordon B. Dodds, chap. 4, "The Fur Trade and Exploration," in Michael P. Malone, ed., *Historians and the American West* (Lincoln: University of Nebraska Press, 1983).

15. Long, *Outlaw*, 218.

16. Quoted in *ibid.*

17. *Ibid.*, 208–17. See also Olsen, *Give a Boy a Gun*, 251–67. Bernhard Goetz had also prepared himself for quick-draw action on the dangerous streets and subways of New York City. See Chapter 4, at note 27.

18. Olsen, *Give a Boy a Gun*, 164, 262–63.

19. Long, *Outlaw*, 232. The jury foreman went on to explain that if Dallas had refrained from shooting both Pogue and Elms in the head as they lay on the ground after being downed by his initial shots the jury would have acquitted Dallas altogether. The jury believed that the head shots contradicted what had been, as they saw it, Dallas's legitimate

claim of justifiable homicide up to the time he put bullets into the heads of the two man. *Ibid.*

20. Long, *Outlaw,* 236.

21. *New York Times,* Nov. 24, 1953, p. 1, col. 2 and p. 20, col. 2–5.

22. On McCarthy and McCarthyism see, among many worthy treatments, David M. Oshinsky, *A Conspiracy So Immense: The World of Joe McCarthy* (New York: Free Press, c. 1983); and Richard M. Fried, *Nightmare in Red: The McCarthy Era in Perspective* (New York: Oxford University Press, 1990).

23. Turner and Musick, *American Dilemmas,* 14–18.

24. James D. Richardson, comp., *A Compilation of the Messages and Papers of the Presidents, 1789–1897* (10 vols.; Washington, D.C.: U.S. Government Printing Office, 1896–99), IV: 388–89. Charles Sellers, *James K. Polk, Continentalist, 1843–1846* (Princeton: Princeton University Press, 1966), 340.

25. Sellers, *James K. Polk, 400.*

26. *Ibid.,* 406–9. K. Jack Bauer, *Zachary Taylor: Soldier, Planter, Statesman of the Old South* (Baton Rouge: Louisiana State University Press, c. 1985), 149.

27. Basler *et al.,* eds., *Collected Works of Abraham Lincoln,* I: 420–22. Don E. Fehrenbacher, *Lincoln in Text and Context: Collected Essays* (Stanford: Stanford University Press, 1987), 3–4. Stephen B. Oates, *With Malice toward None: The Life of Abraham Lincoln* (New York: Harper & Row, 1977), 79–80.

28. In a judicious discussion of the historiography of the Mexican-American War and its origins, Don E. Fehrenbacher noted that "modern American historians have tended to divide the responsibility for the outbreak of hostilities—though not always evenly—between the United States and Mexico, while finding the sources of the war in a combination of Mexican debility and the aggressive energy of the United States." In regard to Polk specifically, "the critical question," Fehrenbacher went on to say, "is whether his desire for California made the difference between war and peace. That is, did it shape the manner in which he handled the crisis with Mexico over Texas and other issues? If the record does not compel an affirmative answer, it clearly forbids a negative one, for there is too much consistency between Polk's actions before the war and the course that he followed after it had begun. His ordering of Taylor's army to the Rio Grande; his almost eager expectation of hostilities as a consequence; his decision to prepare a war message with-

out waiting for hostilities to begin; his inflammatory assertion that American blood had been spilled on American soil; his rejection of [Secretary of State] James Buchanan's proposal to disclaim any intention of territorial aggrandizement . . . ." Fehrenbacher, *Lincoln*, 10, 13–14. See also David M. Pletcher, *The Diplomacy of Annexation: Texas, Oregon, and the Mexican War* (Columbia: University of Missouri Press, c. 1973), 597–98; and Paul H. Bergeron, *The Presidency of James K. Polk* (Lawrence: University Press of Kansas, c. 1987), xiii, 63, 68–69, 72. A cultural history of the war is Robert W. Johannsen, *To the Halls of the Montezumas: The Mexican War in the American Imagination* (New York: Oxford University Press, 1985).

29. Baucr, *Zachary Taylor*, 121 (on Taylor), 63 (quotation from Polk). In his May 11, 1846, message to Congress asking for a declaration of war against Mexico, Polk announced (Richardson, comp., *Compilation of Messages*, IV: 441) that the Mexican general Ampudia had on April 12, 1846, "notified General Taylor to break up his camp [north of the Rio Grande] within twenty-four hours and to retire [northward] beyond the Nueces River." This ultimatim raised the no-duty-to-retreat hackles of both Taylor and Polk.

30. Reinhard H. Luthin, *The Real Abraham Lincoln* (Englewood Cliffs, N.J.: Prentice-Hall, 1960), 273. For Lincoln's overall handling of the Fort Sumter crisis, see *ibid.*, 269, 273–75; and Oates, *With Malice toward None*, 219–26.

31. Jay David, ed., *The Kennedy Reader* (Indianapolis: Bobbs-Merrill, c. 1967), 8.

32. The voluminous scholarship on the containment policy includes John Lewis Gaddis, *Strategies of Containment: A Critical Appraisal of Postwar American National Security* (New York: Oxford University Press, 1982). Generally credited with the formulation of the concept of containment is George F. Kennan. *Ibid.*, chap. 2. Kennan later came to disagree with the American application of containment. *Ibid.* and John Lewis Gaddis, "The Strategy of Containment," in Thomas H. Etzold and Gaddis, eds., *Containment: Documents on American Policy and Strategy, 1945–1950* (New York: Columbia University Press, 1978), 25–37.

33. Harry S. Truman, *Memoirs* (2 vols.; Garden City, N.Y.: Doubleday, 1956), 106. Robert J. Donovan, *Conflict and Crisis: The Presidency of Harry S Truman, 1945–1948* (New York: W. W. Norton, c. 1977), 279–87. Howard Jones, *"A New Kind of War": America's Global Strategy and the Truman Doctrine in Greece* (New York: Oxford University Press, 1989).

34. Donovan, *Conflict and Crisis*, 363–67. Truman, *Memoirs*, II: 122–24, 131, in which Truman noted (131) that in May 1949, in the face of the successful American airlift, it was "the Russians who were ready to retreat"; while Donovan (367) wrote of Truman in regard to Berlin: "He refused to withdraw." Avi Shlaim, *The United States and the Berlin Blockade, 1948–1949: A Study in Crisis Decision-Making* (Berkeley: University of California Press, c. 1983). Richard Collier, *Bridge across the Sky: The Berlin Blockade and Airlift: 1948–1949* (New York: McGraw-Hill, c. 1978). Jean Edward Smith, *The Defense of Berlin* (Baltimore: Johns Hopkins University Press, 1963), chaps. 6–7. At a meeting in late June 1948 to decide whether U.S. forces, pressured by the Soviet blockade, should be kept in Berlin, President Truman stopped discussion by saying: "The United States is going to stay. Period." Smith, *Defense of Berlin*, 109. See also Ann and John Tusa, *The Berlin Airlift* (New York: Atheneum, 1988).

35. Donovan, *Conflict and Crisis*, 287–91.

36. Truman, *Memoirs*, II: 240, 250, 257. Lawrence S. Kaplan, *The United States and NATO: The Formative Years* (Lexington: University Press of Kentucky, c. 1984). Don Cook, *Forging the Alliance: NATO, 1945–1950* (New York: Arbor House, 1989). The Mutual Defense Assistance Act was the American legislative corollary to the North Atlantic Treaty.

37. Robert J. Donovan, *Tumultuous Years: The Presidency of Harry S Truman* (New York: W. W. Norton, c. 1982), 202.

38. Richard F. Haynes, *The Awesome Power: Harry S. Truman as Commander in Chief* (Baton Rouge: Louisiana State University Press, c. 1973), 163–64.

39. Donovan, *Tumultuous Years*, 195–96.

40. *Ibid.*, 197.

41. *Ibid.*

42 Donovan, *Tumultuous Years*, 202.

43. Stephen E. Ambrose, *Eisenhower: The President* (New York: Simon and Schuster, c. 1984), 183 and *passim*. As an alliance, SEATO never gained the strength of its model, NATO, and it quietly expired in 1977. Kaplan, *United States and NATO*, 13. Writing reminiscently after his own presidency, Harry Truman condemned Eisenhower, in effect, for not always following a no-duty-to-retreat policy. Thus Truman accused President Eisenhower of being insufficiently staunch in opposing the Soviet suppression of the Hungarian revolution of 1956 and Fidel Castro's 1959 takeover of Cuba. Harry S. Truman, "He Didn't Like Ike," ed., Margaret Truman, *New York Times Magazine*, Sept, 17, 1989, p. 44.

44. Lyndon B. Johnson, *The Vantage Point: Perspectives of the Presidency,* *1963–1969* (New York: Holt, Rinehart and Winston, 1971), 155. Richard Maxwell Brown, *Strain of Violence: Historical Studies of American Violence and Vigilantism* (New York: Oxford University Press, 1975), 289–95. Robert A. Caro, *The Years of Lyndon Johnson: The Path to the Presidency* (New York: Alfred A. Knopf, 1982), 17–32 and *passim.*

45. Brown, *Strain of Violence,* chap. 8.

46. Johnson, *Vantage Point,* 68.

47. *Ibid.*

48. Johnson's May 1965 foreword to Walter Prescott Webb, *The Texas Rangers: A Century of Frontier Defense* (2nd ed.; Austin: University of Texas Press, 1965), x. Johnson wrote the foreword (ix–xi) for this second edition of a book first published in 1935. A leading American historian and native Texan, Webb, who died in 1963, taught at the University of Texas and was a longtime friend of Johnson.

48. Samuel Eliot Morison, *John Paul Jones: A Sailor's Biography* (Boston: Little, Brown, 1959), 230.

50. C. S. Forester, *The Age of Fighting Sail: The Story of the Naval War of 1812* (Garden City, N.Y.: Doubleday, 1956), 165.

51. Charles Lee Lewis, *David Glasgow Farragut* (2 vols.; Annapolis: United States Naval Institute, 1941–43), II: 269, 469.

52. A. Russell Buchanan, *The United States and World War II* (2 vols.; New York: Harper & Row, 1964), II: 435–37.

53. Bruce Catton, *Grant Takes Command* (Boston: Little, Brown, c. 1968), 223.

54. Robert M. Utley, *Cavalier in Buckskin: George Armstrong Custer and the Western Military Frontier* (Norman: University of Oklahoma Press, 1988), chap. 8.

55. Cora Bell, *The Reagan Paradox: American Foreign Policy in the 1980s* (New Brunswick: Rutgers University Press, 1989). On Reagan's presidential appeal to traditional American values: Robert Dallek, *The Politics of Symbolism* (Cambridge, Mass.: Harvard University Press, 1984); Garry Wills, *Reagan's America: Innocents at Home* (Garden City, N.Y.: Doubleday, 1987); and John Kenneth White, *The New Politics of Old Values* (Hanover, N.H.: University Press of New England, 1988), 50–51, 73, and *passim.*

56. Bob Woodward, *Veil: The Secret Wars of the CIA, 1981–1987* (New York: Simon and Schuster, c. 1987), emphasizes Casey's role.

57. Two scholarly studies with opposing viewpoints are Jiri Valenta and Herbert J. Ellison, eds., *Grenada and Soviet/Cuban Policy: Internal*

Crisis and U.S./OECS Intervention (Boulder, Colo.: Westview, 1986), favoring the overthrow; and Gordon K. Lewis, *Grenada: The Jewel Despoiled* (Baltimore: Johns Hopkins University Press, c. 1987), comdemning it. See also Woodward, *Veil*, 287–300, and Ben Bradlee, Jr., *Guts and Glory: The Rise and Fall of Oliver North* (New York: Donald I. Fine, c. 1988), 172–82.

58. Woodward, *Veil*, 441–46. Bradlee, Jr., *Guts and Glory*, 346–55.

59. The deployment was for the escort of Kuwaiti-owned oil tankers in order to protect them from, especially, Iranian attack as a consequence of the Iran-Iraq war of the 1980s.

60. Reagan's anti-Sandinista policy: Thomas W. Walker, ed., *Reagan versus the Sandinistas: The Undeclared War on Nicaragua* (Boulder, Colo.: Westview, 1987); E. Bradford Burns, *At War in Nicaragua: The Reagan Doctrine and the Politics of Nostalgia* (New York: Harper & Row, c. 1987), a strongly anti-Reagan scholarly study. On covert activity against the Nicaraguan government: Woodward, *Veil*, *passim*, and Bradlee, Jr., *Guts and Glory*, 191–98, 202–3, 213–17, 219–65, 335–37, 356–62, 402–10, 424–27, 429–34, 445–48, and *passim*.

61. On SDI: Philip M. Boffey *et al.*, *Claiming the Heavens* (New York: Times Books, c. 1988). Michael Vlahos, *Strategic Defense and the American Ethos . . .* (Boulder, Colo.: Westview, 1986). By 1989 funding for SDI was significantly lower as a result of technical difficulties that seemed to jeopardize perfection of the system and waning support for heavy defense expenditures in the new post–Cold War era.

62. Tom Wolfe, *The Right Stuff* (New York: Farrar, Straus, Giroux, 1979).

63. *Ibid.*, 387. Emphasis in the passage quoted has been omitted.

64. Bradlee, Jr., *Guts and Glory*, 11.

65. *Taking the Stand: The Testimony of Lieutenant Colonel Oliver North* (New York: Pocket Books, 1987). Bradlee, Jr., *Guts and Glory*, 496–535. North's congressional testimony was the subject of cover stories in all three of the national newsmagazines: *Newsweek,* July 13, 1987; *Time,* July 13, and 20, 1987; and *U. S. News & World Report,* July 13, 1987.

66. Bradlee, Jr., *Guts and Glory*, 506. On Abu Nidal: Yossi Melman, *The Master Terrorist: The True Story of Abu-Nidal* (New York: Adama Books, c. 1986).

67. Bradlee, Jr., *Guts and Glory*, 519–20.

68. However, strong elements in Congress, the news media, and the general population viewed North not as a hero but as a villain whose

role in the Iran-Contra episode subverted the Constitution. See, for example, Bradlee, Jr., *Guts and Glory*, 554. Following a 1988–89 jury trial, Oliver North was, in regard to the aftermath of the Iran-Contra episode, convicted of three felony crimes of obstructing Congress, altering and destroying federal government documents, and receiving an illegal gratuity, but in July 1990 a panel of the U.S. Court of Appeals for the District of Columbia reversed North's conviction on the documents charge and vacated the other two. Prosecutors may well appeal these rulings against the convictions. Eugene (Ore.) *Register-Guard*, July 6, 1989, p. 1A, col. 1–2 and p. 4A, col. 1–5. *New York Times*, national edition, July 21, 1990, p. 1, col. 1 and p. 7, col. 1–6.

69. Bradlee, Jr., *Guts and Glory*, 172–82.

70. *Ibid.*, 289–98.

71. *Ibid.*, 353–55.

72. Tom Clancy, *The Hunt for Red October* (Annapolis: Naval Institute Press, c. 1984), and *Red Storm Rising* (New York: G. P. Putnam's, c. 1986). On Clancy and the appeal of his books to Ronald Reagan, but also, as Clancy himself noted, to millions who voted for Reagan: Patrick Anderson, "King of the 'Techno-Thriller,'" *New York Times Magazine*, May 1, 1988, pp. 53–54, 83–85, and a cover story. "The Art of the Techno-Thriller," *Newsweek*, Aug. 8, 1988, pp. 60–63. Given *The Hunt for Red October* as a 1984 Christmas present, Ronald Reagan read the book, was quoted in *Time*, March 4, 1985, as praising it as "a perfect yarn," and thus boosted it to the top of the best-seller list. *The Hunt for Red October* and *Red Storm Rising* had sold a total of nearly 8,000,000 copies by early 1988. Despite the end of the Cold War in 1989, the popular appeal of *The Hunt for Red October* continued in the early-1990 Hollywood version of the novel—a film that immediately went to the top of the box-office charts despite dismissive reviews by movie critics.

73. Eugene *Register-Guard*, Jan. 6, 1989, p. 3A, col. 3–4. This confrontation took place on Jan. 4, 1989; see *ibid.*, Jan. 5, 1989, p. 1A, col. 1–6 and p. 3A, col. 2–4.

74. Richard S. Lewis, *Challenger: The Final Voyage* (New York: Columbia University Press, 1988).

75. *Public Papers of the Presidents of the United States: Ronald Reagan, 1986* (2 vols.; Washington, D.C.: U.S. Government Printing Office, 1988), I: 109–11.

76. *Newsweek*, May 15, 1989, pp. 20–30.

77. In a recent ruling for the Oregon supreme court Judge Betty

Roberts made clear her dislike of the no-duty-to-retreat doctrine, which, as she saw it, represented skewed values in that it was "based on a policy against making men act as cowards and experience the humiliation of ignominiously running from a physical encounter." Judge Roberts thus spoke for the Oregon state supreme court's decision to uphold the duty to retreat in the 1982 case of *State v. Charles*. In the early 1970s the Oregon state legislature had rejected a duty-to-retreat provision in its revision of the Oregon penal code, choosing to leave the matter up to Oregon case law. In her opinion Judge Roberts held that an earlier decision of the Oregon supreme court—*State v. Rader,* 1919—had been wrongly interpreted as favoring no duty to retreat. *State v. Charles,* 293 Or. 273 (1982). *Willamette Law Review* 19 (Winter 1983):166–69.

78. In regard to gender, for example, a significant turn by females toward violent self-defense in no-duty-to-retreat situations is revealed in a 1988 Gallup poll revealing that one-eighth of American women possess arms. Paxton Quigley, *Armed and Female* (New York: Dutton, 1989).

79. Eugene *Register-Guard,* July 6, 1989, p. 1A, col. 2–5.

80. David M. Reimers, *Still the Golden Door: The Third World Comes to America* (New York: Columbia University Press, 1985).

81. The acculturation of Hispanic immigrants to the notion of no-duty-to-retreat is eased by the ubiquity of *machismo* in their native lands. On *machismo* see, for example, Georgie Ann Geyer, *The New Latins: Fateful Change in South and Central America* (Garden City, N.Y.: Doubleday, 1970), chap. 5. One scholar links a cluster of normative American masculine characteristices to *machismo* in his conception of the seven components that make up what he sees as the "macho presidential style": competitiveness; sports and athletic mindedness; decisiveness; appearance of unemotionalism; strength and aggressiveness; powerfulness; and being "a 'real man' and never 'feminine.' " Yet he notes that these "are not inherently male traits nor are they antithetical to femininity" but that the public has asked presidents from Washington to Reagan to adhere to them. John Orman, *Comparing Presidential Behavior: Carter, Reagan, and the Macho Presidential Style* (Westport, Conn.: Greenwood, 1987), 7–9. A striking example of the acculturative power of such mainstream American values as entrepreneurship is that provided by the Hispanic (Dominican) immigrant teenage members of a typical drug-dealing gang of New York City. Far from being alienated from mainstream American culture, these young third-world immigrants sub-

scribe to the creed of "God Bless America and the Yankee Dollar." Terry Williams, *The Cocaine Kids: The Inside Story of a Teenage Drug Ring* (Reading, Mass.: Addison-Wesley, c. 1987), 24 and *passim*. For a similar finding of the allegiance to mainstream American values by criminous Hispanic immigrant youth: Philippe Bourgois, "Just Another Night on Crack Street," *New York Times Magazine*, Nov. 12, 1989, pp. 53, 60–65, 94.

82. For example, Richard D. Lamm and Gary Imhoff, *The Immigration Time Bomb: The Fragmenting of America* (New York: Truman Talley/E. P. Dutton, c. 1985).

83. International terrorism and its threat to America is beyond the scope of this book, but among a vast scholarly literature on terrorism world wide, see, for example, three recent works: Peter H. Merkl, ed., *Political Violence and Terror* (Berkeley: University of California Press, c. 1986). Paul Wilkinson, Alasdair M. Stewart *et al.*, eds., *Contemporary Research on Terrorism* (Aberdeen, Scotland: Aberdeen University Press, 1987). Walter Laqueur, *The Age of Terrorism* (Boston: Little, Brown, c. 1987). A study of the tradition of American political terrorism in relation to international (or transnational) terrorism is Ted Robert Gurr, chap. 7, "Political Terrorism: Historical Antecedents and Contemporary Trends" in Gurr, ed., *Violence in America* (2 vols.; Newbury Park, Calif.: Sage Publications, 1989), *Volume 2: Protest, Rebellion, Reform.*

84. For the murder of Yusuf Hawkins, see note 37 in Chapter 4.

85. Statement of Devin S. Standard in *New York Times*, national edition, Sept. 2, 1989, p. 13, col. 2–6. Emphasis added.

Index